A POST (

UTAH

Byways

Backcountry drives
for the
whole family

By **TONY HUEGEL**

Cover design, maps, art and production
by Jerry Painter

Photography by Tony Huegel

A Post Co. GUIDEBOOK

Published by the Post Company
P.O. Box 1800, Idaho Falls, Idaho 83403

Edited by Mei-Mei Chan

First edition

Produced in the United States of America.

Library of Congress Catalog Card Number 96-067014
ISBN 0-9636560-8-2

Cover photo: The southern end of the Lockhart Basin Road (*trip 40*).

Disclaimer

This book has been prepared to help you and your family enjoy backcountry driving. However, it is not intended to be an exhaustive, all-encompassing authority on backcountry driving, nor is it intended to be your only source of information about the subject. You must understand that there are risks and dangers that are inevitable when driving in the backcountry. If you drive the routes listed in this book, or any other backcountry roads, you assume all risks, dangers and liability that may result from your actions. The author and publisher of this book disclaim any and all liability for any injury, loss or damage that you, your passengers or your vehicle may incur.

Exercise the caution and good judgment that visiting the backcountry demands. Bring the proper supplies. Remember that the condition of backroads, especially those that are not paved, can and does change. Be prepared for accidents, injuries, breakdowns or other problems, because help is almost always far away.

Acknowledgments

In gathering information for these routes, both before I actually experienced them myself and afterwards, I became indebted to many people. I must express sincere gratitude to them all.

First and foremost are my wife, Lynn MacAusland, and our children, Hannah and Land. They have for years accompanied me on some of America's most rugged and remote backcountry byways, often enduring the kind of rudimentary conditions and hair-raising moments that adventure and discovery entail.

I must express boundless appreciation to many U.S. Bureau of Land Management, U.S. Forest Service, National Park Service and Utah Division of Parks and Recreation staffers statewide. Despite dwindling resources and mounting demands, they took the time to suggest routes at the outset, and then to read over route descriptions prior to publication. They were helpful, courteous and professional, and their contributions cannot be overstated. Any errors or shortcomings that might still exist in this book are my responsibility, not theirs.

I also need to thank Trails Illustrated and the Automobile Club of Southern California (AAA) for providing copies of their outstanding maps.

Many people associated with the Post Company, which publishes my series of backcountry touring guidebooks, provided enormous amounts of technical expertise, patience, talent, skill and hard work to bring this project to fruition. Publisher Jerry Brady endorsed the vision. Executive Editor Mei-Mei Chan diligently kept the project moving, as she has done throughout the expansion of the series. In *Utah Byways'* final stages, she demonstrated remarkable skill in editing the text and maps. And once again, Jerry Painter's graphics skills have produced exceptional results.

Publicist Michael Dobrin deserves my gratitude for providing assistance, support and enthusiasm that helped make the research possible. Finally, I must thank Toyota, whose legendary sport-utility vehicles have never failed, over thousands of rugged backcountry miles, to bring me and my family home safe and sound.

Contents

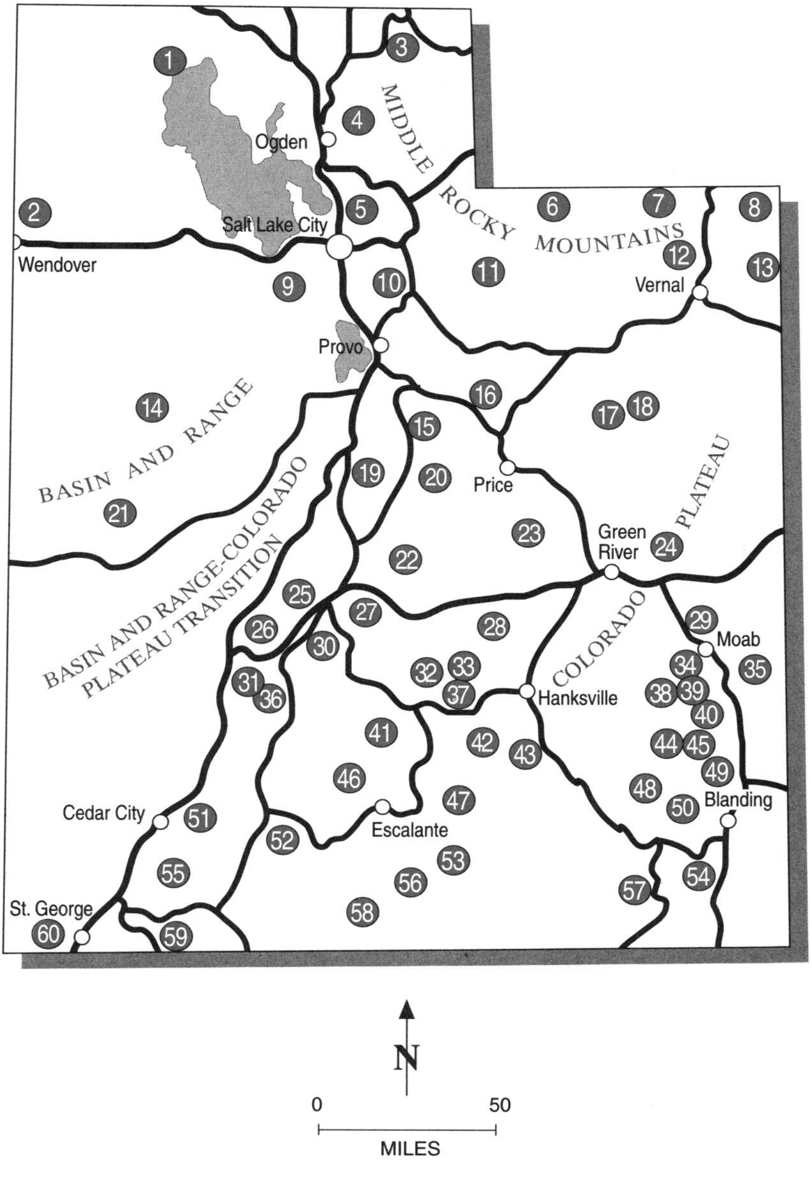

Ogden
Salt Lake City
Wendover
Provo
Vernal
Price
Green River
Moab
Hanksville
Blanding
Escalante
Cedar City
St. George
MIDDLE ROCKY MOUNTAINS
BASIN AND RANGE
BASIN AND RANGE-COLORADO PLATEAU TRANSITION
COLORADO PLATEAU
N
0
50
MILES

Appendix

Trail descriptions

Describing backcountry tours can be subjective. Much of the assessment of a route's beauty, difficulty and even how long it takes depends on the individual's experience, likes and dislikes, perceptions, circumstances and the stops one makes along the way. I've tried to bring some objectivity to the various categories I've used to describe each drive, but that can only go so far. Anyway, here's what's behind each category:

LOCATION: Where the drive is.

HIGHLIGHTS: What's best about the drive.

DIFFICULTY: Subjective. I assumed you are not a serious four–wheeler, but just somebody in a modern sport–utility vehicle who's looking for reasonably safe adventure. The ratings are: *easy*, which means it's a real cruise, perhaps on a graded dirt and gravel that won't require four-wheel drive; *moderate*, which means you'll need four-wheel drive occasionally, the going will be slow, and you can expect rough spots, stream fordings, ruts, etc.; and *difficult*, which means rough and slow, using four-wheel drive most of the time, and a higher likelihood that you'll scrape your undercarriage's protective skid plates.

TIME & DISTANCE: The approximate time it takes to complete the drive, excluding travel time getting to the starting point and stops you might make along the way. Since odometer accuracy varies among vehicles, your measurements of distances might differ from mine somewhat.

GETTING THERE: This will direct you to the starting point.

THE DRIVE: Details of the trip, such as what turns to take, where you'll end up, how far it is from here to there, and what you'll see. My geologic descriptions often include the abbreviation MYA, for million years ago.

REST STOPS: Where you can stop for a picnic, to camp, see a historic or cultural site, visit a museum, etc.

SPECIAL NOTES: Rules, restrictions or recommendations you need to keep in mind.

GETTING HOME: Varies according to where home is. But there are usually common exit points leading to highways.

MAPS: Each trip recommends specific maps and other materials. I recommend a number of maps, including those produced by the U.S. Forest Service, Bureau of Land Management (BLM) and Trails Illustrated. *Indian Country*, published by AAA affiliate Automobile Club of Southern California (ACSC), is an outstanding reference for southern Utah. An excellent statewide map is *Recreational Map of Utah*, published by GTR Mapping. They're widely available. The Utah Travel Council (UTC) publishes a series of five maps for the state that are very good as well. All are widely available at Forest Service and BLM offices, and retail outlets. The addresses section toward the back of the book lists map sources.

INFORMATION: A telephone number you can call for road conditions and other information. **All of Utah is area code 801.**

ALSO TRY: A route in the area that is not described in detail.

Map symbols

Point of interest	■	Hiking trail	dashed line
Paved road	solid line	Forest road	3S01
Easy dirt road	double line	Interstate highway	5
Primitive road	dashed double line	U.S. highway	101
Camping	▲	State highway	1
Lake		North indicator	N
Stream			
Mountain			
Ranger station			
Picnic area			
City or town	○		

Trips indicated in color

- Paved road
- Easy dirt road
- Primitive road

Guide to trip highlights

Mt. biking

Rock art

Photo opportunities

Camping

Hiking

Arches

Picnicking

Restaurant

Historic sites

Wildlife viewing

Ruins

Rock hounding

INTRODUCTION

Swinging Bridge, Brown's Park

Discovering Utah's outback

"If you ever come this way it will scare you to death to look down it. It is about a mile from the top down to the river and it is almost straight down, the cliffs on each side are five hundred feet high and there is just room enough for a wagon to go down. It nearly scared me to death. The first wagon I saw go down, they put the brake on and rough locked the hind wheels and had a big rope fastened to the wagon and about 10 men holding back on it, and then they went down like they would smash everything. I'll never forget that day. When he was walking down, Willie looked back and cried and asked me how we would get back home."

From a letter by Elizabeth Morris Decker, a Mormon pioneer in Utah with the 1879-1880 Hole-in-the-Rock expedition.

Utah, a state of deserts, mountains, rivers, canyons and courage, was a formidable frontier for Brigham Young's brave pioneers. Today, adventuresome motorists who trade monotonous freeways for Utah's scenic, historic and unpaved backcountry roads can get a taste of what Elizabeth Morris Decker and those like her experienced, but without the danger and hardship they confronted. While edging down steep switchbacks high above the Colorado River or along mountain ridgelines at the brink of the Great Basin remains an exhilarating adventure, crossing Utah's outback is today far easier and safer than anything little Willie could have imagined.

With ownership of sport-utility vehicles expanding rapidly, families, seniors, individuals with disabilities — almost anyone — can explore places of unrivaled natural splendor and dramatic human history more comfortably, safely and conveniently than ever before. Whether for an hour, an afternoon, a day or a weekend, motorists with suitable vehicles can easily experience Utah's extraordinary wildlands and get back home with no greater concern than whether the line at the car wash will be too long.

Like the rest of America, much of Utah has been tamed by paved roads and multi-laned highways. But a huge and spectacular wild side survives, reachable by a seemingly endless selection of unpaved backcountry roads. Many are graded, maintained county roads. Others are rudimentary two-tracks or wash bottoms through exotic red-rock labyrinths. Some are notable not only for scenery but for their historic, even legendary, place in the American experience. A handful are part of the U.S. Bureau of Land Management's system of National Back Country Byways. Many are included in the state of Utah's Scenic Backways program, while others follow segments of the Great Western Trail, a multiple-use corridor that will stretch from Mexico to Canada.

Utah is a place of countless wonders and contrasts. For example, driving to the Golden Spike National Historic Site, where a pair of steam locomotives recall the linking of the continent by rail in 1869, you'll pass Thiokol's sprawling aerospace facility. In colorful canyon country, mountain bikers, jeepers and other backcountry touring enthusiasts navigate benchlands, canyons and washes on Cold War-era uranium prospecting trails that follow old stock trails, which in turn followed old Indian trails. Some motorists speed across the Great Basin on Interstate 80. Others drive the old Pony Express and stagecoach trail, south of the interstate. Jet-engine "cars" set world land speed records on the same salt flats once dreaded by pioneers in plodding wagon trains.

Silently but continuously, a tug of war rages between Utah's great deserts and its forested mountains and lush Alpine meadows, with the front lines often so close that you can cross from one into the other in a few miles. The Earth's crust is being ceaselessly buckled, lifted, folded and distorted by forces of incomprehensible power and violence. Yet when you look down on all that dynamic geology from the Bull Creek Pass National Back Country Byway, in the soaring Henry Mountains, the world will seem quiet and still.

In places mountains of igneous rock — among them the landmark La Sal, Abajo and Henry mountains — stand where, in their earlier molten form, they had squeezed up through faults in the thick layers of sedimentary rock. Hardened and defiant of erosive forces, today they tower above restless expanses of more acquiescent sandstone. Salt formations thousands of feet thick, the remains of a primordial sea, squirm beneath the mass of accumulated sediments, leading to the creation of Arches National Park's sandstone statuary. In northeastern Utah the state's highest mountains, the huge Uintas, extend east-west in a region where mountain ranges typically trend north-south.

Most of eastern and southern Utah occupies the Colorado Plateau, a spectacular region uplifted some 65 million years ago. Named for the river that drains it through a system of sinuous tributaries, it is famous for its smaller plateaus, richly colored canyons, imposing cliffs and monoliths formed of the sands of ancient desert dunes. You'll be enthralled by meandering gorges scoured by patient rivers like the Colorado, Green, San Juan and San Rafael. The geologic waves of the Great Basin meet the Colorado Plateau along dramatic escarpments of mountain ranges and plateaus that form Utah's high central spine. There, roads undulate along mountain ridges more than 11,000 feet above sea level. On the Kaiparowits Plateau, part of the larger Colorado Plateau Province, Smoky Mountain smolders with underground coal fires as hot as the political fight over how much of the Kaiparowits, and the rest of unspoiled Utah, should remain forever in its natural state.

While crowds fill the motels and restaurants during Moab's Easter Jeep Safari, the Mardi Gras of four-wheeling, you can still find a quiet place to focus binoculars on centuries-old ruins left silent by the mysterious disappearance of the Anasazi Indians, ancestors of modern Pueblo Indians. Or you can ponder the inscrutable messages behind images that native people scratched and painted on rock faces thousands of years ago. Today, tourists pay good money to float rivers that in 1869 imperiled the lives of explorer John Wesley Powell and his companions. In Bullion Canyon (a.k.a. Canyon of Gold), where the search for riches goes back to the days of Spanish explorers, tourists are now the ore.

Tangible evidence of Utah's unique natural and cultural past is everywhere. The ruins of Pony Express stations, the cemeteries along the old Transcontinental Railroad, trilobite fossils, petrified logs and sandstone outcrops scarred by wagon wheels bring even the most ancient history alive. Some of Brown's Park's history was written by outlaws like the infamous Wild Bunch. At Dance Hall Rock, where members of the Hole-in-the-Rock expedition held morale-building dances while others scouted a route through the wilderness, one can almost hear the music, see the dancers. If you are alone at Hole-in-the-Rock, you'll hear the commotion of wagons being lowered down the perilous crack in the 2,000-foot cliff overlooking the Colorado River where Lake Powell lies today. You'll hear echoes of poor Willie, too, if you try.

With five national parks, six national monuments, six national forests, two national recreation areas, 45 state parks, a national historic site and almost 23 million acres of publicly owned land managed by the U.S. Bureau of Land Management, Utah has an unsurpassed array of wonders. Backcountry roads, whether through high-walled sandstone canyons or along the crests of sky-scraping plateaus, offer adventurers in modern sport-utility vehicles the chance to experience Utah at its wild best.

Camping in Canyon Country

Touring backcountry byways

Traveling Utah's remarkable network of unpaved backroads is one of the most rewarding and exciting ways to see a state with truly dramatic natural and human history. But you must take precautions and use good judgment to assure a safe and memorable experience, to avoid injury to yourself and your passengers and damage to the land and your vehicle.

In case you're new to adventure motoring on backcountry roads, here are some tips that will help you safely experience the thrills of exploration and discovery.

KNOW WHERE YOU'RE GOING. The maps in this book are not intended for route finding. They are only at-a-glance maps intended to give you an idea of where the drives are. Each route description includes a map that I recommend for greater detail and route finding. The recommended maps typically include background about the area's natural and human history, and important information, such as rules and regulations, about the lands they cover. Government maps outline wilderness areas, where mechanized travel is prohibited, and identify both publicly and privately owned lands. But some are out of date. That can mean you'll find road numbers that no longer apply, campgrounds that have become picnic areas only, even roads that are now closed or whose quality is misrepresented.

When buying U.S. Forest Service maps, be sure they are the latest available. Many national forests are replacing old, outdated maps, but visitor centers and retailers sometimes still sell the old ones. Maps can be purchased at national forest and Bureau of Land Management offices, U.S. Geological Survey and Utah Geological Survey outlets and information centers. Many addresses and telephone numbers are listed in the back of this book. Outdoor equipment stores, map and travel stores, bookstores and many other retail outlets carry maps as well.

Various government agencies that manage publicly owned lands are developing a series of 24 maps for Utah, titled Interagency Recreation Travel Maps, that will be released over the next few years. As of this writing (May 1996) the initial release was due out soon. I use USGS topographic maps only occasionally, because of the expense and because many routes would require multiple maps. I also don't always need the kind of detail they provide. The BLM publishes a series of topographic maps, available from BLM offices, that depict surface and mineral management status. They are good, but they aren't really aimed at the recreation and travel market and can be difficult to read.

The Utah Travel Council (UTC) publishes five very good and inexpensive multipurpose maps that include mileages, points of interest and lots of information and background. Maps published by AAA affiliates can be good. *Indian Country*, published by AAA affiliate Automobile Club of Southern California (ACSC), is excellent for touring southern Utah. Besides its accurate depiction of backcountry roads, it is packed with information. It is sold at many retail outlets, but is free to members. Trails Illustrated, GTR Mapping and Canyon Country Publications publish maps that are especially good as well. A full appreciation of Utah cannot be attained without some understanding of the astounding geology that confronts visitors. So I highly recommend bringing a copy of Lehi F. Hintze's excellent *Geologic Highway Map of Utah*, published by the Department of Geology at Brigham Young University, in Provo.

Whichever maps you choose, study them before you leave. Learn your route before you start out. Be sure to bring the maps with you. Keep track of where you've been along the way, and be aware of what's to come.

Most of the routes in this book are designated as either Utah Scenic

Backways or Bureau of Land Management National Back Country Byways. While the BLM routes are generally well-marked, only some of the Utah Backway routes are. Never assume that signs will guide you to or along the routes. Those that have been put in place are often damaged, destroyed or removed by vandals, especially the gun-toting kind who use them as targets.

BE CAREFUL. The best advice is to avoid traveling alone. There's no security like more than one vehicle. But the reality is that when you're on vacation, or off for a day or weekend, you'll probably have little choice but to go alone. Many of Utah's unpaved backroads are fairly well-traveled, however, because they remain important ways to get from one place to another.

Backcountry travel can be done alone safely, with proper precautions, preparation and due recognition of the potential hazards. But you must recognize that there are risks, just as there are risks in hiking backcountry trails.

Many of the roads in this book are about as safe, easy and well-maintained as unpaved public roads can be. Some are rudimentary two-tracks. Others are quite popular, so you might have company. Never assume that you have the road to yourself. Many of these roads are narrow with blind curves, and sometimes people forget that there are others out there. The closest I've ever come to head-on collisions has been on remote, one-lane backcountry roads. You'll often be sharing these roads with jeepers, mountain bikers, folks on ATVs and motorcycles, even hikers. One time in the Henry Mountains I rounded a curve and suddenly came upon dozens of pack-laden Scouts hiking up the road. In such circumstances, stop and ask if there are others ahead. Sometimes people on ATVs and motorcycles will signal with their fingers how many more are behind them.

The north end of the Lockhart Basin Road *(trip 40)* has a segment that is quite challenging and can inflict some degree of damage if you're not careful and experienced. In such situations, which are few in this book, use your low-range gears and plan your route. Have someone spot you through. In some areas, like the high Colorado Plateau, the soil often has a high clay content. The road surface is dangerously slick when wet, and quickly turns to mud. The wet clay clings to tires, clogs the treads and turns them into useless donuts. Attempting to drive in those conditions is not only hazardous for you and your vehicle, it also ruins the roadbed, leaving severe ruts when it finally dries. If you get caught in a rainstorm, stop, let it pass, then wait an hour or so to let the road surface dry out some before proceeding. Don't try to rush out of the hills when the roads are muddy. You will get stuck, or worse.

It's important to remember that the condition of these roads can, and does, change. You should call the appropriate authority before setting out to be sure the route is driveable, although I must warn you that knowledgeable people are often difficult to reach. Sometimes routes are so remote that understaffed agencies rarely are able to get out there and inspect them.

Consider the time of day before you set out. Is it getting late? You might be better off delaying until morning. Don't get caught out there at night unless you've planned an overnight stay.

The best seasons for backcountry touring are usually the same as they are for hiking, backpacking and mountain biking, although air conditioning, heaters and the ability to carry supplies for more contingencies can make adverse conditions tolerable. The mountains and plateaus east of Utah's high central spine will generally be open by July, depending on weather and location. But even in late summer you might find roads still blocked by snowbanks on shaded north-facing slopes. I think early fall is the best time to explore Utah. The roads are drier, the aspens are turning, the sunlight has a brassy hue, the air is crisp and clear, and the deserts are pleasant. But do avoid the mountains in hunting season, when hunters and their vehicles are everywhere. Winter snows typically close high country routes. Desert regions, like Canyon Country and the Great Basin, which can get very hot in summer, are best visited in spring and fall, perhaps even early winter.

You must be especially careful when venturing into the deserts in summer, when extremely hot temperatures and flash floods are very real and perilous threats. Definitely avoid narrow, high-walled canyons in late summer, typically the worst time for flash floods caused by sudden downpours.

Always be prepared for sudden weather changes, and to spend a few days out there in case you get stuck or lost, or your vehicle breaks down. Carry adequate survival supplies, including water, for the number of people you have along.

Don't be tempted by excessively steep, rocky or sandy stretches. Know your vehicle. Don't overestimate what it can do. Many 4x4 owners will admit that they never got stuck so often or so badly before they bought a vehicle they thought could go anywhere. Always remember that help is a long way off. Wear your seat belt. Have children in proper safety restraints. Check the weather forecast before setting out, and watch for changes.

FOLLOW THE RULES. There are some, written and unwritten, even in places where it's likely no one will be looking. The intent behind them is simple: to keep you safe, and to preserve these places from destructive activities that scar the roads, damage the environment, deface or damage archaeological and historic sites, disturb wildlife, and interfere with other lawful activities such as livestock grazing, mining and logging. Misconduct and mistakes can result in personal injury, damage to your vehicle, areas being closed and legal penalties.

It's important to be aware of rules that apply in the areas you'll be visiting, especially if you'll be on roads across lands managed by the national park service, or which cross federally designated wilderness areas. Those areas usually are under more restrictions than lands managed by the U.S. Forest Service and Bureau of Land Management.

Here are some things to keep in mind:

• Your vehicle must be street legal to take these drives. Obey all traffic laws.

• Never drive in designated wilderness areas or wilderness study areas, which are usually marked. Mechanized travel, including on motorcycles and mountain bikes, is not allowed in wilderness areas unless a legal route for such travel has been designated. Peavine Corridor *(trip 48)* is such a road. You must always remain on established routes designated for motor vehicle use. *Never leave the established road, make a new trail, or follow in the tracks of some irresponsible person who did.*

• Do not touch, alter, collect, remove or in any other way disturb archaeological or historic artifacts and sites, in which Utah is especially rich. They are irreplaceable national treasures. Native American sites have great significance to Indian people. Show respect. Vandalization of sites, structures and artifacts, intentional and unintentional, is a serious problem, even though they are protected by federal laws. The Archaeological Resources Protection Act of 1979 offers a reward for information leading to a conviction. If you see any illegal activity, report it to the authorities. In short, leave sites and artifacts alone. Some sites, like ghost towns (e.g. Sego, *trip 24*) or other historic ruins, may be on private land. View them from the road. Never touch rock art, or create your own. Never enter or even walk close to an ancient rock structure unless it is designated for public tours. If you find an artifact while exploring a side canyon in, say, Canyonlands National Park, don't disturb it. But do report it to a ranger. Moving it might damage it. Also, its location and position can provide important information for archaeologists. Do not use archaeological or historic sites for picnics or camping. The more time people spend at these sites, the greater the likelihood of damage. Also, collecting or removing any objects — rocks, fossils, petrified wood, plants, etc. — from national parks and monuments is not allowed. Whether land is publicly or privately owned, ask before you act.

• In the deserts you'll see a fragile light- or dark-colored crust, called cryptobiotic crust, covering the ground. It appears to be a thin mineral crust, but it is actually a living, self-sustaining biological unit. Its name, in fact, means "hidden life." It is essential to stabilizing desert soils, and helps to create and maintain suitable conditions for desert plants and healthy ecosystems. Once damaged or destroyed it takes many decades to recover. Yet people often walk, bike or drive on it thoughtlessly, a high crime in this country. Instead, travel only on exposed rock (called slickrock in canyon country), in washes and on designated trails and roads.

• Obey regulatory and private property signs.

• Leave someone with a copy of your map showing the routes you plan to take. Let the person know when you'll return, and whom to call if you don't. Be sure to check in with that person when you return. Invite a friend to come along in his or her vehicle if you can.

• If you camp, the general rule is to leave no trace that you've been there. Camp only in established campsites, whether developed or primitive. Camp on more resilient mineralized soil, rather than soft grassy areas, at least 200 feet from the banks of streams, ponds and lakes to avoid damage and pollution. In desert areas, particularly Utah's regions of exposed sandstone, wood fires are not recommended. In national parks they may even be illegal; be sure to check. If you want to have a campfire where they are legal, bring your own wood. Use a fire pan to avoid blackening the ground.

• Increasing visitation to Utah's spectacular, remote and undeveloped desert lands has meant more people answering the call of nature where nature is unable to deal with solid human waste. Feces and toilet paper, which don't easily decompose in such conditions, are a critical issue. In some places the amount of human feces (urine alone doesn't pose the same kind of problems) being deposited has become a real problem. If, for example, you visit Lockhart Canyon, a spur off the Lockhart Basin Road (*trip 40*), you'll see many feeble and misguided attempts to let the elements do what they cannot. In such remote areas where there are no facilities you must use a portable, washable toilet. You can find them at RV supply and department stores. They needn't be very expensive, or even elaborate. Some people just use old metal ammunition boxes, lined with plastic. Portable toilets have become essential to preserving the arid backcountry. But if you must bury your waste, dig a hole 6-8 inches deep (preferably beneath a pinyon pine or juniper tree where fragile cryptobiotic crust is not present) at least 300 feet from any water source, sandy wash or trail. Carry out toilet paper in a sealed container; do not burn it.

• Leave gates as you find them. Don't disturb wildlife or livestock.

• Take out only what you bring in. Clean up after yourself and those who came before you. Haul out your trash.

• Be extremely careful around old mining operations. They're very dangerous, especially for children. View them from a distance. Never enter shafts, tunnels or holes.

• Avoid parking on grass; hot exhaust systems can ignite fires. Avoid steep hillsides, stream banks and meadows.

• If you get stuck or lost, stay with your vehicle unless you're certain that help is nearby. Your vehicle will be easier to find than you will be. It will provide shelter, too.

• Remember that the miners, loggers and settlers who carved roads through the mountains, forests and deserts of Utah over the last century didn't have you and your safety in mind. Spurs from the main roads can be very rough. If so, ask yourself if it's worth the risk to you, your passengers and your vehicle. It probably isn't.

If you're particularly interested in preserving the privilege of exploring backcountry byways, you might join Tread Lightly!, Inc., an organization founded to promote environmentally responsible use of off–highway vehicles. It is based in Ogden, Utah. Call 1-800-966-9900.

BE PREPARED. Here's a basic checklist of some things to bring.

❑ Food and drinks. Remember that stores will be far away, and deserts are hot and dry in summer. Many backcountry campgrounds don't have potable water, or any water at all. If you plan to camp, bring plenty for drinking, cooking and washing.
❑ A full fuel tank; carry several gallons of extra fuel in a full, well–sealed container.
❑ A good first aid kit, with plenty of ointment and bandages for the inevitable scraped knees and elbows.
❑ Very good tires, a good spare and jack, tire sealant, air pump, pressure gauge, and a small board to support the jack on dirt. I've gotten multiple flats in a single day, even on some of Utah's best graded dirt roads.
❑ Supplies, like sleeping bags and warm clothing, for spending the night in case you must.
❑ Basic tools, including jumper cables, duct tape, electrical tape, baling wire, spare fuses, multipurpose knife, high-strength tow strap, fire extinguisher, shovel and a plastic sheet to put on the ground. An assortment of screws, washers, nuts, hose clamps and such could come in handy, too.
❑ Portable toilet
❑ Maps, compass
❑ Extra eyeglasses and keys
❑ Camera (still or video), film or video tape, tripod, binoculars
❑ Trash bags
❑ Flashlight or head lamp, extra batteries
❑ Matches and firewood
❑ Roadside emergency reflectors, flares, windshield scraper
❑ Reflective space blanket, useful in treating shock and highly visible to searching aircraft
❑ Altimeter, just for fun
❑ Watch
❑ Hats and clothing suitable for adverse weather
❑ Sunscreen and insect repellent
❑ Toilet paper, paper towels, wet wipes

I keep much of this stuff ready to go in a large plastic storage container. Sometimes I bring my mountain bike as a backup vehicle in case I get into a bind. I also use it to reach places that might damage my vehicle. Think about getting a CB radio, even though their transmitting range is limited. These days a cellular telephone can be handy, too, depending on where you're going.

I also have some tips on what to wear:

Forget shorts. Why would anyone expose his or her legs to brush, rocks, bugs, drying air and burning sun? Long pants and a shirt with breast pockets and sleeves you can roll up or down as needed are best. I also recommend high-topped leather boots with lug soles. If you're like me, you're going to do a lot of scrambling around to get that perfect camera angle. Ankle-high boots let debris in.

LEARN THE NECESSARY SKILLS. There are some driving techniques that can help you get where you're going and back again safely. They can also help you avoid damaging the roads.

Learn how to work your four-wheel-drive system before setting out. Think ahead as you drive; engage 4wd before you actually need it. When in doubt, scout ahead. Walk uncertain stretches of trail before you drive them. If the roadbed is rough, lower your tire pressure to 18-20 psi. The softer tires will absorb more of the punishment. In sand, try 15 psi. That'll help them spread out and float on the surface instead of sinking in. The problem is that if a place to air them back up again is far off, you'll need either a hand pump or a small electric air compressor, like those available at department stores, to get your tires back up to proper inflation as soon as possible when you return to pavement.

On terrain with large rocks, lowered pressure will give the tires better grip by letting them wrap around more of the rocks' surface. On especially rough and rocky stretches place your tires on a line of high spots, thus keeping your undercarriage as high as possible above obstacles. When going through rocks or badly rutted stretches, keep your hands loose on the steering wheel, at 10 and 2 o'clock. Keep your thumbs on top of the wheel. Otherwise, if a front tire hits a rock or rut, the steering wheel could be jerked in an unexpected direction, possibly injuring a thumb with a steering wheel spoke.

Try not to spin your tires, which digs up the soil and could get you stuck.

In difficult situations low-range gears will provide both greater control and the high engine revs needed at slow speeds to keep from stalling. I use mine a lot. Use them to climb or descend steep hills and to inch carefully through tight spots. Avoid traversing steep hillsides if you can. Even if the road goes that way, use good judgment. Stop if you're not confident it's safe. Don't try to turn around on a steep hillside; back out. When climbing a steep hill, or going through mud, snow or sand, don't stop midway. Momentum can be everything; keep moving. If you stall going up a hill and must get out of the vehicle, put it in low-range first gear or reverse, set the parking brake and solidly block the wheels. When you try to get going again, play the parking brake against the clutch (if you have one) so you don't roll backwards. (This is one of many situations that demonstrate the superiority, in my view, of automatic transmissions for backcountry travel.)

If you must back down a steep hill, use low-range reverse for greater control. Don't clutch. Also use low range to ease yourself down loose terrain. If your engine bogs down often in high range, switch to low range. Remember that vehicles driving uphill have the right of way, if practical, because it's usually easier and safer for the vehicle going downhill to back up the hill.

Have someone guide you through difficult spots. If the road has deep ruts, straddle them, letting them pass beneath the vehicle while the wheels ride high on the sides. Check your vehicle's clearance before driving over obstacles. Cross obstacles at an angle, one wheel at a time. Don't let anything hit the big round parts, called "pumpkins," of your front and rear axles. Cracking or punching a hole in one will let oil drain out and expose the gears to dust and dirt. Run a tire over an obstacle if it's not too large, rather than letting it pass beneath the drivetrain.

Avoid crossing streams, if you can, so you don't stir up sediment. If you must cross a stream, do so only at an established crossing. Inspect streams before crossing. Use a stick for checking the depth, comparing the depth to your vehicle. It's best to ford slowly to reduce the amount of sediment your tires stir up. It also will make less of a wake, thus minimizing erosion of the streambanks. Do not attempt to cross a road or streambed during a flash flood. Be aware of where your engine's air intake is. It may not be high enough to ford deep water. If it isn't, it'll suck water into the engine. Then you'll have very serious problems.

If you get stuck, calmly analyze the situation. With thought and work, you'll probably get out. If a tire is spinning, try this: Jack up the vehicle and back-fill the space beneath it, building a base high enough to help you get a rolling start. If you're in sand, dampen it with water to firm it up. Lower the vehicle and remove the jack. If you get high-centered, meaning your undercarriage is lodged on something high and your tires have daylight between them and the ground, take out your jack and the little board you brought to set it on. Carefully jack up the vehicle, little by little, placing rocks, dirt and other materials under each suspended tire to build a higher base for it to rest on. You can also dig out the undercarriage if it's safe to do so.

If you reach a point where there are several routes to choose from and none has a sign, follow what appears to be the most heavily used route.

MAINTENANCE & ACCESSORIES. Today's sport-utility vehicles are built to take families places that sedans, vans and station wagons either cannot go, or shouldn't. Despite their comforts, they are rugged transport. Equipped with four-wheel drive, protective steel skid plates, high ground clearance and all-terrain tires, they can go from the showroom straight into the hills without modifications. They are also far more reliable and comfortable than their predecessors of, say, 15 or 20 years ago. Reliability, durability, capability and comfort are paramount.

My family's Toyota 4Runner has a 5-speed manual transmission. The Toyota Land Cruiser I used to research this book had an automatic. I prefer the latter for driving the outback. Manuals are more responsive and give better fuel mileage. But in many off-highway situations, especially when slowly crawling uphill among large rocks, automatic transmissions work best. Unlike manuals, they don't require three legs to keep the accelerator, brake pedal and clutch going simultaneously while you're trying to pick the right gear and keep from stalling or rolling up or down a hill out of control.

A glance at any four-wheel-drive magazine makes it obvious that there is a huge accessories market. Are those add-ons necessary? It depends on how much, and what type, of adventure motoring you plan to do. The routes in this book don't require vehicle modifications. However, you can start out thinking you're just going to do an easy cruise only to discover that road conditions have deteriorated and greater capability is warranted.

Most of the routes in this book are easy in good weather and won't require the use of four-wheel drive. But some do have challenging moments. Others are long and, to varying degrees, have an element of unpredictability. I strongly recommend auxiliary headlights, because the sun will go down at times before you return to civilization. If you camp, I recommend a roof-top clamshell container. Open racks will hold more, but your gear will be exposed to dust, rain, bugs and everything else airborne. I've had no need for oversize tires and lift kits. But the best all-terrain tires are the wisest investment you can make. All-season highway tires are inadequate. Heavy-duty shock absorbers are a good idea. But brush guards seem silly to me, except as mounts for auxiliary lights. Locking differentials, a.k.a. lockers, greatly improve traction by equalizing power to driving wheels and eliminating the differential's tendency to transfer power to the wheel with the least traction. (One wheel is spinning while the other is dead still. Sound familiar?) I've equipped my 4Runner with a locker activated by compressed air, not because I want to challenge and defeat whatever nature puts in my way, but because I'm usually exploring alone or with my wife and children. I cannot afford to get stuck. Lockers work. The best ones are factory-installed options. I don't have a winch, but there have been times when I wished I did.

Backcountry roads can give even the toughest SUV quite a workout. So you've got to give yours more attention than you might be accustomed to giving a car.

Start with your owner's manual. (It's in the glove compartment, right?) You might see two maintenance categories intended for two basic driving conditions: severe, and everything else.

Since you bought this book, you probably fall into the severe category, so do more maintenance. For example, changing oil is a remarkably cheap and effective way to prolong engine life. It is not the place to skimp. Do it no later than every 3,000 miles, sooner if you drive particularly dusty roads. Instead of getting a lube job at 15,000 miles, get one no later than every 7,500 miles, or immediately after returning from a dusty drive or after deep water crossings. Don't neglect gearbox oils, wheel bearing grease, brake and power steering fluids and coolant. Follow your owner's manual.

Inspect your air filter at least every 3,000 miles. It's cheap and easy to clean or replace.

Check the tires often. No part of your SUV will take a greater beating than they will. Inspect them, including your spare, closely before, during and after your drive. If you pass through an old mining area, you're likely to get a nail in one or more tires. Depending on its location and how deflated the tire has become, it might be best to leave the nail in. Pulling it out will prevent it from tearing up the tire's insides, but it also will let the remaining air out. Get it repaired as soon as possible. Never drive without a serviceable spare.

When you get back to town, head for the car wash. Don't bring home the mud, dirt and debris that has collected underneath. The transportation of spores, insects and other organisms to distant geographic regions and ecosystems via dirty off-highway vehicles raises serious concerns. Thoroughly clean the vehicle. Put extra effort into the undercarriage, particularly the wheel wells.

READ. You'll enjoy your Utah adventures much more if you know something about the geology, flora, fauna and history. Bookstores, visitor centers and other places have many fine titles to choose from. This book is not intended to be an exhaustive guide to exploring Utah. The "References & recommended reading" section in the back lists some good books that have helped me understand, explore and enjoy Utah.

HAVE FUN! You can easily justify the expense of a sport-utility vehicle, especially in a state with so many spectacular unpaved backroads. And as you travel tell me what you've found, whether it's mistakes in the book or additional trips and tips you'd like to see added in future editions. Write to me in care of the Post Company, P.O. Box 1800, Idaho Falls, ID, 83403.

Salt Creek Canyon, Canyonlands National Park

Making it fun for all

Trying to keep kids, especially teenagers, happy on car trips is always tough. But there are some things you can do to make touring the backcountry fun and interesting for them, too.

Probably the best advice I can give is this: Don't just drive. Stop, and stop often. Watch for wildlife. (I've seen bears in the road.) In Canyon Country, scanning cliffs for ancient rock art and structures can be a rewarding game. Just remember the rules about preserving these national treasures: never touch rock art, enter or in any way disturb ancient structures.

Recreational rock collecting with hand tools is permitted on lands managed by the U.S. Bureau of Land Management, but not on lands managed by the National Park Service. Inquire with the appropriate agency before you dig. Don't forget to bring a magnifying glass.

If Utah is about anything, it's about geology and Western history. Bring some good reference books along so you can enjoy Utah's human and geologic story. I think it's especially interesting to know the story behind place names. Get some good books on identifying wildflowers, birds, insects, vegetation and animals in the region as well. They're all available at local bookstores and visitor centers.

Make a photocopy of the area on the map where you'll be going. Get each child an inexpensive compass. Let them help you navigate and identify peaks, creeks, historic sites and other landmarks. Let each child pack his or her favorite books and toys, but don't cram the car with stuff. And don't forget the sunscreen.

Bring at least one personal cassette player. Before leaving, go to your local public library and check out some children's cassette tapes. Better yet, buy some. You'll make good use of them for years to come.

Books on tape, something I listen to myself on long highway drives, are great diversions for children, too. Many video rental stores carry them.

Other items that have bought us quiet and good humor in the back seat are an inexpensive point-and-shoot camera the kids can use, and inexpensive binoculars. My son, Land, likes to have his own notebook and pencil so he can pretend he's taking notes about our journeys just like dad.

If you have a responsible, licensed teenage driver on board, let him or her drive now and then. The sooner a teen learns backcountry driving skills, the longer he or she will remain an eager participant. Someday you may need an experienced co-pilot.

Of course, you must bring snacks, preferably the nutritious, non-sticky kind, and refreshing drinks. There will be plenty of bumps on your adventures, so be sure cups have secure tops that you can poke straws through. Plastic garbage bags, paper towels, changes of clothing, wet wipes and pillows for the sleepy are good to have along, too.

Safety is always a concern. Hazards exist. In many places you'll come across old mine sites. Don't let children anywhere near them. For that matter, adults should stay clear of them, too. If you want a closer look, use your binoculars. Never attempt to get close to wildlife, either.

Whether you travel with children or not, make the drive part of a day that draws on the huge range of experiences Utah has to offer. Plan a picnic. See the sights. Hike to a hilltop. Ride your mountain bikes. And do something civilized when the drive is over: Go out to dinner.

Author's favorites

Utah has so many world-class adventure roads, each with its unique appeal, that deciding which are my favorites was enormously frustrating. I didn't want to list "the best," because each of us has our own preferences, likes and dislikes. Still, I thought you might like to know which of the 60 routes I've described are, to me, among the most exciting and rewarding.

White Rim Road *(trip 38)*: This is my all-time favorite, in part because Canyonlands National Park and the surrounding area is where my family and I got started in backcountry touring. In my opinion, the White Rim Road's remoteness, the vast scale of its exotic red-rock scenery and the contrast between the powerful geology and the fragile ecology make it one of the most remarkable backcountry roads anywhere.

Transcontinental Railroad *(trip 1)*: Driving this National Back Country Byway is literally experiencing a mythical moment in American history. The race to reach Promontory Summit and the drama of hammering in the "golden spike" there in 1869 is part of the American legend. Now you can drive the actual bed of this historic route across a remote stretch of the Great Basin, passing abandoned town sites, lonely cemeteries and crumbling trestles along the way.

Pony Express Trail *(trip 21)*: This long and remote route also lets the adventuresome motorist relive a legendary moment in American history. You'll really get to know the awesome expanse of the Great Basin as you follow the trail used by Pony Express riders and stagecoaches. Ruins of Pony Express and stage stations help bring it all back to life.

Skyline Drives *(trips 5, 15 & 20)*: The routes I call Skyline Drives I, II & III are utterly magnificent. The high-elevation scenery is unsurpassed. I also especially like the variety they offer, from easy graded two-lane dirt to narrow mountainside ledges. In addition to top-of-the-world views, Skyline Drive I is especially appealing because of its convenient proximity to Salt Lake City and other Wasatch Front population centers.

Inspiration Point *(trip 4)*: This is an ideal road for sport-utility vehicles, with outstanding vistas. It culminates high in the dramatic Wasatch Range at a vista point with a truly breathtaking view. This route, too, is relatively close to Wasatch Front cities and towns.

THE DRIVES

Inspiration Point

On the way to Cummings Parkway

Transcontinental Railroad

LOCATION: Goes west from Golden Spike National Historic Site at Promontory Summit west of Brigham City, along the northern shore of the Great Salt Lake to Lucin.

HIGHLIGHTS: Experience the Great Basin by driving on the actual bed of the historic transcontinental railroad. Informational signs explain the sights. Old town sites, cemeteries, etc., all protected by state and federal laws. (Don't disturb anything.) At Golden Spike two replica steam locomotives operate daily May 1 through the first weekend of October. "Last spike" reenactments are held each May 10 (free).

DIFFICULTY: Easy. The rail bed is obvious throughout the drive. Watch out for eroded spots. Spikes can cause flats. Avoid washed-out sections, unsafe trestles and culverts. No services or water. Muddy when wet. Hot summers, cold winters. Much of the actual rail bed is paralleled by well-maintained dirt and gravel roads.

TIME & DISTANCE: 8 hours; 90 miles.

GETTING THERE: Take exit 368 from I-15 at Brigham City. Take U-83 northwest for 18.7 miles; turn west toward Golden Spike, another 8 miles. I start west of the visitor center, where the gravel road begins. Set your odometer at 0.

THE DRIVE: From Promontory Summit, where the eastbound Central Pacific RR met the westbound Union Pacific on May 10, 1869, parallel the rail bed for 7.5 miles through high desert where the pale vistas have changed little, if at all, for millennia. Imagine gazing from the window of a sooty rail car as it rolled across the raw expanse. Begin driving on the rail bed beyond the BLM's National Back Country Byway sign. Signs explain how busy the Promontory Branch was until 1904, when it was bypassed by the shorter, more economical Lucin Cutoff across the lake. As traffic on the Old Line dwindled, towns at Kelton (1869-1942) and Terrace (1869-1910) died out. In 1942 the rails were moved to military depots for service in WWII. Many relics remain: collapsed trestles, graves, ties, spikes. Keep right at the Y at 16.6, leaving the rail bed where it's washed out. Go left at the next two Ts. At a bend 0.4 miles beyond the second T, take the two-track to the left to return to the rail bed. 3 miles from Kelton go left toward (but not to) the Hogup Mountains. In 3.3 miles go right (west) on a two-track toward Terrace and Lucin (no services).

REST STOPS: Golden Spike. Primitive camping on BLM land.

GETTING HOME: From Lucin it's almost 50 dirt and gravel miles south to I-80 at Wendover; or 5 miles north to Utah Highway 30, which you can take to I-80 or I-84.

MAPS: USGS *Brigham City*. UTC's Northern Utah.

INFORMATION: BLM, Salt Lake Field Office, 977-4300; Golden Spike National Historic Site, 471-2209.

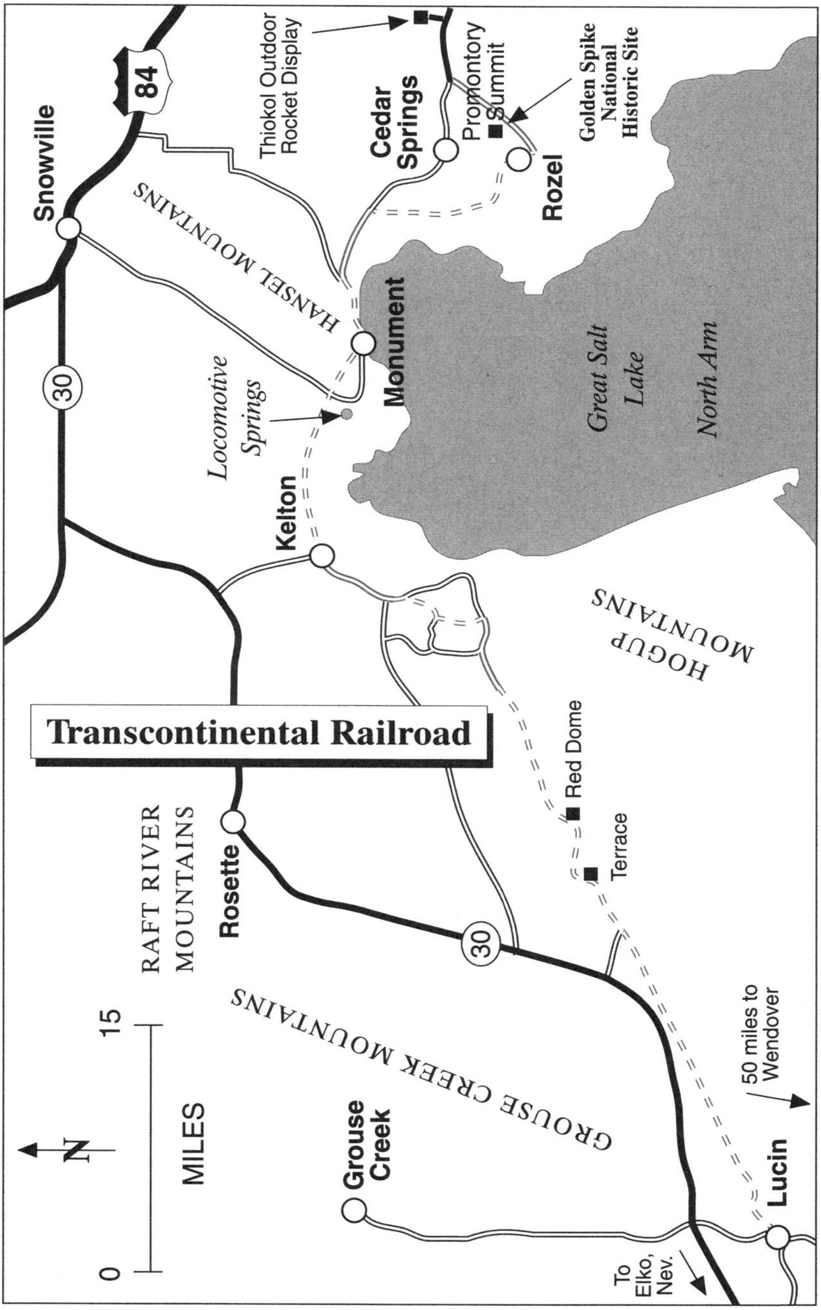

Transcontinental Railroad
Snowville
84
30
Thiokol Outdoor Rocket Display
Cedar Springs
Promontory Summit
Rozel
Golden Spike National Historic Site
HANSEL MOUNTAINS
Monument
Locomotive Springs
Great Salt Lake
North Arm
Kelton
HOGUP MOUNTAINS
Red Dome
Terrace
Rosette
RAFT RIVER MOUNTAINS
GROUSE CREEK MOUNTAINS
30
50 miles to Wendover
Lucin
Grouse Creek
To Elko, Nev.
N
MILES
0
15

Silver Island Mountains Loop

LOCATION: Northeast of Wendover; just north of the Bonneville Salt Flats near the Nevada border.

HIGHLIGHTS: This National Back Country Byway loops around the base of a historic range with jagged volcanic peaks that loom above the Great Salt Lake Desert. Convenient side trip off I-80. Beautiful in the golden light of late afternoon.

DIFFICULTY: Easy on a dirt and gravel road.

TIME & DISTANCE: 2.5 hours or more, depending on whether you explore side routes; 54 miles.

GETTING THERE: Take the Bonneville Speedway exit from I-80 about 2.7 miles east of Wendover. Follow the signs for the speedway. Where the paved road angles right toward the speedway, go left onto unpaved Leppy Pass Road. There may be a sign for the Silver Island Mountains. Soon you'll see the route, a good dirt and gravel road, branch off to the right. (This also is the turnoff for the local dump.) Set your odometer at 0 here.

THE DRIVE: Silver mining gave this range its name. Salt Flats racers loaned their names to the major peaks. The range was once the bottom of an ancient sea that was eventually lifted high above sea level. Volcanic activity later covered much of the limestone with lava flows such as those to your left, around Leppy Pass and Volcano Peak. The mountains still bear the mark of ancient Lake Bonneville's shoreline. In the 19th century, mountain men, explorers and wagon trains crossed these mountains. Among them was the ill-fated 1846 Donner-Reed Party, which crossed the pass that bears the party's name at the northern end of the route. You'll follow a graded road northeast past jumbled mountains at the edge of the vast Salt Flats. At mile 11 you'll pass the left turn to Silver Island Pass. By mile 25 you're angling west. As you climb up Donner-Reed Pass you'll see the Pilot Range to the west, across a dry lakebed. Pilot Peak was a beacon for pioneer travelers crossing the desert. At 33.4 you'll see a signpost marking the Hastings Cutoff, a pioneer route west. At mile 55 rejoin Leppy Pass Road, then go left toward I-80 and Wendover.

REST STOPS: Lots of primitive campsites.

GETTING HOME: I-80 to Salt Lake City (120 miles).

MAP: Recreational Map of Utah.

INFORMATION: Bureau of Land Management, Salt Lake Field Office, has a flyer with a map, 977-4300.

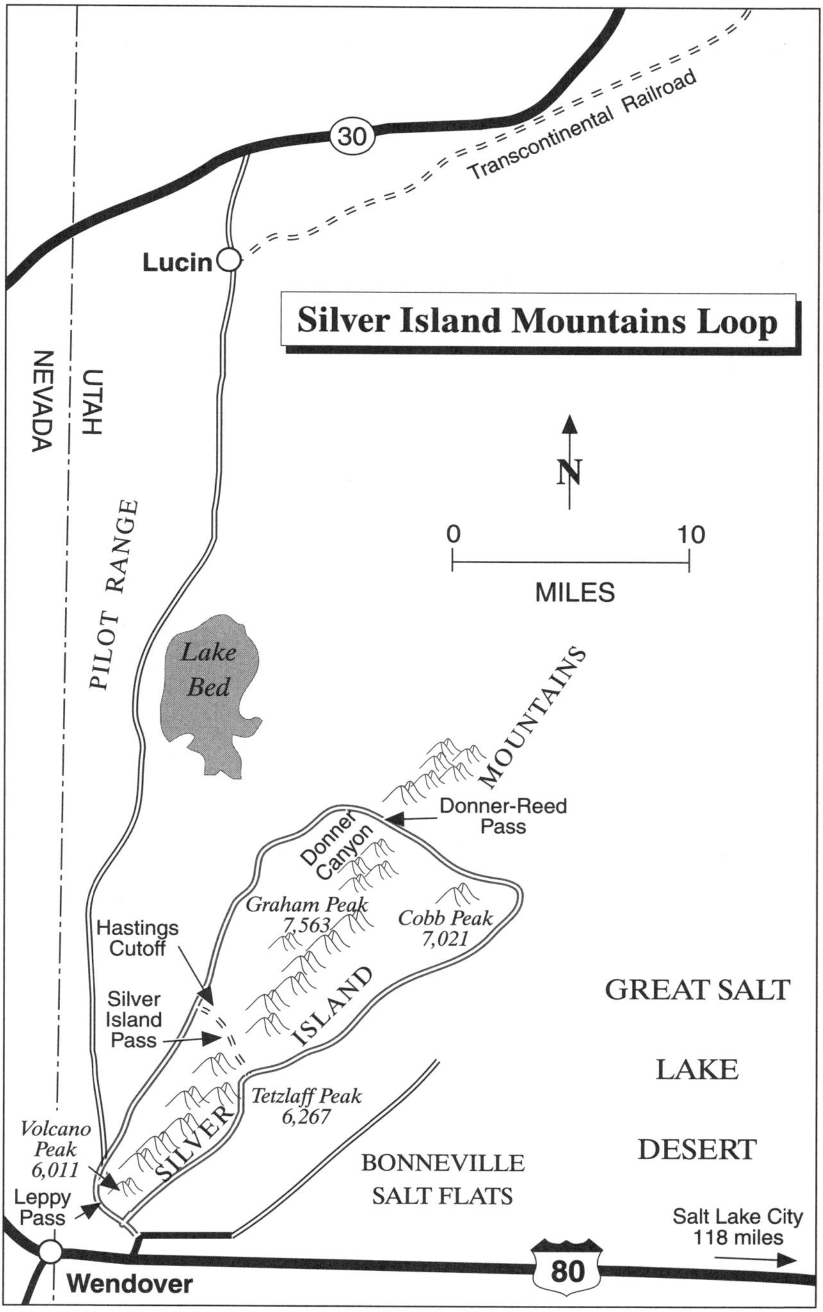
Silver Island Mountains Loop
30
Transcontinental Railroad
Lucin
NEVADA
UTAH
N
0
10
MILES
PILOT RANGE
Lake Bed
MOUNTAINS
Donner-Reed Pass
Donner Canyon
Graham Peak 7,563
Cobb Peak 7,021
Hastings Cutoff
Silver Island Pass
ISLAND
GREAT SALT
LAKE
DESERT
Tetzlaff Peak 6,267
SILVER
Volcano Peak 6,011
Leppy Pass
BONNEVILLE SALT FLATS
Salt Lake City 118 miles
Wendover
80

TRIP 3

Hardware Ranch Road

LOCATION: Wasatch Range southwest of Bear Lake.

HIGHLIGHTS: Fascinating canyons; pastoral valleys; rolling hills; aspens & pines; wildlife. Ends at Bear Lake Summit. Returning to Logan on U.S. 89 through Logan Canyon makes a great loop.

DIFFICULTY: Easy to moderate. At least one stream crossing, several more during spring runoff. Very slick and possibly impassable when it rains. Closed in winter from Hardware Ranch north to the sinks area.

TIME & DISTANCE: 2.5 hours; 41 miles.

GETTING THERE: From Hyrum, take paved U-101 between the steep walls and cliffs of Blacksmith Fork Canyon 15.5 miles to Hardware Ranch, where the asphalt ends. Watch for a Utah Scenic Backway sign.

THE DRIVE: Hardware Ranch, once owned by Brigham City hardware dealer Alonzo Snow, is now a largely state-owned wildlife management area where elk feed in winter. At Hardware Ranch the road, No. 054 (a.k.a. Bear Lake Rd.), turns to hard-packed dirt, rocky and rutted in places as you turn north through rolling hills of grass, sagebrush, pinyon and junipers. About 6.8 miles beyond the pavement, shortly before reaching a slope of loose rock at a bend in the road, turn left onto road 105. Follow this narrow, winding road, Danish Dugway, down a canyon. After 1.2 miles, cross Saddle Creek and veer right (north). (The trail to the left, along Left Hand Fork, is a rough, unmaintained jeep trail.) If the creek seems too high and fast, you can return to 054 and go through Strawberry Valley for 4.1 miles, turning left at a Y toward Saddle Creek Spring, where you'll reach road 105 after 2.3 miles. If you cross the creek, follow Saddle Creek up a canyon lined with rock spires. Continue north at the intersection you'll reach after about 3.5 miles, passing through Hell's Hollow and Log Cabin Hollow, and groves of pines and large aspens. Not far from U.S. 89 you'll pass an open area of sinks caused by water seepage and erosion.

REST STOPS: Local campgrounds; check the map. Limber Pine Nature Trail a quarter-mile east of the end at U.S. 89.

GETTING HOME: U.S. 89 southwest through scenic Logan Canyon to Logan.

MAP: Wasatch-Cache National Forest, Ogden & Logan Ranger Districts (1994).

INFORMATION: Logan Ranger District, 755-3620.

Hardware Ranch Road

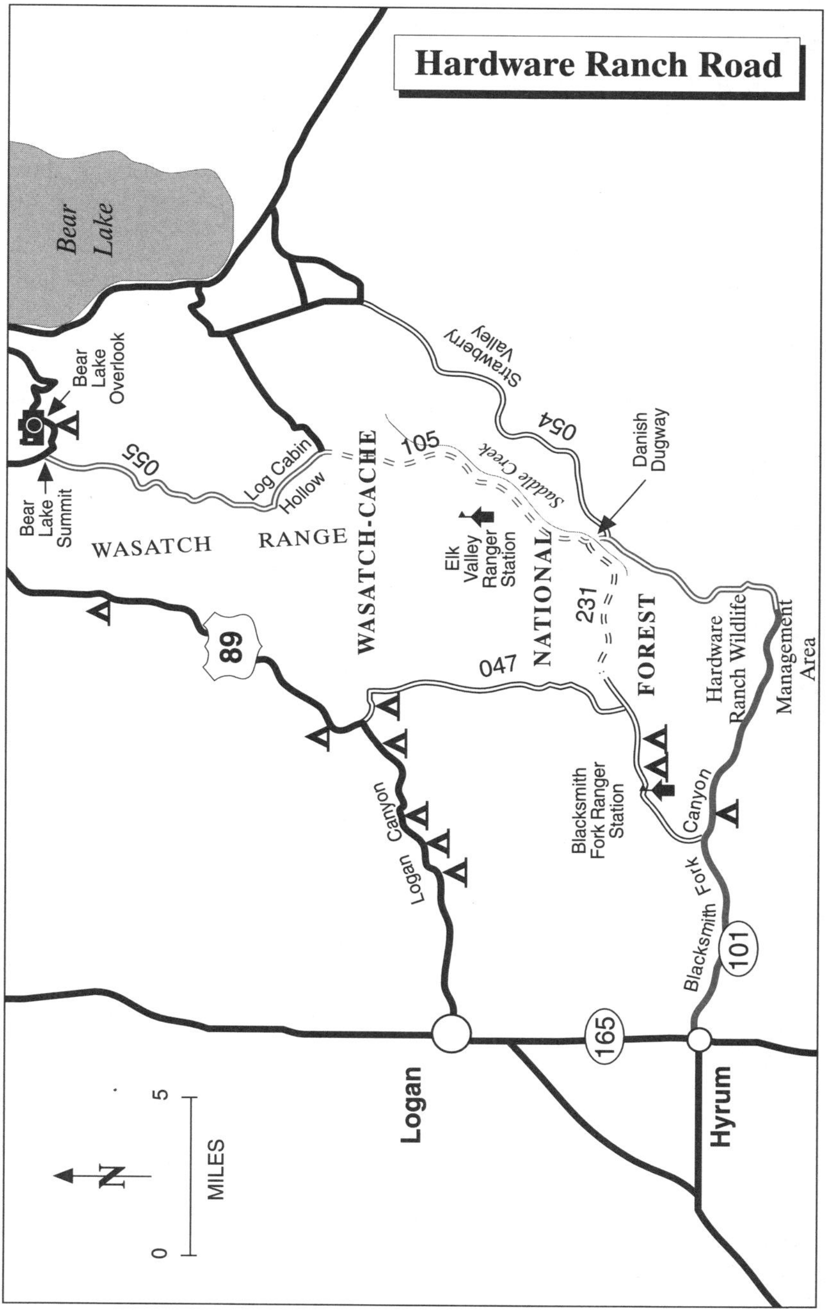

TRIP
4

Inspiration Point

LOCATION: Wasatch Range east of I-15, between Ogden and Brigham City. Wasatch-Cache National Forest.

HIGHLIGHTS: As you climb more than 4,000 feet, you'll enjoy superb high-elevation scenery, from shady forests to the spine of the Wasatch Front, the flats of the Salt Lake Valley and the expanse of the Great Basin Desert.

DIFFICULTY: Easy-moderate. Closed by snow in winter.

TIME & DISTANCE: 5 hours; 30 miles with spurs.

GETTING THERE: In Mantua, about 4 miles east of Brigham City on U.S. 89/91, zero your odometer and follow Main Street south through town. Keep left at the Y at a small city park. Keep right at the Mormon church.

THE DRIVE: The two-lane dirt and gravel road will soon narrow to a single lane that is quite rocky and rutted. The road, 084, climbs through shady forest, providing fine views of valleys east of the Wasatch Range. About 7.3 miles from Mantua you'll reach a saddle. The road will dip down the other side, becoming rougher. Keep left; the right fork goes a short distance down some moguls to a pond. Eventually you'll reach a pass at 9,300 feet elevation, where there's a sign for Willard Basin, up ahead. Uncontrolled fires and abuse of the land denuded this basin earlier this century, causing destructive floods. Environmental restoration work in the 1930s has stabilized it and restored its beauty. (Note the terracing on the slopes.) The road angles left of the sign; you'll see spurs that go short distances to the north and south that are worth exploring. The main road loops around Willard Basin, passing a small waterless campground at the site of a Depression-era Civilian Conservation Corps camp. Scan the slopes around you for bighorn sheep, which have even been seen at the campground. In a couple of miles you'll climb to 9,400 ft. at Inspiration Point, just below the mountain named, like the town below, for Richard Willard, a counselor to Mormon leader Brigham Young. Here is one of Utah's most spectacular, top-of-the-world views, from the forested Wasatch Range across the pale Great Basin Desert to the west.

REST STOPS: Willard Basin; park & playground at the city building in Mantua; small park at the Y on South Main.

GETTING HOME: Return to Mantua. I-15 north or south; U.S. 89/91 to Logan.

MAP: Wasatch-Cache National Forest, Ogden & Logan districts.

INFORMATION: Ogden Ranger District, Union Station Information Center, 625-5306.

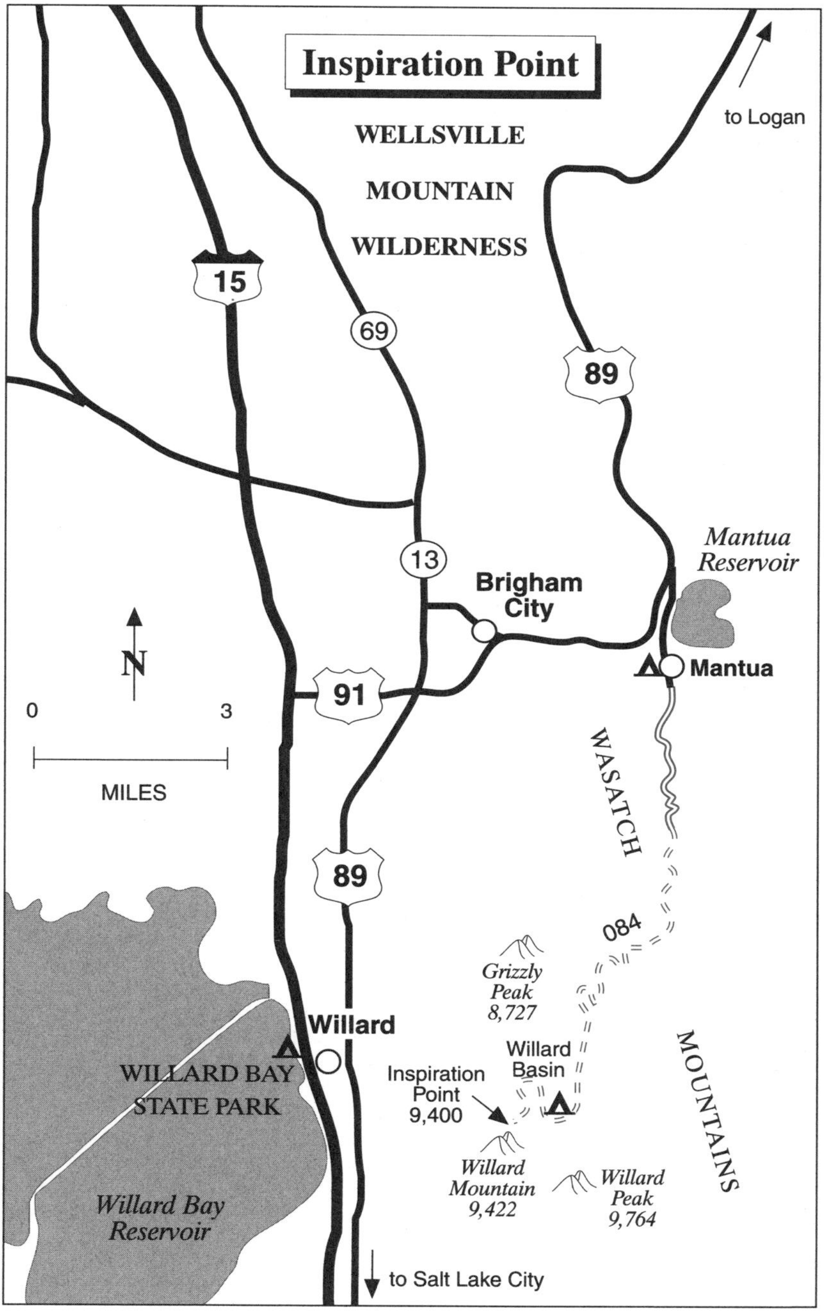

Inspiration Point
to Logan
WELLSVILLE
MOUNTAIN
WILDERNESS
15
69
89
13
Brigham City
Mantua Reservoir
Mantua
N
0
3
MILES
91
WASATCH
89
084
Grizzly Peak 8,727
Willard
Willard Basin
WILLARD BAY STATE PARK
Inspiration Point 9,400
MOUNTAINS
Willard Mountain 9,422
Willard Peak 9,764
Willard Bay Reservoir
to Salt Lake City

TRIP
5

Skyline Drive I

LOCATION: East of I-15 on the crest of the Wasatch Range, between Bountiful and Farmington.

HIGHLIGHTS: Awesome vistas from atop the abrupt escarpment of the Wasatch Front across the seemingly lifeless Great Salt Lake Desert and Great Basin Desert. A magnificent and popular drive close to major urban centers.

DIFFICULTY: Easy. A good, narrow and serpentine dirt and gravel road. Many blind curves. Some narrow sections. Closed in winter. It's usually open July 1 to sometime in October, depending on weather.

TIME & DISTANCE: 2-3 hours depending on how much time you spend enjoying the views; 23 miles.

GETTING THERE: You can take this north-south route starting at either Bountiful and going north, or at Farmington and going south. (Both are off I-15.) I start at Bountiful. Follow 400 North (Utah 106) toward the large B on the mountainside east of Bountiful. Turn left (north) onto 1300 East at a stop sign. Pass below the B, go through a subdivision and angle right. The pavement ends at a dirt parking area on a hillside north of Bountiful's Mormon Church temple. Skyline Drive angles sharply to the left (north). There may be a sign for the campgrounds along the way. There may also be a Utah Scenic Backway sign, and a sign for Old Ward Canyon Road. Set your odometer to 0. From Farmington, go east on State Street, then left (north) on 100 East to Farmington Canyon.

THE DRIVE: The views to the west of the Great Basin's pale desert flats and waves of mountain ranges are absolutely spectacular. At mile 3.4 you'll reach Ward Canyon Overlook, the first of a number of scenic pullouts. At about mile 7.2 you'll see a parking area on the right, where the Sessions Mountains Road (805) angles south along the eastern slope, providing excellent views of valleys and ranges to the east. In another 3.5 miles you'll see Bountiful Peak Overlook, with an inspiring view of the Great Basin and Wasatch Range from almost 9,000 feet. You'll descend from here. At mile 14.6, at a T, the road to the right (600) is closed. (It goes to an electronic site atop Francis Peak.) The route winds down steep-walled Farmington Canyon past road cuts exposing the Farmington Canyon Complex, a Precambrian-era formation at least 2 billion years old. The road is paved by about mile 21.3. Go south to State Street in charming Farmington.

REST STOPS: Pullouts and vista points along the way, as well as campgrounds at the north end. Refer to the forest map.

GETTING HOME: I-15 north or south.

MAP: Wasatch-Cache National Forest, Salt Lake Ranger District (1994 edition).

INFORMATION: Salt Lake District, 943-1794.

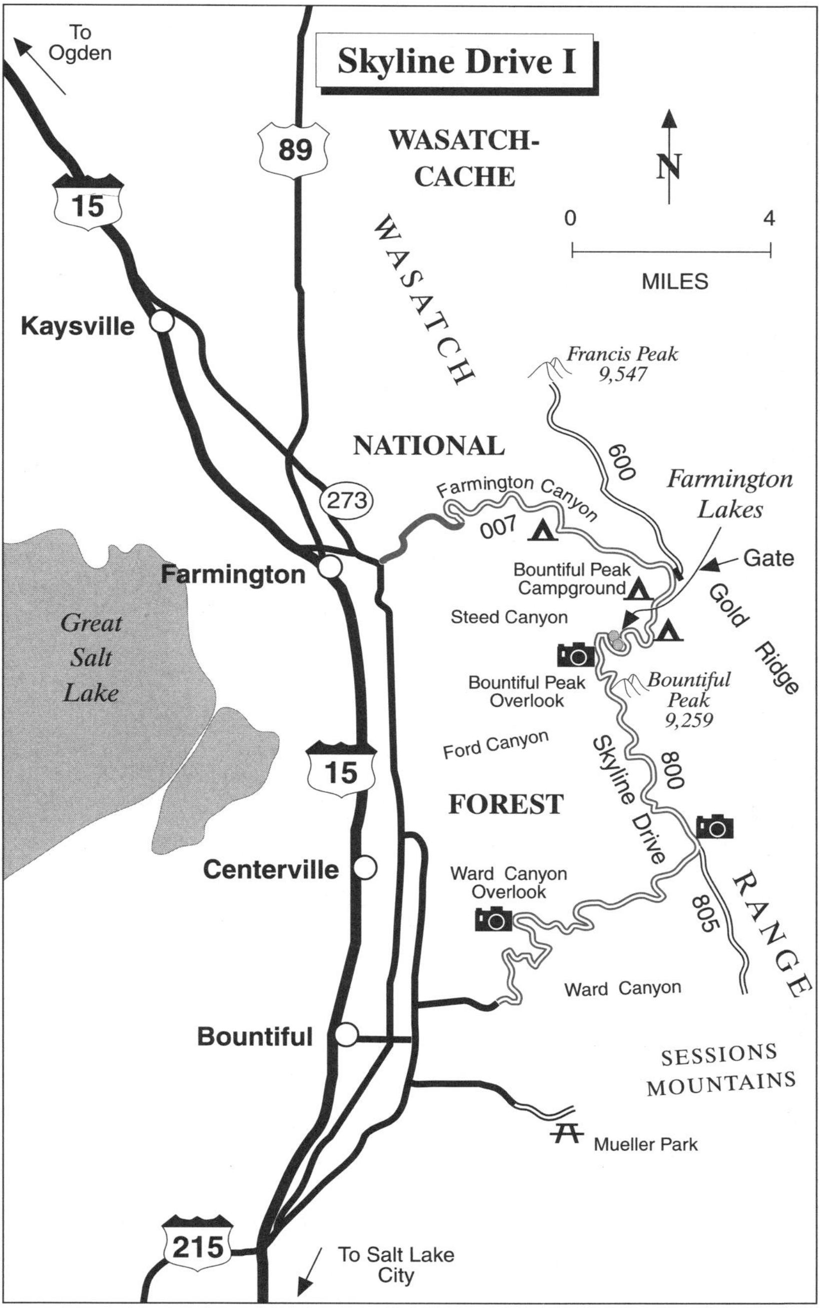
Skyline Drive I
To Ogden
89
WASATCH-
CACHE
N
0
4
MILES
15
WASATCH
Kaysville
Francis Peak
9,547
NATIONAL
600
Farmington
Lakes
Farmington Canyon
273
007
Gate
Farmington
Bountiful Peak
Campground
Gold
Ridge
Steed Canyon
Great
Salt
Lake
Bountiful Peak
Overlook
Bountiful
Peak
9,259
Ford Canyon
Skyline Drive
800
15
FOREST
Centerville
Ward Canyon
Overlook
805
RANGE
Ward Canyon
Bountiful
SESSIONS
MOUNTAINS
Mueller Park
215
To Salt Lake
City

TRIP 6

North Slope Road

LOCATION: South of the Wyoming border on the north slope of the Uinta Mountains. Wasatch-Cache National Forest.

HIGHLIGHTS: High and remote; historic ruins; lush meadows; lakes, streams, fishing; wildlife.

DIFFICULTY: Easy. Closed in winter.

TIME & DISTANCE: 6 hours; about 90 miles.

GETTING THERE: From U-150 at East Fork & Bear River campgrounds, take 058 east toward Black's Fork River, named in the 1820s for Arthur Black of the Ashley Fur Co.

THE DRIVE: For 11 miles the road is very good as you drive through forest toward 10,235-foot Elizabeth Pass. You'll see fantastic vistas of canyons, cliffs and peaks salted with snowfields. At mile 14 you'll pass an old log building, the remains of one of the area's early-20th century logging camps where "tiehackers" cut railroad ties. At 16.2 Little Lyman Lake Campground will be to the left; a short distance farther, road 063 branches right to the West Fork of the Black's Fork. This side trip passes through a gorgeous valley with some private land. It ends in 6.7 miles at a trailhead after you ford the West Fork. Continuing on 058, about 8.2 miles from the West Fork turnoff you'll see road 073, initially a more rudimentary road, on the right. You'll take it, but for now go toward Meek's Cabin Reservoir. Soon you'll see a cluster of log ruins, the old Black's Fork Commissary, a lumber camp (1870-1930) and government commissary. Road 073 is rough as it climbs through lodgepole pines, passing more log ruins. In about 5.5 miles road 074 branches north to Suicide Park (2.5 miles), where three tiehackers who are believed to have committed suicide are buried. 073 improves greatly from here. When you reach 075 you can go north to Mountain View (27 miles) or continue to China Meadows (where the road becomes 072) and Stateline Reservoir. 2.5 miles beyond the reservoir road 017 branches right. You can continue to Mountain View, 22 miles north, or go right to Lonetree, 20 miles away on a good road.

REST STOPS: Many campsites. A pit toilet at the start. Bear River Service, north of the starting point, has supplies.

GETTING HOME: Wyoming Highway 414 north to I-80.

MAP: Wasatch-Cache NF, Evanston & Mt. View Districts.

INFORMATION: Evanston District, (307) 789-3194; Mountain View District, (307) 782-6555. Bear River Ranger Station 642-6662, June-Oct., is south of the starting point on U-150.

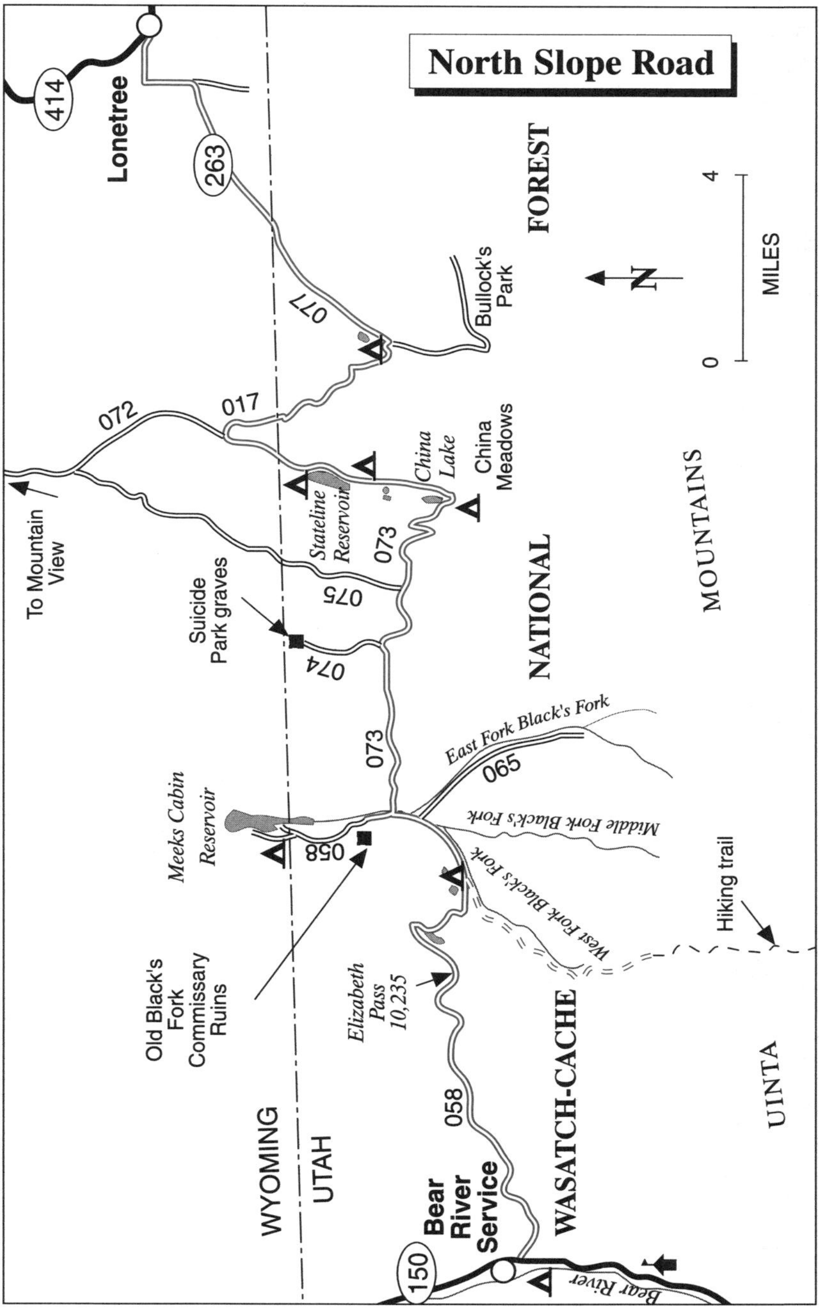

North Slope Road
414
Lonetree
263
077
Bullock's Park
FOREST
0
4
MILES
N
072
017
To Mountain View
China Lake
China Meadows
Stateline Reservoir
073
075
Suicide Park graves
074
NATIONAL
MOUNTAINS
East Fork Black's Fork
065
Middle Fork Black's Fork
West Fork Black's Fork
Meeks Cabin Reservoir
058
Hiking trail
Old Black's Fork Commissary Ruins
Elizabeth Pass 10,235
WASATCH-CACHE
UINTA
WYOMING
UTAH
Bear River Service
150
Bear River

Sheep Creek Loop

LOCATION: Uinta Mountains west of Flaming Gorge National Recreation Area.

HIGHLIGHTS: Aspen and pine forest (much of it clearcut), Honslinger Draw, Sheep Creek Canyon Geologic Area.

DIFFICULTY: Easy on a good, mostly two-lane dirt and gravel road. Road down into Honslinger Draw is one lane.

TIME & DISTANCE: 2.5 hours; 48 miles. Add an hour and 13 miles for the geologic area.

GETTING THERE: You can go in either direction, starting off highway U-44 south of Manila and heading west, or off U-43 at McKinnon, Wyo., going south, then east. I do the latter.

THE DRIVE: From the store at McKinnon go south through farmlands on a good road (it becomes forest road 221) into Utah's forested Uintas. After 6 miles you'll climb through aspens and pines. Enter Uinta NF at about mile 6.7. At 13.2, after the road bends east, you'll see on the right the turnoff for Spirit Lake, road 001. It passes meadows and logged areas for 5.8 miles to end at about 10,000 feet elevation, at a small lake set against an amphitheater of iron-colored mountains. There's a campground, and you'll be charmed by homey Spirit Lake Lodge. On 221 continue east past areas of former lodgepole pine forest, both logged and burned. Almost 36 miles from the Spirit Lake spur you can go right on road 005 to visit restored Ute Mountain Lookout, a national historic site and Utah's last working lookout. Soon you'll reach an intersection. You can go left to the fantastic Sheep Creek geologic tour, which exposes a billion years of multicolored rock strata. But go right on narrow road 539 for the plunge into Honslinger Draw, where there's a campground. Take the geologic tour after reaching the highway, 2.4 miles from the canyon. Go north on U-44 for 3.2 miles to the tour turnoff.

REST STOPS: Refer to your map for campgrounds. Spirit Lake Lodge has cabins, cafe, row boats, horse rides, pack trips. Picnic sites along the geologic tour (road is paved).

GETTING HOME: North to Manila & I-80; south to Vernal.

MAPS: Ashley National Forest; Trails Illustrated's *Flaming Gorge/Eastern Uintas.*

INFORMATION: Flaming Gorge District, 784-3445. For the geologic area tour get the brochure *Wheels of Time.*

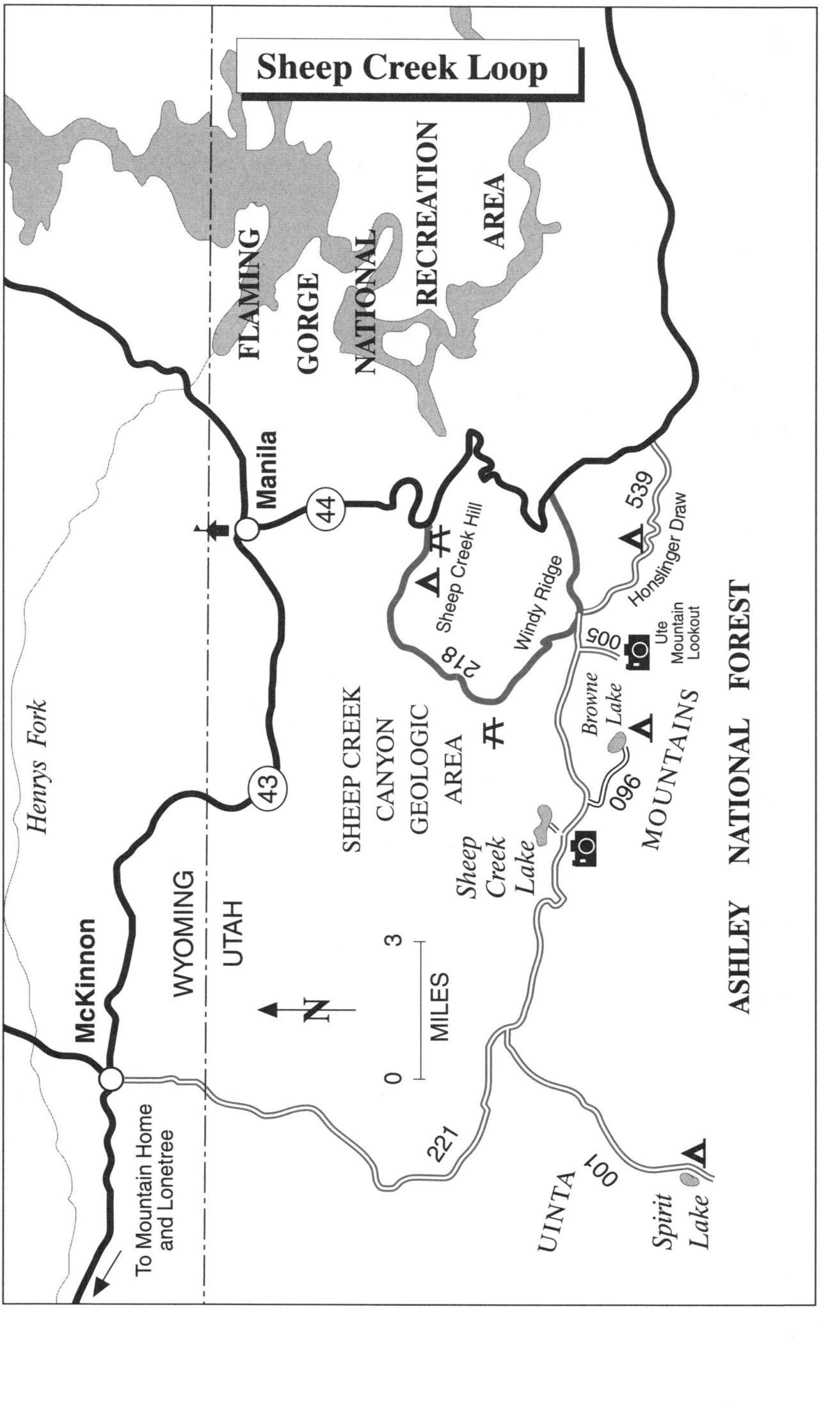

Sheep Creek Loop
FLAMING GORGE NATIONAL RECREATION AREA
Manila
44
Sheep Creek Hill
Windy Ridge
218
539
Honslinger Draw
005
Ute Mountain Lookout
Browne Lake
096
Sheep Creek Lake
SHEEP CREEK CANYON GEOLOGIC AREA
UINTA MOUNTAINS
ASHLEY NATIONAL FOREST
001
Spirit Lake
221
0 3
MILES
N
43
Henrys Fork
WYOMING
UTAH
McKinnon
To Mountain Home and Lonetree

TRIP 8

Brown's Park

LOCATION: In Utah's northeastern corner.

HIGHLIGHTS: Magnificent vistas; narrow Crouse Canyon; "swinging bridge"; John Jarvie Historic Site; outlaw country.

DIFFICULTY: Easy.

TIME & DISTANCE: 3 hrs; 78 miles starting at Vernal.

GETTING THERE: In Vernal take Vernal Ave. (U.S. 191) north about a half-mile from Main Street. Turn right at 500 North, toward Diamond Mountain, Jones Hole and Brown's Park. Set your odometer at 0. About 3 miles farther keep left (veering north) at the junction.

THE DRIVE: The narrow paved road climbs to Diamond Mountain Plateau, providing a panorama of geologic turmoil. At a Y 7.7 miles from U.S. 191/Vernal Ave., take the left branch, toward Diamond Mt. The right goes to Rainbow and Island Parks *(trip 13)*. In about 18 miles you'll be on the plateau's rim, at about 7,500 feet elevation. In about 7 more miles you'll see the left turn to Brown's Park. It's a good dirt road through a vast landscape with a sweeping view of Utah's restless geology. Continue through rounded sorrel mountains and broad rolling valleys. 5.6 miles from where the dirt began you'll pass the turnoff to Crouse Reservoir. In 8 miles descend into Crouse Canyon, named after settler Charlie Crouse, on a one-lane road between high red cliffs. You'll emerge in amber-colored Brown's Park, a 40-mile east-west valley stretching into Colorado and Wyoming. (The origin of "Brown" is unclear.) Snaking through it is the Green River. Indians, mountain men, explorers, settlers, even The Wild Bunch outlaws fill the valley's history. The road enters Colorado, passes through a waterfowl refuge, then crosses the river on a one-lane suspension bridge. At a paved stretch of Hwy. 318 go west toward the Jarvie site, 10 miles. Dirt resumes at the Utah line. The Jarvie property, home of murdered settler John Jarvie, was the trading and social hub for 100 miles around from 1880-1909. Beyond it you'll climb Jesse Ewing Canyon, also named after a settler, then cross an underground natural gas storage facility at Clay Basin. The last 10 miles to U.S. 191 are paved.

REST STOPS: Camp at Crouse Reservoir; 2 camping areas near the Jarvie Historic Property, which has tours 7 days a week May-October, 10 a.m. to 5 p.m.

GETTING HOME: U.S. 191 to I-80 or Vernal.

MAPS: Recreational Map of Utah; get the brochure *Flaming Gorge, Brown's Park, Diamond Mt. Loop* at the Vernal Welcome Center, 235 East Main, 789-4002.

INFORMATION: BLM, Vernal Field Office, 781-4400. Jarvie Historic Property (BLM), 885-3307.

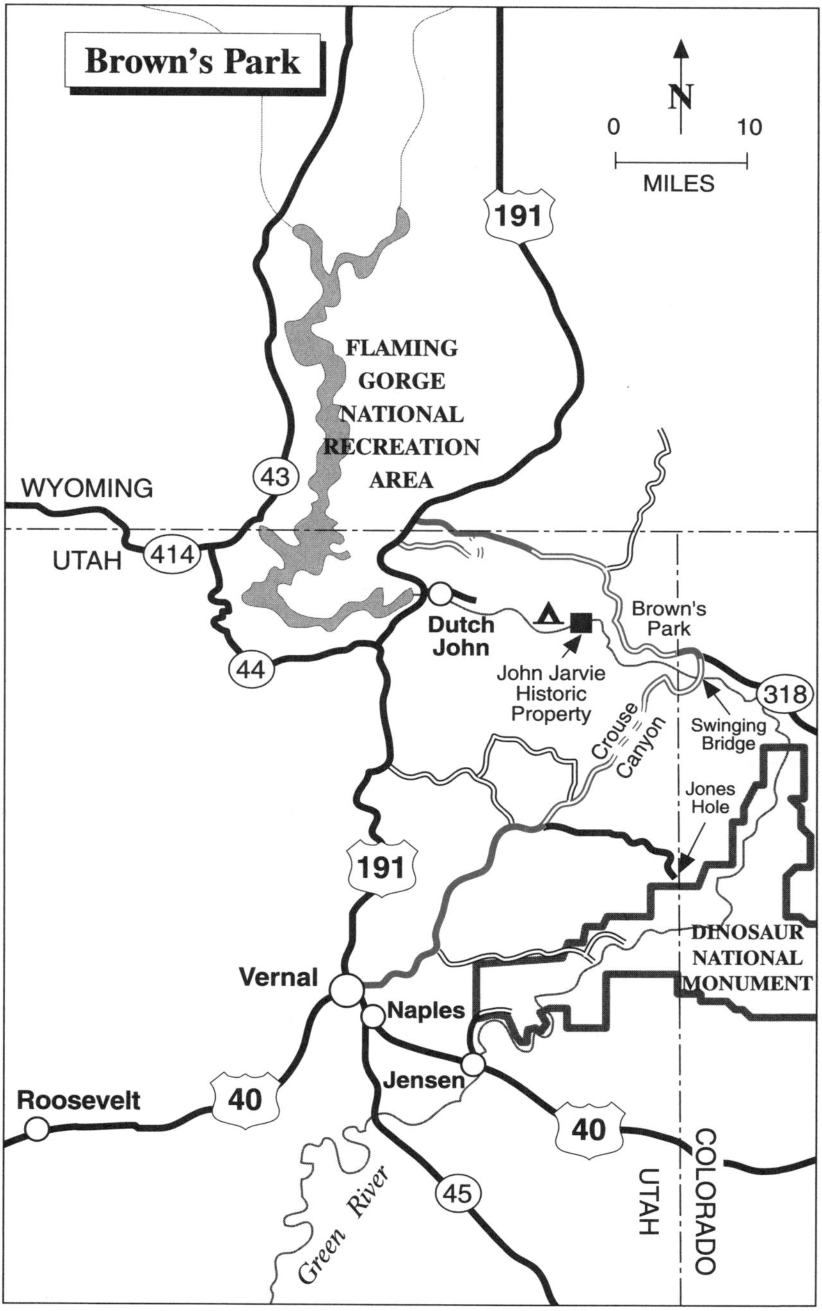
Brown's Park
N
0
10
MILES
191
FLAMING
GORGE
NATIONAL
RECREATION
AREA
43
WYOMING
UTAH
414
Dutch
John
Brown's
Park
John Jarvie
Historic
Property
44
318
Crouse
Canyon
Swinging
Bridge
Jones
Hole
191
DINOSAUR
NATIONAL
MONUMENT
Vernal
Naples
Jensen
Roosevelt
40
40
45
Green River
UTAH
COLORADO

TRIP 9

Middle Canyon Road

LOCATION: Between Tooele & Riverton; Oquirrh Mountains.

HIGHLIGHTS: After climbing 3,800 feet you'll reach an overlook above the world's largest open-pit copper mine. Great views across the Salt Lake Valley to the Wasatch Range, and from the Great Salt Lake south to Utah Lake.

DIFFICULTY: Easy, but possibly hazardous in bad weather. Some sharp, steep and blind turns. Closed in winter.

TIME & DISTANCE: 1.5 hours; 26.5 miles.

GETTING THERE: Go in either direction. I start in Tooele at Main and Vine. Set your odometer at 0; go east on Vine.

THE DRIVE: As you drive the paved, two-lane road east from Tooele you'll see up ahead a deep gash in the mountains, which have suffered from logging, smelter pollution and other problems. Their name, Oquirrh, is Goshute Indian, and has several meanings, including wooded mountain. By mile 2.7 you'll be in narrow Middle Canyon. Its lower reaches are forested with box elder and maple, its higher reaches with firs and aspens. Notice the jagged rock outcrops. At 3.7 you'll see some picnic spots on the right. At 6.8 the pavement ends, and the graded but washboarded dirt road narrows to a little more than one lane. Climb fairly steeply, navigating switchbacks and eroded spots. By mile 8.3 you'll reach Butterfield Pass, at about 8,400 feet. Ahead, where the road drops down the eastern side, is a long view toward the Wasatch Range. Go left here, driving 2.5 miles to a vista point high above Kennecott Copper's mammoth Bingham Canyon Mine. The elevation here is about 9,400 feet. Listen to the low hum of the operation as huge trucks haul ore from the pit. Watch your speed on the winding descent from Butterfield Pass through aspens and pines. At mile 17.6 pavement resumes at the Butterfield Reclamation Area, at the base of a huge tailings pile. In a couple more miles you'll be in Riverton.

REST STOPS: Picnic spots with tables along the way, east of Tooele. The overlook.

GETTING HOME: From Riverton, go east to I-15. From Tooele, go north to I-80.

MAP: Recreational Map of Utah.

INFORMATION: Tooele County Road Dept., 882-9204.

ALSO TRY: South Willow Road, 5 miles south of Grantsville (northwest of Tooele). A lovely 14.8-mile (round-trip) drive through forest and high-walled narrows in the Stansbury Mountains. Nice campgrounds.

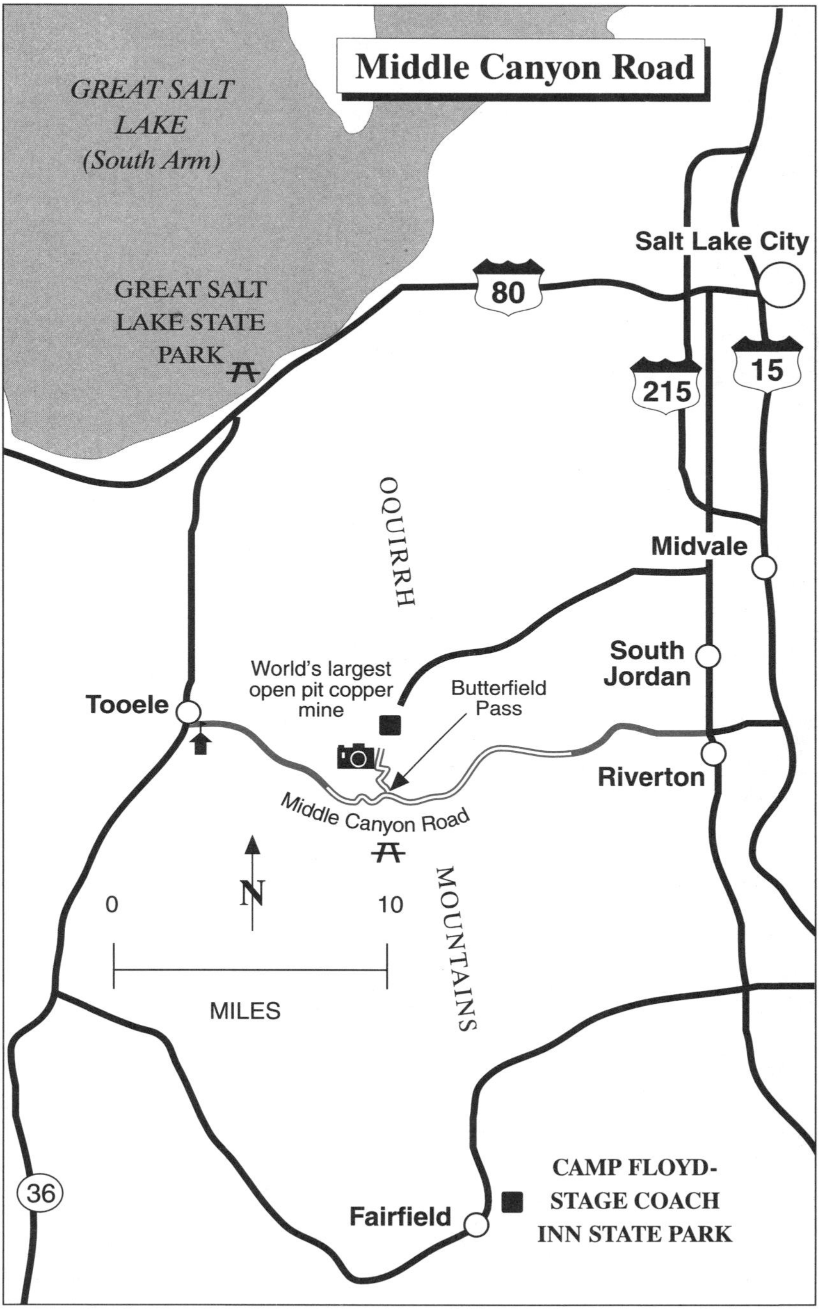
Middle Canyon Road
GREAT SALT LAKE (South Arm)
GREAT SALT LAKE STATE PARK
80
Salt Lake City
215
15
OQUIRRH
Midvale
South Jordan
World's largest open pit copper mine
Butterfield Pass
Tooele
Riverton
Middle Canyon Road
N
0
10
MILES
MOUNTAINS
36
Fairfield
CAMP FLOYD-STAGE COACH INN STATE PARK

TRIP
10

Cummings Parkway

LOCATION: Wasatch Mountain State Park.

HIGHLIGHTS: 8,000-ft. ridge with views of 11,750-foot Mt. Timpanogos. Park has many amenities. Cascade Springs.

DIFFICULTY: Easy to moderate.

TIME & DISTANCE: 2.5 hours; 26 miles.

GETTING THERE: This north-south road can be taken in either direction. It's arguably more scenic going north to south, but then one must go up a rocky stretch. So I go south to north, starting south of Midway. From U-113 turn west onto Tate Lane. Go right after a half-mile onto Stringtown Road, then left onto Cascade Springs Road. Reset your odometer.

THE DRIVE: The good dirt and gravel road, bordered by a rustic fence of lodgepole pine, crosses farmland as it approaches the mountains. As you climb to Decker Pass you'll enjoy an expansive view of Heber Valley. At mile 5.6 you'll be at Cascade Springs. Here the road becomes paved. In another 0.4 mile, at a sharp left bend in the road, turn right (north) onto a dirt road, toward Little Deer Creek CG and Wasatch Mountain State Park. In 2.75 miles, before you reach the campground, you'll see your route branch off to the right. Watch for a sign saying Tibble Fork Jeep Trail and Snake Creek. This is Cummings Parkway. The road switchbacks up to a ridge, providing views of Mt. Timpanogos. Drive north on the crest of the ridge. 5.7 miles from where you turned, the Tibble Fork jeep trail, road 085, branches to the left. (It's moderate overall, but there is a difficult rocky stretch through some narrows. It's 11 miles to Tibble Fork Reservoir.) Go right toward Midway. In 2.5 miles the road will become very rocky. It would be a rough uphill stretch in the opposite direction, but it's only about 150 yards long. At paved Snake Creek Road, go right toward the visitor center, 2 miles farther.

REST STOPS: Cascade Springs has water and restrooms; no tables. Take a 20-minute walk around the springs, which daily produce more than 7 million gallons of water that flows over travertine ledges and through a series of pools. Little Deer Creek CG ($3 day use; $9 overnight) has water and flush toilets. Play golf at the state park. Let the kids fish for rainbow trout in the pond at the visitor center. The easy drives on good dirt and gravel roads to Park City and Brighton are beautiful, too.

GETTING HOME: U-224 north to Park City and I-80; U.S. 189 south to Provo.

MAPS: *Wasatch Mountain State Park & Vicinity* flyer, available from the park; Wasatch-Cache National Forest's Salt Lake District map (1994); Trails Illustrated's *Uinta National Forest.*

INFORMATION: Wasatch Mountain State Park, 654-1791.

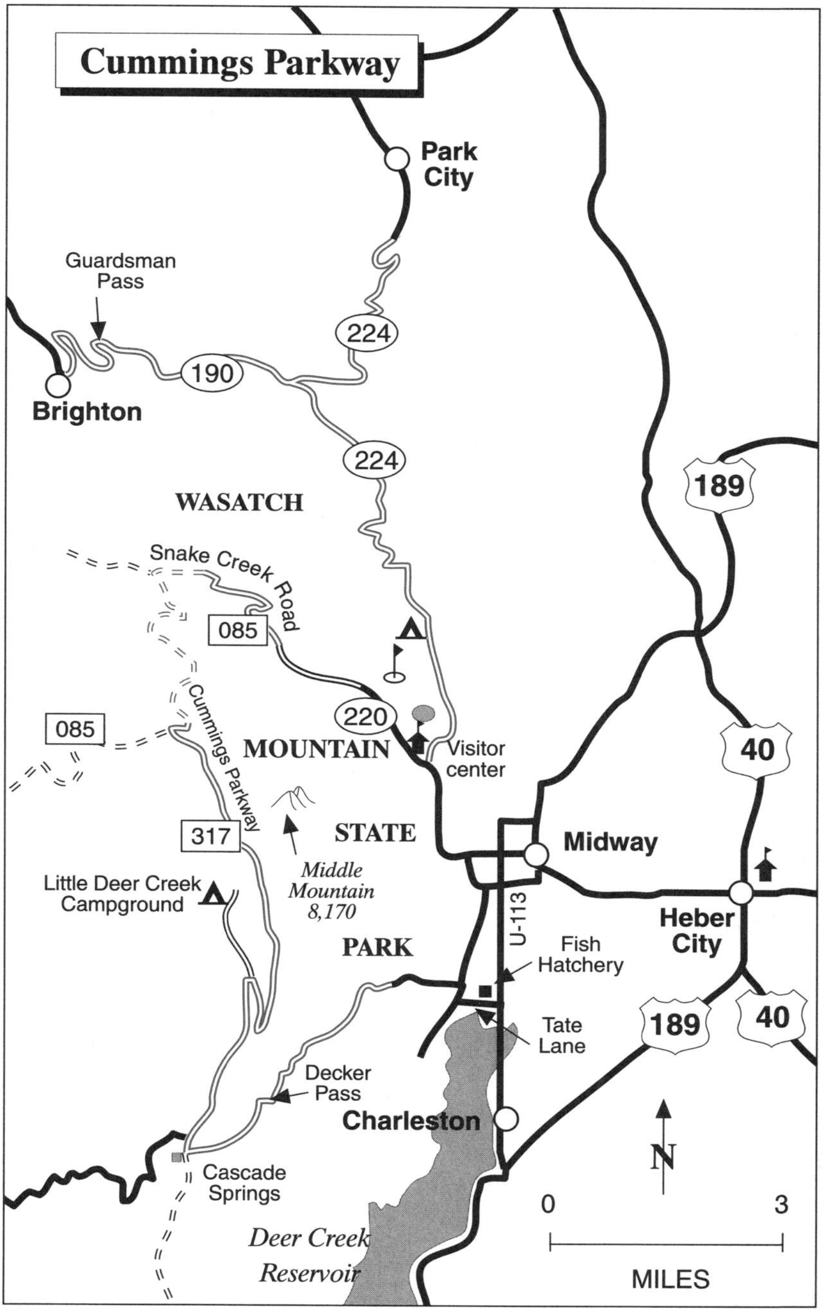
Cummings Parkway
Park City
Guardsman Pass
224
190
Brighton
224
WASATCH
Snake Creek Road
085
189
220
085
Cummings Parkway
MOUNTAIN
Visitor center
40
STATE
317
Midway
Middle Mountain 8,170
Little Deer Creek Campground
U-113
Heber City
PARK
Fish Hatchery
Tate Lane
189
40
Decker Pass
Charleston
N
Cascade Springs
0
3
Deer Creek Reservoir
MILES

Broadhead Meadows

LOCATION: East of Kamas off U-150; Wasatch-Cache National Forest.

HIGHLIGHTS: A fun and pretty drive on a rudimentary road that passes along the edge of a high, pristine Alpine meadow crossed by a meandering stream. Named after a settler. A convenient loop off scenic U-150.

DIFFICULTY: Moderate.

TIME & DISTANCE: An hour or less; 5 miles.

GETTING THERE: Take U-150 21.6 miles east of Kamas. The turnoff for Murdock Basin Road, No. 137 on the right (east) side of the highway, is well-marked.

THE DRIVE: 1.4 miles after you turn off the highway onto the old logging road through second-growth lodgepole pine forest, you'll see rough and narrow road 416 go left to Broadhead Meadows. There might be a sign. (The very rough Murdock Basin Road continues to a basin with high Alpine lakes.) Road 416 is a somewhat rocky, undulating one-lane road through shady forest. 1.3 miles later you'll reach a Y. You might see on a tree a small arrow pointing right. It goes a short distance to the edge of a lush meadow protected by a rustic log fence and traversed by an exceptionally pretty creek. Continuing on the main road, you'll soon see a pretty pond, and the peaks of Murdock Mountain, which rise to 11,212 ft. The meadows are at about 9,600 ft. Beyond them you'll cross a brook, then the road begins to descend, too soon for me, to the highway.

REST STOPS: The right at the Y takes you to a wonderful place to stop for lunch, or to walk through the meadow. No facilities. Upper Provo Bridge Campground is along the highway between where you go in and where you come out. The Provo River Falls overlook is about 2.4 miles north of where you rejoin the highway.

GETTING HOME: U-150 back to Kamas, or north to Evanston, Wyo., and I-80.

MAP: Wasatch-Cache National Forest, Kamas Ranger District.

INFORMATION: Kamas Ranger District, 783-4338.

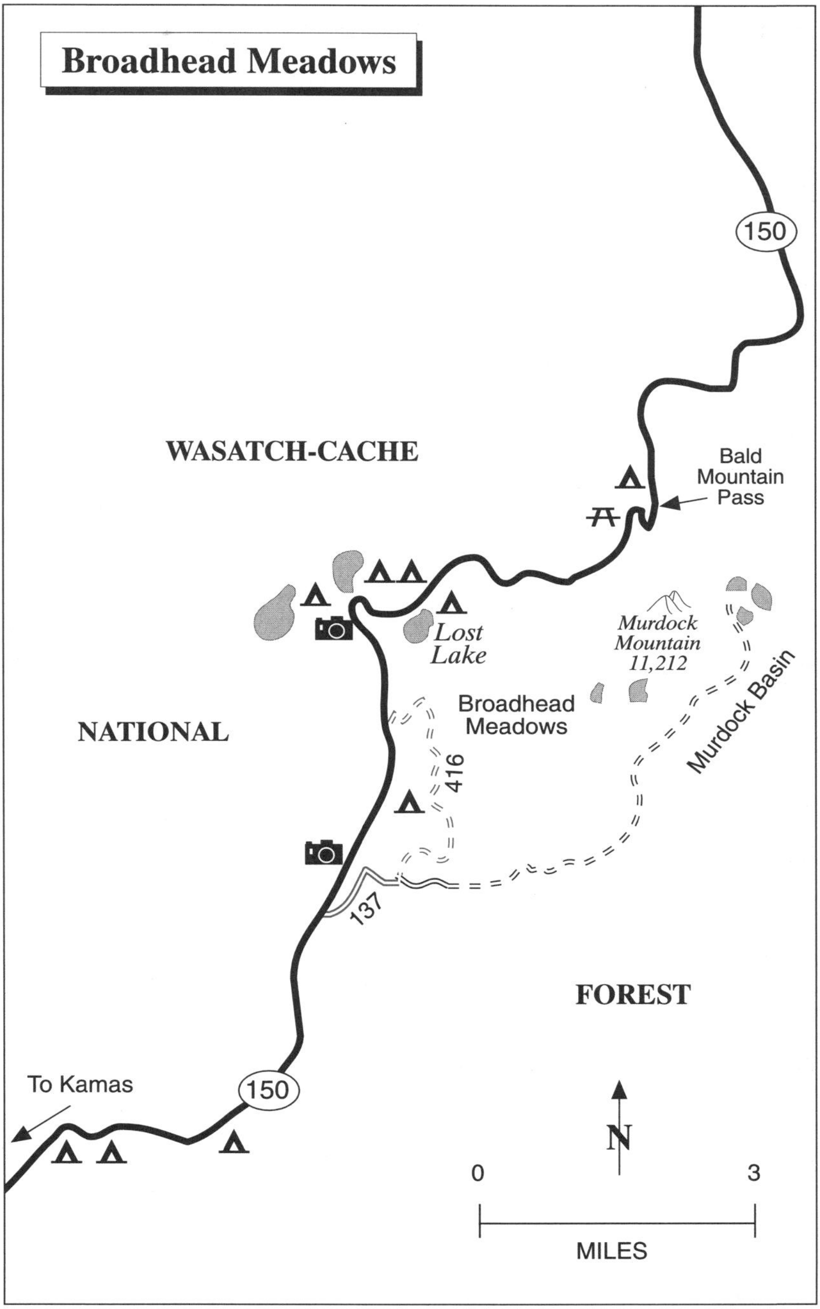
Broadhead Meadows
150
WASATCH-CACHE
Bald
Mountain
Pass
Lost
Lake
Murdock
Mountain
11,212
Broadhead
Meadows
Murdock Basin
NATIONAL
416
137
FOREST
To Kamas
150
N
0
3
MILES

TRIP 12

Red Cloud Loop

LOCATION: Uinta Mountains north of Vernal.

HIGHLIGHTS: Meadows, lodgepole pine forest (much clearcutting, however), wildlife, petroglyphs, canyons, vistas.

DIFFICULTY: Easy on a good road. Logging trucks.

TIME & DISTANCE: 4-5 hours & 60 miles including the sidetrip to Horseshoe Park and visits to the petroglyphs.

GETTING THERE: Take U.S. 191 about 18 miles north of Vernal. Turn west on road 018, and set your odometer to 0.

THE DRIVE: At the start you can look south across the Uinta Basin, beyond the uplift of the uniquely east-west trending Uinta Mountains. Follow the paved road 3.4 miles; go left at the sign for the Red Cloud Loop. The road becomes graded gravel, meandering through hills of aspen, grass and sagebrush. Turn left again at mile 4.1. Soon you'll pass lodgepole pine forest and pretty meadows. At mile 9.1 you'll see Kaler Hollow CG. About 4 miles farther is the turnoff to a somewhat better one, Oak's Park. Go left in another 3.3 miles, toward Dry Fork. Soon you'll see a small, more appealing campground on the North Fork of Ashley Creek. Beyond Lily Pad Lake you'll reach Dry Fork Overlook, where you can gaze across the Uinta Basin. From there you'll wind down through scenic Brownie Canyon. 8 miles from the overlook turn right onto road 031 up Dry Fork Canyon toward Horseshoe Park. In 1.7 miles you'll pass the Dry Fork Nature Trail. At an open area a small road goes left. Just beyond the gate scan the cliffs on the right for a small arch. A short distance farther, also on the right, is a small cave you can easily climb to. Back on 018, continue through magnificent Brownie Canyon. When the asphalt resumes you've left the national forest. Go left at a T. Watch for the sign on the left for McConkie Ranch (see Rest Stops). Vernal is 10 miles.

REST STOPS: Toilet at the start. Campgrounds. Dry Fork Picnic Area near the end, south of the national forest boundary, on the right. For $2 you can see rock art at McConkie Ranch. Remember the Maine County Park is near the end of the drive. 1.5 miles before the park is a turnout on the right; follow a trail around the cliff to see more petroglyphs.

GETTING HOME: Return to Vernal and U.S. 191 & U.S. 40.

MAPS: Ashley National Forest; Trails Illustrated's *Flaming Gorge/Eastern Uintas.*

INFORMATION: Vernal Ranger District, 789-1181. At Vernal's Utah Field House of Natural History on Main Street get the *Indian Petroglyphs* and *Red Cloud Loop* brochures.

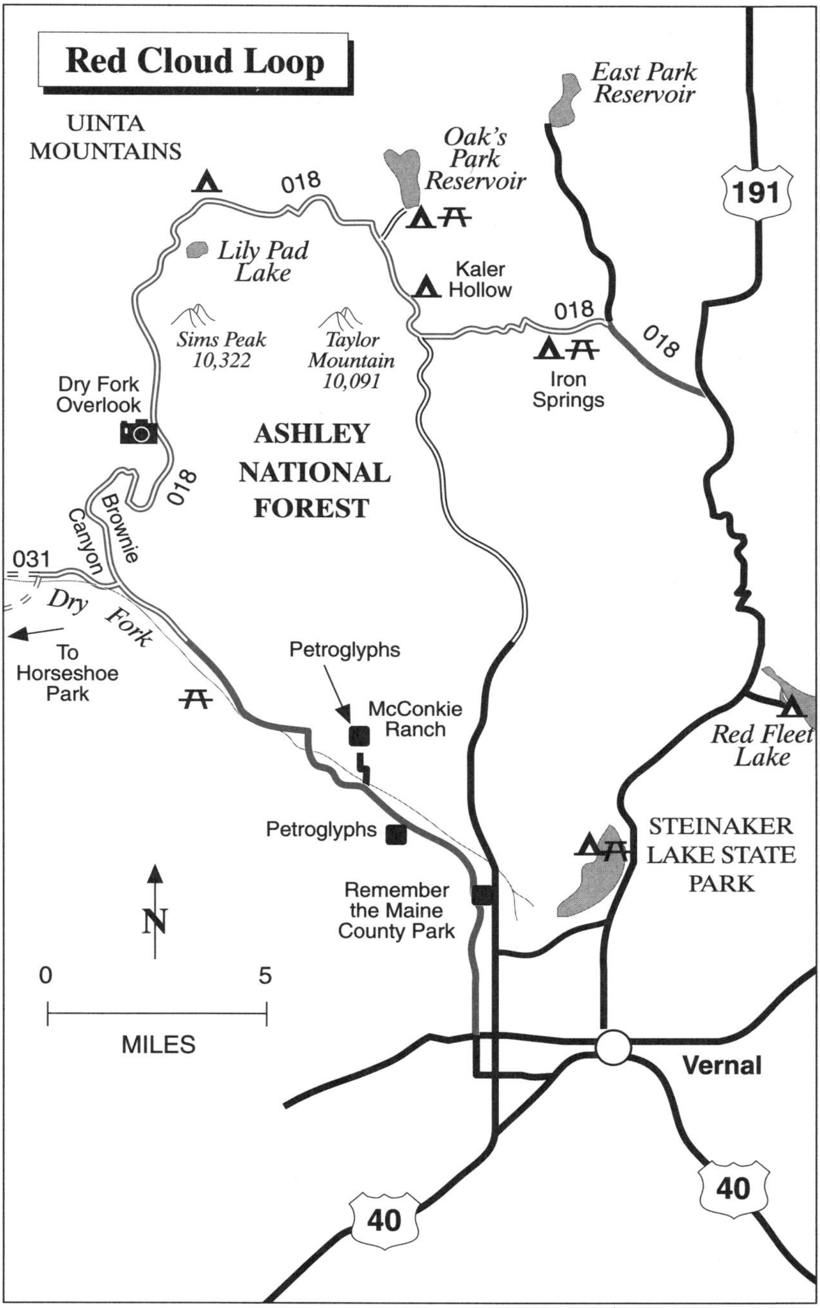

Red Cloud Loop
UINTA MOUNTAINS
East Park Reservoir
Oak's Park Reservoir
018
191
Lily Pad Lake
Kaler Hollow
018
018
Sims Peak 10,322
Taylor Mountain 10,091
Iron Springs
Dry Fork Overlook
ASHLEY NATIONAL FOREST
018
Brownie Canyon
031
Dry Fork
To Horseshoe Park
Petroglyphs
McConkie Ranch
Red Fleet Lake
Petroglyphs
STEINAKER LAKE STATE PARK
Remember the Maine County Park
N
0
5
MILES
Vernal
40
40

TRIP
13

Rainbow and Island Parks

LOCATION: Dinosaur National Monument. A spur off Brown's Park *(trip 8)* that ends at the Green River.

HIGHLIGHTS: Dramatic scenery, like Split Mountain Canyon. McKee Spring petroglyphs. Historic Ruple Ranch.

DIFFICULTY: Easy. Many wash crossings, dips, blind curves. Impassable when wet. Best in fall. The road leads to a launch site for boat trips; watch for vehicles with wide loads.

TIME & DISTANCE: 2.5 hours; about 42 miles round-trip starting at the road to Jones Hole.

GETTING THERE: In Vernal take U.S. 191 north from Main St. Turn right (east) at 500 North, toward Jones Hole and Brown's Park. In 3 miles keep left (north) at a junction. About 4.7 miles farther take the right branch toward Rainbow and Island parks (the main road continues to the Brown's Park road and Jones Hole). Reset your odometer to 0. You can also reach this route from Quarry Visitor Center north of Jensen.

THE DRIVE: The narrow road becomes dirt and gravel as it passes through badlands. It soon angles south. In 2.2 miles go left, or east (there may be a sign). From here, the drive north of Split Mountain's dramatic anticline presents fascinating color contrasts, with the pale greens and yellows of high-desert vegetation, the tans of the soil, and reds and grays of the massive uplifts. By mile 7.3 you'll see on the left The Reef, a sharp line of rock thrusting upward like fingertips. You'll reach the monument boundary at mile 12, at McKee Springs. Near the entrance sign are outstanding petroglyphs. Scan the cliffs for human-like figures and geometric shapes. (Never touch rock art.) At mile 13.9 you'll reach the turnoff to Rainbow Park, a mile to the right at the Green River. There you can peer into the maw of Split Mountain Canyon, where the river has scoured a high-walled passage through the mountain. (Boaters need permits.) From the turnoff to Rainbow Park continue 5 miles to Island Park. But after 1.5 miles detour to the right up a hill, to Island Park Overlook. At Island Park are the remains of historic Ruple Ranch. The Ruples were the first to settle in the area, in the 1880s. (Historic sites and artifacts are legally protected. Don't disturb or take anything.)

REST STOPS: 2 shady but waterless campsites at Rainbow Park (carry out your trash). Quarry Visitor Center.

GETTING HOME: Return to Vernal, or backtrack and continue to Brown's Park and U.S. 191.

MAPS: Recreational Map of Utah. Get Dinosaur National Monument's flyer, *Island Park and Jones Hole Areas.*

INFORMATION: Dinosaur National Monument, (970) 374-3000; Quarry Visitor Center, 789-2115; BLM, Vernal Office, 781-4400.

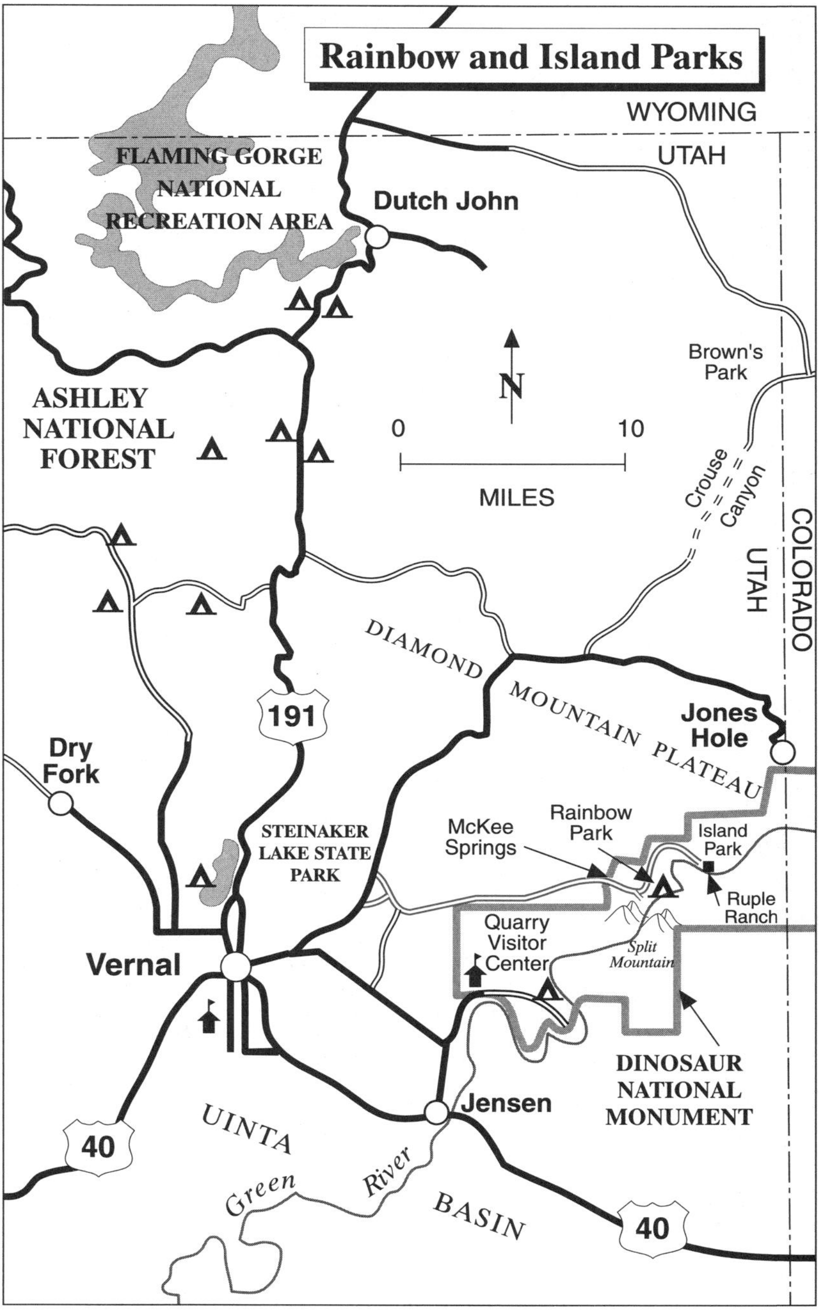
Rainbow and Island Parks
WYOMING
UTAH
FLAMING GORGE
NATIONAL
RECREATION AREA
Dutch John
Brown's
Park
ASHLEY
NATIONAL
FOREST
N
0
10
MILES
Crouse
Canyon
COLORADO
UTAH
DIAMOND
MOUNTAIN PLATEAU
191
Jones
Hole
Dry
Fork
STEINAKER
LAKE STATE
PARK
McKee
Springs
Rainbow
Park
Island
Park
Ruple
Ranch
Quarry
Visitor
Center
Split
Mountain
Vernal
DINOSAUR
NATIONAL
MONUMENT
Jensen
UINTA
BASIN
40
Green
River
40

TRIP
14

Fossil Beds Loop

LOCATION: House Range west of Delta.

HIGHLIGHTS: Recreational trilobite fossil collecting; awesome geology and vistas. A.k.a. Notch Peak Loop, after the 9,655-foot peak with a 2,700-foot cliff. Best spring and fall.

DIFFICULTY: Easy. Side canyons are moderate. Notch Peak, Swasey Peak & Howell Peak are in wilderness study areas where mechanized travel is not allowed. Hot in summer.

TIME & DISTANCE: 5-6 hours & 75 miles or more with side trips; 2.5 hours & 53.4 miles for the loop alone.

GETTING THERE: Take U.S. 6/50 west 42.1 miles from the western edge of Delta into the Sevier Desert. Go north at the Utah Scenic Backway sign. Set your odometer at 0.

THE DRIVE: These mountains reveal a Paleozoic record from 400 to 500 million years ago, when trilobites and other marine invertebrates left their imprints in primordial ooze. At mile 4.3 continue north at the Y toward 9,678-foot Swasey Peak and Antelope Springs/Wheeler Amphitheater. At 15.1 pass the road up Marjum Pass, part of old U.S. 6/50 until it was bypassed in 1949. There's an intersection at mile 19.9, at a pond. Go northwest toward Swasey Peak, Antelope Springs & Dome Canyon (a.k.a. Death Canyon, after pioneers who froze to death there). By mile 21 you'll be in Wheeler Amphitheater. Soon you'll see U-Dig Fossils, a commercial trilobite quarry (season 4/15-10/15). (Don't trespass on posted mining claims.) A bit farther is another intersection. To the left is Dome Canyon Pass and spectacular Dome Canyon. To the right 4.4 miles, past Sinbad Springs' ponderosa pines, the road ends at Sinbad Overlook, with a fantastic view into Nevada. To the northeast is Swasey Peak. Park among the limber pines and relatively young bristlecone pines; climb south along the rim of the cliff through the trees to a summit at 8,600 ft. with an awesome vista 4,000 ft. above Tule Valley. The road down Dome Canyon winds west between massive cliffs with side canyons to explore. At the carcass of an old truck, go left (south). 6.8 miles farther is the left to magnificent Marjum Canyon and Marjum Pass. Take it 3.2 miles; on the left (north side of the road) will be a two-track up a side canyon. Follow it a short distance, then walk about 30 yards. On the left you'll see the cliff dwelling occupied by hermit Robert Stinson from 1920-1945. U.S. 6/50 is 13.9 miles south on the main road.

REST STOPS: Primitive camping. Bring water, toilet. Trilobites are easy to find (hand tools only). Dig where others have. Drive up to Miller Cove (turn left 4.3 miles north of U.S. 6/50) then to Sawtooth Cyn. for the 2.5-3-hour hike past ancient bristlecone pines to Notch Pk. (refer to the BLM map).

GETTING HOME: Return to Delta.

MAPS: BLM's Tule Valley map; USGS *Notch Peak*; also see BLM's *House Range & Warm Springs Recreation & Vehicle Guide.*

INFORMATION: BLM, Fillmore Field Office, 743-6811. U-Dig Fossils, 864-3638.

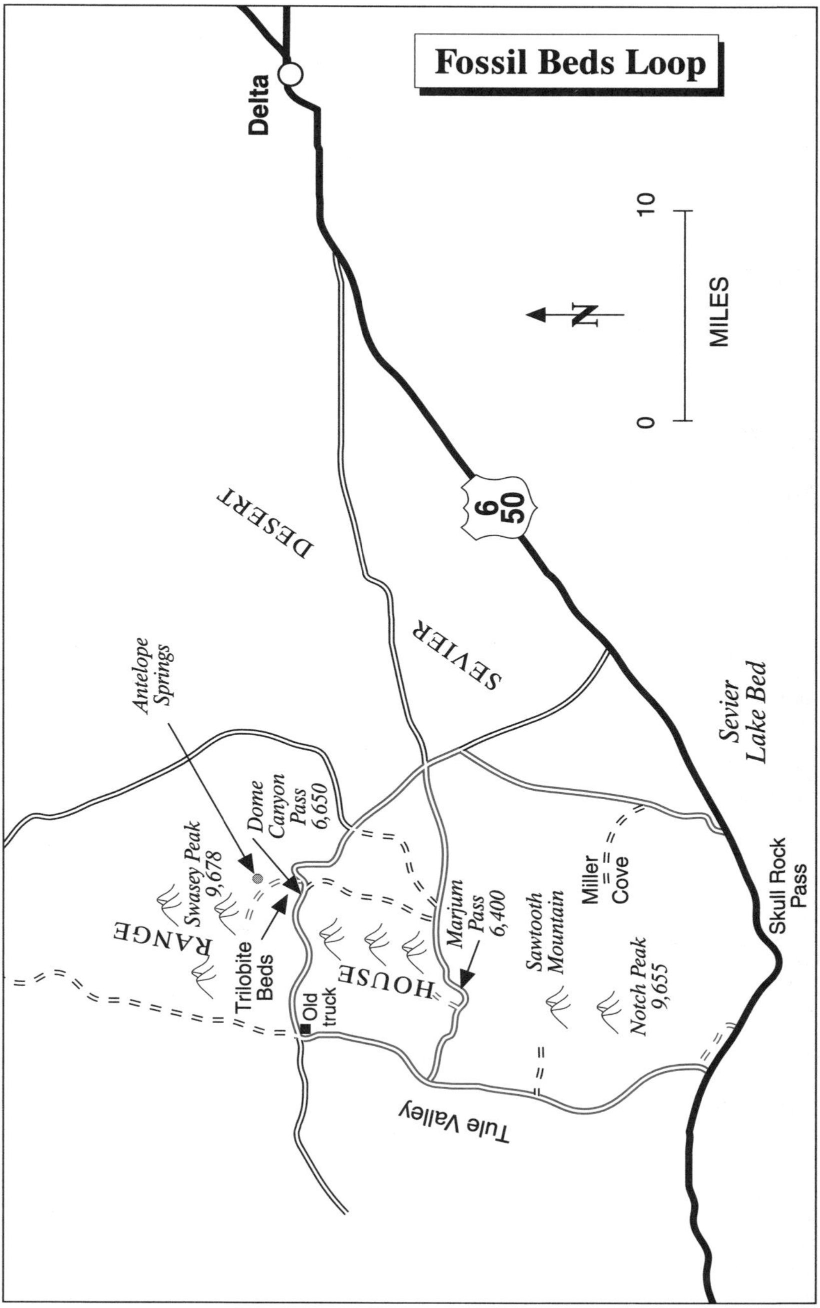
Fossil Beds Loop
Delta
0
10
MILES
N
6
50
DESERT
SEVIER
Sevier Lake Bed
Antelope Springs
Dome Canyon Pass 6,650
Swasey Peak 9,678
HOUSE RANGE
Trilobite Beds
Old truck
Marjum Pass 6,400
Sawtooth Mountain
Miller Cove
Notch Peak 9,655
Skull Rock Pass
Tule Valley

TRIP
15

Skyline Drive II

LOCATION: Southeast of Provo, between U.S. 6 and U-31.

HIGHLIGHTS: Serene and scenic high-elevation cruise atop the Wasatch Plateau. Endless vistas of mountains, valleys and deserts. Aspens, pines, cottonwoods, broad Alpine meadows. Many good places to pull off the road and enjoy the view. This is a leg of the Great Western Trail and Adventure Highway. Mid-summer wildflowers displays, depending on weather.

DIFFICULTY: Easy; a very good dirt and gravel road.

TIME & DISTANCE: 1.5 hours; 28 miles.

GETTING THERE: This north-south route can be taken in either direction, beginning or ending on U.S. 6 southeast of Spanish Fork. I go south. Take U.S. 6 to the Tucker rest area, about 30 miles southeast of I-15. Go between the picnic area and the building, angling left. You'll follow road 150. Reset your odometer.

THE DRIVE: The Left Fork of Clear Creek is on your left as you drive a one-lane road through cottonwoods, pines and aspens. At mile 2.7, where you enter Manti-La Sal National Forest, you'll begin climbing rapidly to the top of the Wasatch Plateau. You were at about 6,200 feet elevation at the rest area. By mile 10 you're over 10,000 feet, meandering south among rolling, pastoral mountaintops that melt into Plateau Country to the east. To the west lie the gray mountains and alkali flats of the Great Basin Desert. To the north rises the dramatic escarpment of the Wasatch Range and the uplift of the uniquely east-west trending Uinta Mountains. The road is two lanes in sections, and well-maintained. Do watch your speed, because the gravel tends to roll, causing tires to lose their grip. At mile 28.2 you'll reach pavement. A short distance farther is U-31, a designated scenic byway. If you want more high-elevation adventure, try rougher, longer Skyline Drive South, which I call Skyline Drive III *(trip 20)*. Go left (south) on U-31, then right after 4.9 miles where road 150 resumes.

REST STOPS: Tucker rest area has shady picnic sites. Many undeveloped campsites along the way. Developed Gooseberry Campground. Fishing at Lower Gooseberry Reservoir near the end of the drive. Fairview Museum.

GETTING HOME: U-31 west to Fairview and U.S. 89.

MAP: Manti-La Sal National Forest; Sanpete, Price districts.

INFORMATION: Sanpete Ranger District, 283-4151; Price Ranger District, 637-2817.

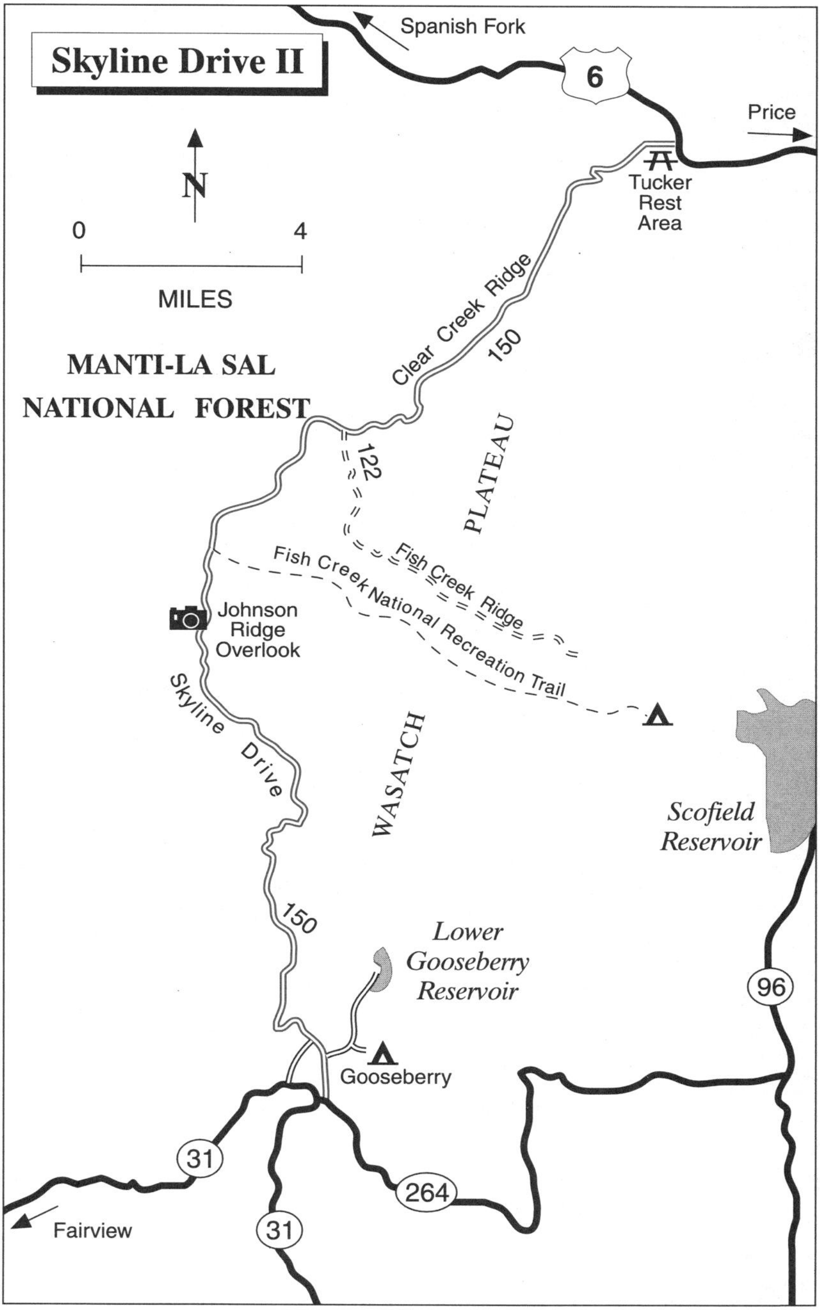
Skyline Drive II
Spanish Fork
6
Price
Tucker Rest Area
N
0
4
MILES
MANTI-LA SAL NATIONAL FOREST
Clear Creek Ridge
150
122
PLATEAU
Fish Creek Ridge
Fish Creek National Recreation Trail
Johnson Ridge Overlook
Skyline Drive
WASATCH
Scofield Reservoir
150
Lower Gooseberry Reservoir
96
Gooseberry
31
264
31
Fairview

TRIP
16

Reservation Ridge

LOCATION: Between U.S. 6 & U.S. 191 north of Helper.

HIGHLIGHTS: An enchanting drive along a high ridge, on a road of uneven quality with remarkable vistas. Particularly appealing because of its proximity to three highways. Has a perfect mix of pine and aspen forest, meadows and distant vistas, and glimpses of wildlife early in morning or evening. If you begin or end at U.S. 40, you can take in Strawberry Pinnacles, sedimentary formations at the confluence of Strawberry River and Red Creek.

DIFFICULTY: Easy to moderate. Can be very rutted. Extremely slick when wet. Best summer, early fall.

TIME & DISTANCE: 2 hours; 27 miles.

GETTING THERE: You can go several ways. I start off U.S. 6 near Soldier Summit and end at U.S. 191. The turnoff for Uinta National Forest road 081 is on the east side of U.S. 6, 0.7 mile south of the summit. Another option: From U.S. 40 about 3 miles west of U-208, go south on Red Creek Road a.k.a. Strawberry Pinnacles Road. Go south to the pinnacles, then west on road 149 up Timber Canyon to the ridge.

THE DRIVE: This tour quickly becomes very pretty, especially in the brassy autumn light of late afternoon, as you drive through hills of grass and sagebrush toward mountains forested with aspens and pines. The road forks at mile 0.6; keep right. It narrows to a single lane as you drive up a canyon through aspens that promise autumn beauty. By mile 7.6 the view west down the canyon you've come up extends across range after distant range. A mile farther and you're on Reservation Ridge, at about 8,800 feet. The views are fantastic. To the east, beige hills roll toward the Strawberry River drainage in the Uinta Basin and the West Tavaputs Plateau. To the south and west, mountains and valleys spread like a rumpled woolen blanket to the horizon. Road 147 south on the crest of the ridge provides a relaxing cruise among mountaintops and through aspen groves, although the undulating one-lane road can be rough in spots. By mile 17 you'll ascend to 9,700 feet, and then begin the gradual descent to Avintaquin Campground, at 25.5. U.S. 191 is a couple miles farther.

REST STOPS: Primitive campsites. Avintaquin Campground. Western Mining & Railroad Museum in Helper; College of Eastern Utah Prehistoric Museum in Price.

GETTING HOME: U.S. 191 south to U.S. 6 near Helper or north to U.S. 40 at Duchesne.

MAP: Ashley National Forest.

INFORMATION: Uinta National Forest, Spanish Fork District, 798-3571; Ashley National Forest, Duchesne Ranger District, 738-2482, and Roosevelt Ranger District, 722-5018.

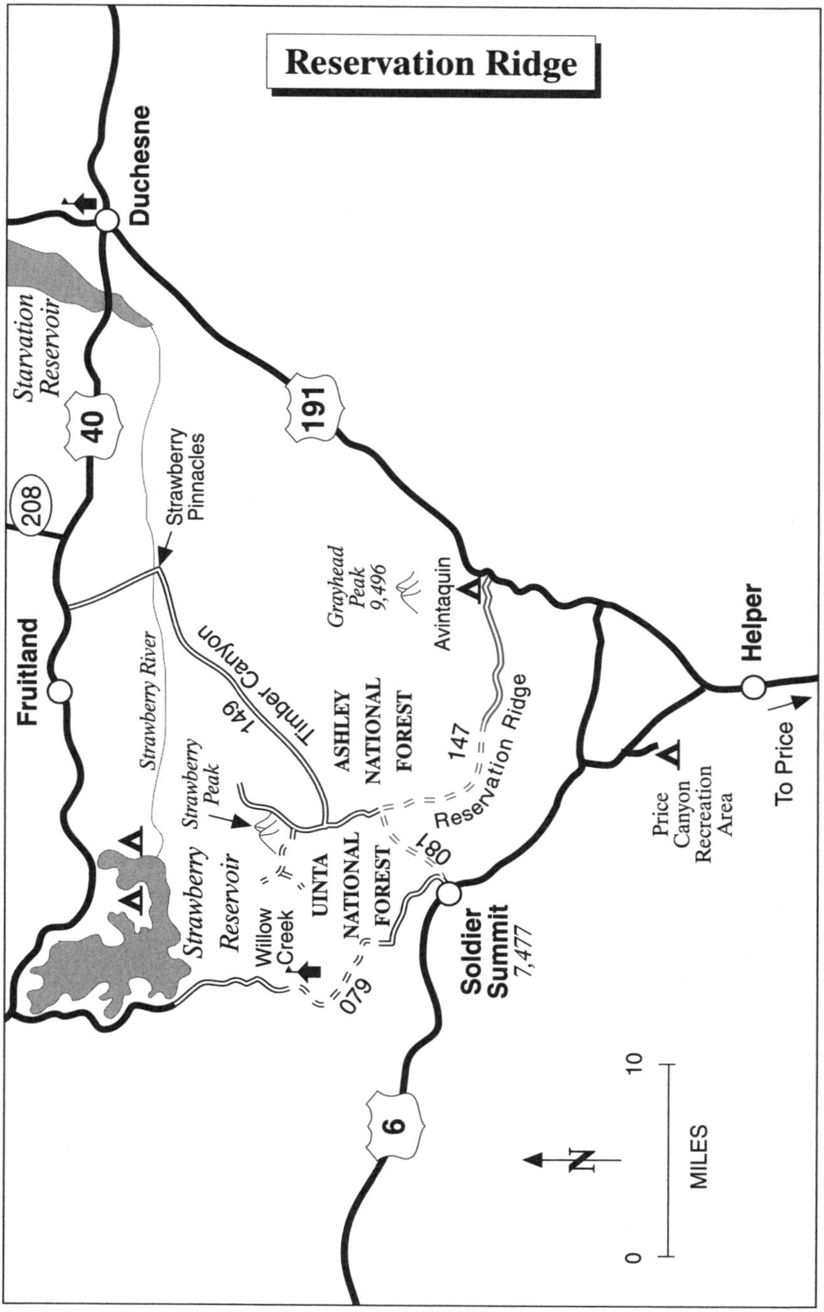
Reservation Ridge
Duchesne
Starvation Reservoir
40
191
208
Strawberry Pinnacles
Fruitland
Strawberry River
Grayhead Peak 9,496
Avintaquin
Helper
To Price
Price Canyon Recreation Area
149
Timber Canyon
ASHLEY NATIONAL FOREST
147
Reservation Ridge
Strawberry Peak
Strawberry Reservoir
Willow Creek
UINTA NATIONAL FOREST
081
079
Soldier Summit 7,477
6
N
0
10
MILES

TRIP 17

Nine-Mile Canyon

LOCATION: Northeast of Wellington; south of Myton.

HIGHLIGHTS: Incredible array of Fremont Culture (300-1250 A.D.) and later Ute Indian rock art. Ancient ruins, too. The road was built in the 1880s by the all-black 9th U.S. Cavalry. Old stage stop, homesteads and telegraph poles. Towering red cliffs. Bring binoculars.

DIFFICULTY: Easy. Side canyons are rougher.

TIME & DISTANCE: 5-6 hours; 80-100 miles.

GETTING THERE: From U.S. 6/191 go north on Soldier Creek Rd., just east of Wellington. You'll enter the canyon in 20 miles. 1.4 miles west of Myton on U.S. 40, go south onto 5550 West toward Sand Wash. Drive south on the historic and scenic road through Wells Draw and Gate Canyon to Nine-Mile Canyon Road, about 31 miles. I start at U.S. 6/191.

THE DRIVE: Nine-Mile Canyon, more than 40 miles long, is named after the creek running through it. 12.4 miles from the highway you'll pass Soldier Canyon Mine; the asphalt ends. The dirt and gravel road climbs to a 7,300-ft. summit as it approaches West Tavaputs Plateau. 1.5 miles beyond Minnie Maud Creek you'll see an old log cabin on the left, on private property. 3.4 miles farther, at a turnout on the left where the road bends, is a panel of rock art. 3.2 miles farther stop and scan the cliffs above. About two-thirds of the way up, at the base of a crack, is an ancient granary. In a mile you'll pass Harper, once a stagecoach stop. 3.5 miles beyond the turnoff to Sand Wash and Myton you'll see the spur to the top of Prickly Pear Canyon, a worthwhile detour. 2.3 miles farther down Nine-Mile, before a cattle guard, is a cave with pictographs. Near the corral beyond the cave are more petroglyphs. At a Y cross the bridge to the right. In 1.2 miles, shortly before a BLM sign, a rock outcrop will be above to your right, bearing an extraordinary hunting scene. Left at the Y takes you 5.2 miles down Nine-Mile to Frank's Canyon. A moderate, scenic spur up Frank's ends in 5 miles at the road to Sand Wash *(trip 18)*.

REST STOPS: No facilities or services after Myton and Wellington.

GETTING HOME: East or west on U.S. 40. U.S. 6 north to I-15 at Spanish Fork, south to I-70 west of Green River.

MAPS: BLM's Price Surface Management Status map. The Castle Country Travel Council has a detailed brochure. Also get the booklet *The Pioneer Saga of the Nine Mile Road.*

INFORMATION: BLM in Price, 636-3600; in Vernal, 781-4400. Castle Country Travel Council, 1-800-842-0789.

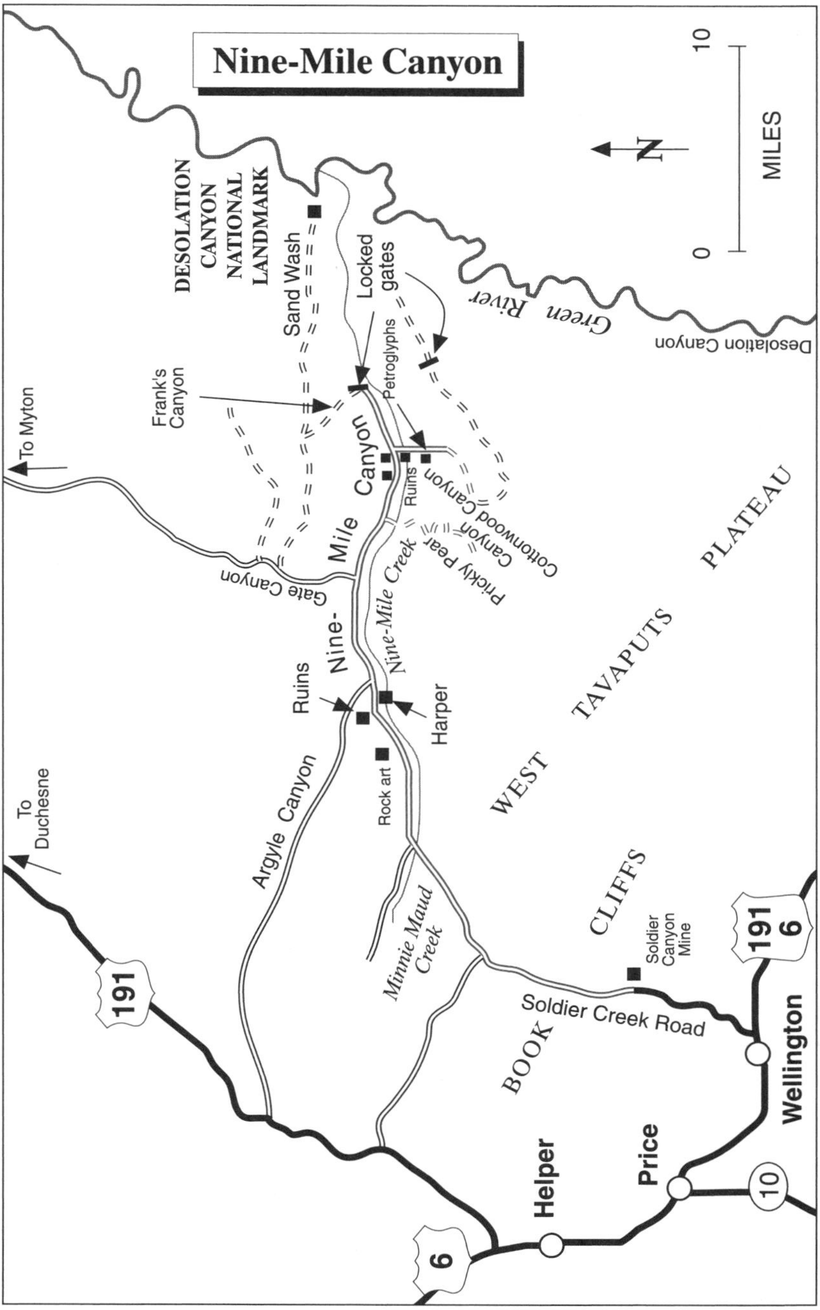
Nine-Mile Canyon
DESOLATION CANYON NATIONAL LANDMARK
Sand Wash
Locked gates
Petroglyphs
Frank's Canyon
To Myton
Green River
Desolation Canyon
N
0
10
MILES
Nine-Mile Canyon
Ruins
Cottonwood Canyon
Prickly Pear Canyon
Nine-Mile Creek
Gate Canyon
Ruins
Harper
Rock art
Argyle Canyon
To Duchesne
Minnie Maud Creek
WEST TAVAPUTS PLATEAU
BOOK CLIFFS
Soldier Canyon Mine
Soldier Creek Road
191
191
6
6
10
Wellington
Price
Helper

TRIP 18

Sand Wash

LOCATION: West Tavaputs Plateau, south of the Uinta Basin. North of Nine-Mile Canyon.

HIGHLIGHTS: Towering cliffs. Magnificent view from an overlook above the Green River, upriver from remote Desolation Canyon. Historic buildings at Sand Wash. Near Nine-Mile Canyon *(trip 17).*

DIFFICULTY: Easy. Sharp stones often cause flats.

TIME & DISTANCE: 3.5 hours; 63 miles.

GETTING THERE: There are several ways to do this. Make an 85-mile loop from U.S. 40/191 near Myton; go south from U.S. 40/191 to conclude at Nine-Mile Canyon; or start at Nine-Mile, going north to U.S. 40/191. I do the latter.

THE DRIVE: In Nine-Mile Canyon is a T intersection. The road north, Price-Myton Road, is a well-maintained dirt and gravel road up eroded Gate Canyon. Etched in the sandstone at the mouth of the canyon is Fremont Culture (300-1250 A.D.) rock art. Driving up the canyon you'll see names and dates from the late 1880s. 4.8 miles from the intersection a sign signals the right turn to Sand Wash on the Wrinkle Road, which passes through a rock-hounding area. Drive along Myton Bench, which drops off in the distance where the Green River has cut through the rock to separate West and East Tavaputs Plateaus. Lofty sandstone cliffs dominate the bench. Now and then the road edges to the brink of a tributary of the river canyon. To the southeast the river flows through Desolation Canyon, named in 1869 by John Wesley Powell, who led the first exploratory float trip down the Green and Colorado rivers. In 1969 the canyon was designated a natural historic landmark because, of all the canyons Powell explored, it has changed least. About 12 miles from the Price-Myton Rd. you'll see the moderate 5-mile 4x4 spur on the right descending down Frank's Canyon to Nine-Mile Canyon. About 8 miles farther a spur branches right, past an airstrip to a spectacular viewpoint at the edge of the bench. The road to Sand Wash is about a mile farther. Once a ferry crossing, it's now an entry point for the multi-day float through the canyon (permit required). At the main road, go right (north) and climb out of the canyon onto a bench, then wind through hills and draws. 25 miles from Sand Wash go left at an intersection. In 9.7 miles you'll be at the road to Nine-Mile Canyon. Go right to U.S. 40/191.

REST STOPS: Campground at Sand Wash (very buggy). No water. There's a nature trail. Visit the historic buildings, too.

GETTING HOME: U.S. 40/191 west to I-80.

MAP: Recreational Map of Utah.

INFORMATION: BLM, Vernal Field Office, 781-4400.

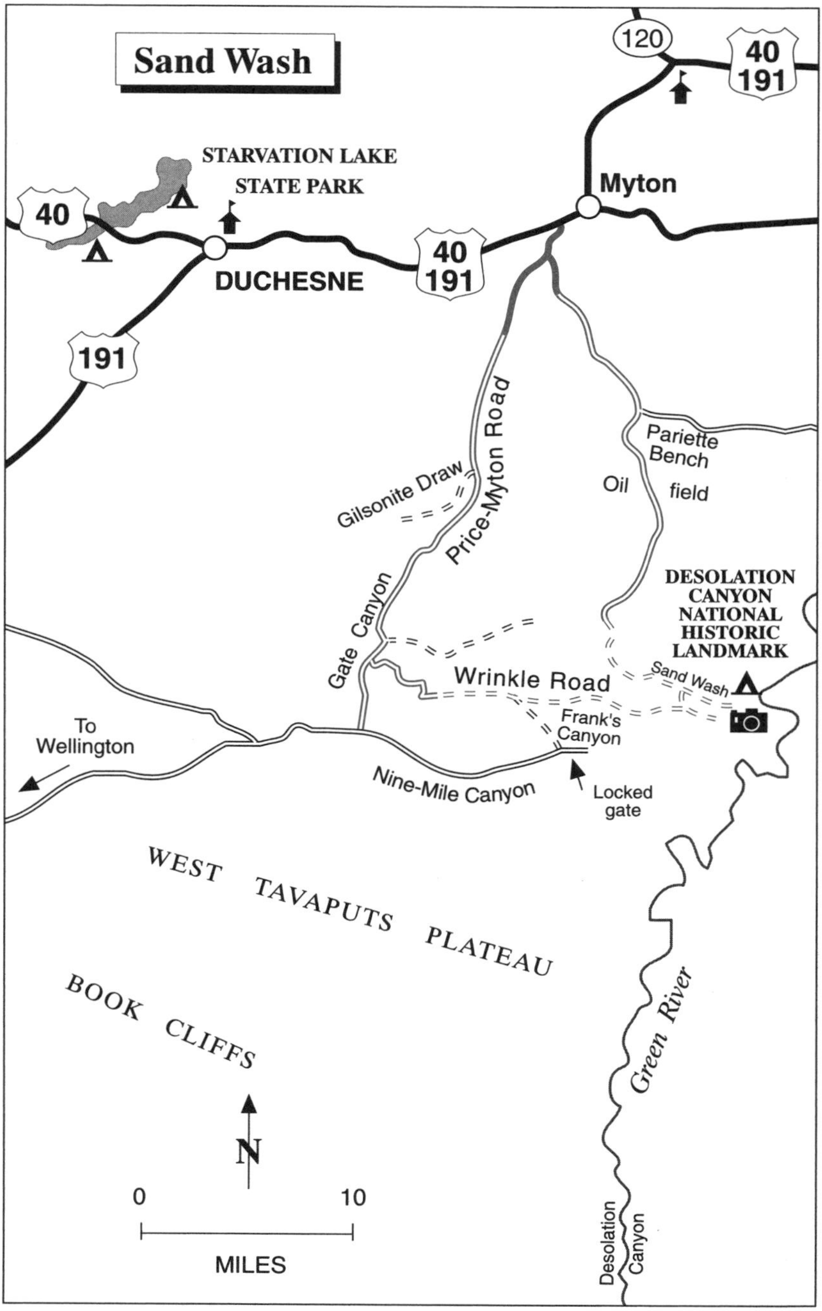
Sand Wash
120
40
191
STARVATION LAKE
STATE PARK
Myton
40
DUCHESNE
40
191
191
Price-Myton Road
Pariette
Bench
Oil
field
Gilsonite Draw
Gate Canyon
DESOLATION
CANYON
NATIONAL
HISTORIC
LANDMARK
Wrinkle Road
Sand Wash
To
Wellington
Frank's
Canyon
Nine-Mile Canyon
Locked
gate
WEST TAVAPUTS PLATEAU
BOOK CLIFFS
Green River
N
0
10
MILES
Desolation
Canyon

TRIP
19

Chicken Creek

LOCATION: San Pitch Mountains south of Nephi, east of Levan. Part of Uinta National Forest that is administered by Manti-La Sal National Forest.

HIGHLIGHTS: Excellent autumn drive through a narrow, rugged canyon with exposed rock and forested with pines, aspens, maples and other deciduous trees. Side canyons to hike up. Fine views.

DIFFICULTY: Easy.

TIME & DISTANCE: 1.5 hours; 16 miles.

GETTING THERE: You can take this east-west route in either direction, beginning or ending at Levan or Wales. I start at Levan, on U-28 south of Nephi and east of I-15. In Levan, turn east off U-28 (Main Street) onto First South Street. My mileages begin here.

THE DRIVE: As you follow the paved road toward the mountains you can see the canyon ahead. At mile 1.5 there is a Y; left is to Pigeon Creek, so go right, toward Wales. Here the road surface becomes dirt and gravel, just a bit more than one lane, although you will travel over short paved segments. Note the exposed, yellowish sedimentary rock on the canyon's north wall. At mile 4.2 look ahead and to the right, and you'll see a small waterfall. At 4.5 the road, now No. 101, enters Uinta National Forest. By 5.2 the roadbed becomes somewhat rougher, though it remains a good road. At 5.8 Chicken Creek Campground is on the right, with water and pit toilets. From here the road climbs steadily, and becomes rockier. At 6.7, the canyon's walls reveal that these mountains are composed of a jumble of rocks, stones and sediment collectively called conglomerate, mostly lakebed deposits laid down in the Mesozoic era (66-208 MYA). At mile 8.2 a trail on the left goes up pretty Reddick Canyon. Continue straight at mile 12, where road 157 to Wales branches right, heading down Wales Canyon toward a magnificent view of Sanpete Valley and the Wasatch Plateau. The scene soon will be framed by the rock walls of a gap you'll drive through. At mile 16 asphalt resumes, at the hamlet of Wales.

REST STOPS: Chicken Creek Campground.

GETTING HOME: Take U-132 north to Nephi & I-15, or go south to U.S. 89, continuing on to Manti, Salina and I-70.

MAP: Manti-La Sal National Forest, Sanpete Ranger District.

INFORMATION: Sanpete Ranger District, 283-4151.

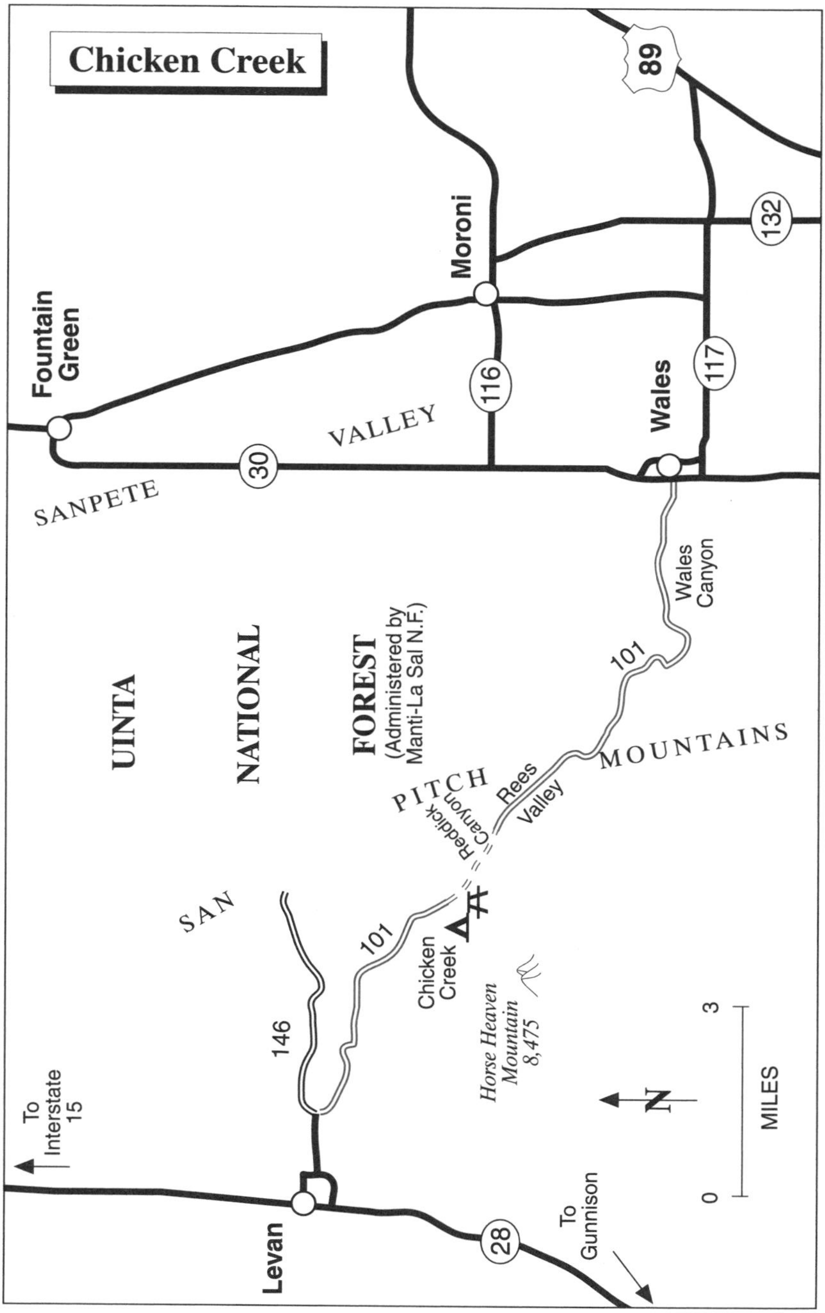
Chicken Creek
89
132
Moroni
Fountain Green
116
117
Wales
SANPETE VALLEY
30
UINTA NATIONAL FOREST
(Administered by Manti-La Sal N.F.)
Wales Canyon
101
SAN PITCH MOUNTAINS
Rees Valley
Reddick Canyon
101
Chicken Creek
Horse Heaven Mountain 8,475
146
To Interstate 15
Levan
28
To Gunnison
N
0
3
MILES

Skyline Drive III

LOCATION: North of I-70, between U.S. 89 and U-10.

HIGHLIGHTS: A.k.a. Skyline Drive South. Awesome vistas from the Great Basin to the Colorado Plateau. Varied road conditions, including narrow ledges, add to the exhilaration of reaching 10,900 feet on the Wasatch Plateau. Great mountain biking.

DIFFICULTY: Easy to difficult depending on where you start. North end can be extremely muddy and rutted. At mile 23 the road crosses a north-facing slope that can be blocked by snow well into summer.

TIME & DISTANCE: 6 hours; 76 miles.

GETTING THERE: If the weather has been dry for some time, letting the road dry out, you can start on U-31 at the Sanpete Valley Overlook and go south. Expect severe ruts. Easier accesses are the serpentine, 15-mile gravel road from Ephraim east up Ephraim Canyon; or the 37-mile drive from Castle Dale, on U-10, west on U-29/Forest Hwy. 8 past Joe's Reservoir. I start at U-31, from which you can drive the entire route.

THE DRIVE: This leg of road 150 is more rugged and even more spectacular than the route I call Skyline Drive II *(trip 15)*, which starts 4.9 miles farther north on U-31. The route begins high above Sanpete Valley. You'll pass a number of lush, U-shaped glacial basins. At about mile 20 you'll pass North & South Tent Mountains, both of which exceed 11,200 feet. At 22.3 cross a sharp divide at about 10,600 feet, and a short distance farther cross the ridge. The road improves from here, though it's still one lane as you cross an exposed, rocky landscape of rolling mountaintops and Alpine meadows. At 43.9 you'll reach Hightop, the highest point on the drive. The sign says it's 10,897 feet; the map says 10,904. Descend to Twelve-Mile Flat, and go left at the campground toward Gunnison Valley. 10.3 miles farther road 290 angles right (west), descending toward Mayfield. Follow the two-track that continues ahead into the woods. Soon you'll enter Fishlake National Forest, where road 150 becomes road 001. In 6 miles road 001 (from here scenic Willow Creek Road) goes right (west) 25 miles toward U.S. 89. Skyline Drive, road 009, continues south down Salina Canyon to I-70 (13 miles).

REST STOPS: Twelve-Mile Flat Campground.

GETTING HOME: I-70 west to I-15, east to Green River.

MAPS: Manti-La Sal National Forest, Sanpete & Price ranger districts; Fishlake National Forest, Richfield Ranger District.

INFORMATION: Manti-La Sal National Forest, Sanpete District, 283-4151; Price District, 637-2817; Ferron District, 384-2372; Fishlake National Forest, Richfield District, 896-9233. Get a copy of *Auto Tour; Great Basin Experiment Range,* from the Forest Service. They also can be found in boxes along the way.

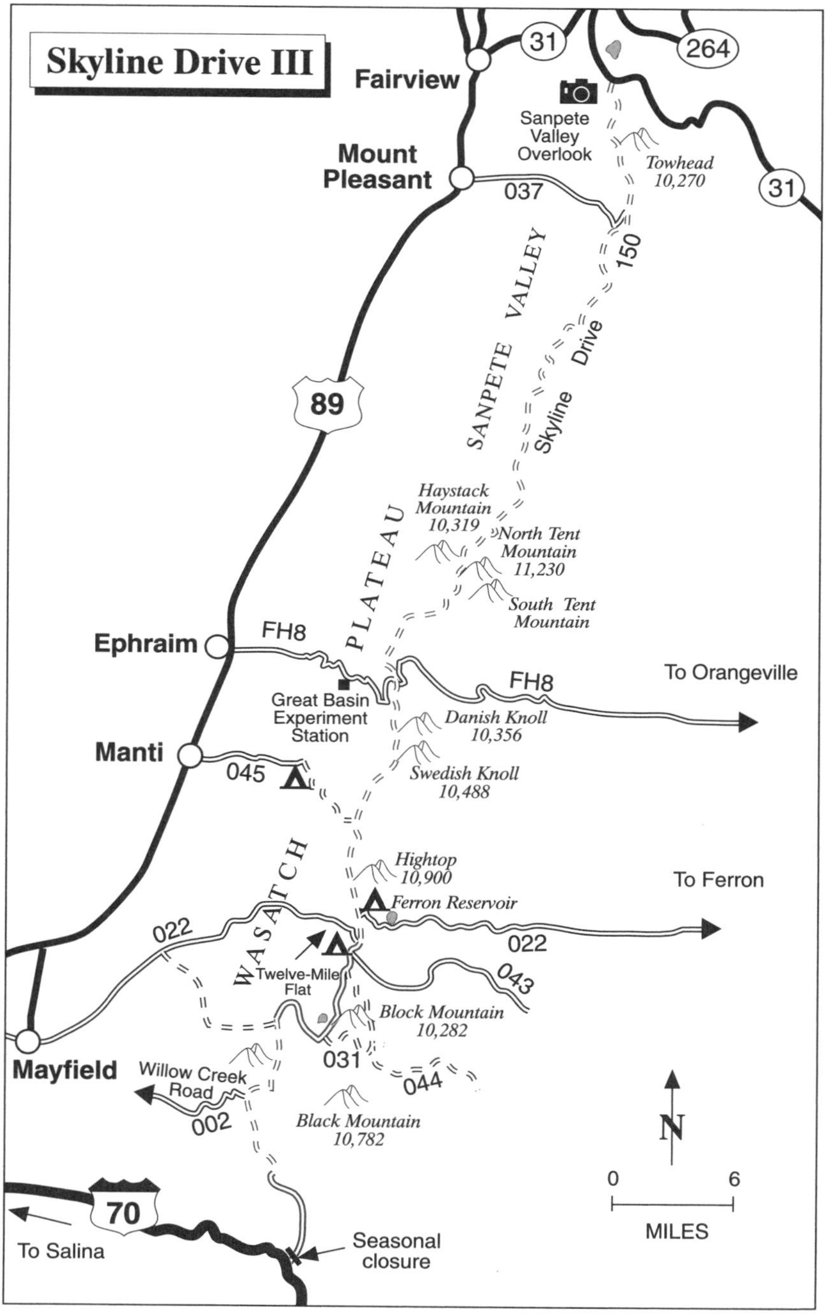
Skyline Drive III
Fairview
31
264
Sanpete
Valley
Overlook
Towhead
10,270
Mount
Pleasant
037
31
150
SANPETE VALLEY
Skyline Drive
89
Haystack
Mountain
10,319
North Tent
Mountain
11,230
South Tent
Mountain
PLATEAU
Ephraim
FH8
To Orangeville
FH8
Great Basin
Experiment
Station
Danish Knoll
10,356
Manti
045
Swedish Knoll
10,488
WASATCH
Hightop
10,900
To Ferron
Ferron Reservoir
022
022
Twelve-Mile
Flat
043
Block Mountain
10,282
Mayfield
Willow Creek
Road
031
044
002
Black Mountain
10,782
N
0
6
MILES
70
To Salina
Seasonal
closure

TRIP
21

Pony Express Trail

LOCATION: Fairfield to Ibapah, between I-80 & U.S. 50/6.

HIGHLIGHTS: National Back Country Byway across the Great Basin. Interpretive sites and ruins help you relive the legend created during the Pony Express' 19 months of operation, 1860-61, and the days of stagecoach travel. Waterfowl at Fish Springs National Wildlife Refuge.

DIFFICULTY: Easy dirt and gravel road. No services. Prepare for desert travel. Flash floods possible during storms.

TIME & DISTANCE: 6 hours; 133 miles.

GETTING THERE: South of Salt Lake City take U-73 to Camp Floyd-Stagecoach Inn State Park. Reset your odometer.

THE DRIVE: From the park, where there's an information kiosk and museum, take U-73 southwest to Five-Mile Pass. Turn left onto Faust Rd. At mile 18.9 you'll reach U-36. Go left (south) on the highway for a half-mile, then right at the sign onto a dirt and gravel road. Climb to 6,192-ft. Lookout Pass. Visit the cemetery where a stagecoach station operator's beloved dogs lie buried with three people. Continue through basin and range desert, across sloping valleys interrupted by range after range. At 45.2 you'll reach reconstructed Simpson Springs Station. Cross the Dugway Range, and at about mile 70 you'll pass the Dugway Geode Beds rock-collecting area. At mile 85 is marshy Fish Springs NWR, which has an 11-mile auto tour (best April & Sept.). Continue to Callao, at the base of the Deep Creek Range, topped by 12,087-ft. Ibapah Peak. 1.7 miles south of the T intersection is one of several 4x4 roads that ascend the benchlands of this towering range, the only one in the interior of the Great Basin in Utah with an abundance of water. (The upper reaches are a wilderness study area. Mechanized travel is restricted to roads in the southern foothills, on the east slope's benchlands, and Toms, Middle, Trout, Birch & Granite Canyons.) The Pony Express route goes right (north) at the T in Callao. 5.2 miles north of the T keep right at the Y, where the road becomes a single lane. Soon you'll see, on the left as you enter Overland Canyon, the ruins of Canyon Station, built after Indians killed the agent and four soldiers in 1863 at the original station site in the canyon. In 5.9 miles go left at a T; the adventure ends in 6 miles. (6 miles to the right from this T is Gold Hill ghost town.)

REST STOPS: Picnic areas at Camp Floyd (fee), Lookout Pass and Fish Springs. Simpson Springs CG (dry; $2 fee per vehicle). A dry but free campground 4 miles south of Callao. Recreational rock & mineral collecting at Dugway Geode Beds.

GETTING HOME: Go north to U.S. 93A, Wendover, I-80.

MAPS: Recreational Map of Utah; BLM's *House Range & Warm Springs Recreation & Vehicle Guide.*

INFORMATION: BLM, Salt Lake Office, has a brochure, 977-4300; Camp Floyd-Stagecoach Inn State Park, 768-8932; Fish Springs National Wildlife Refuge, 831-5353.

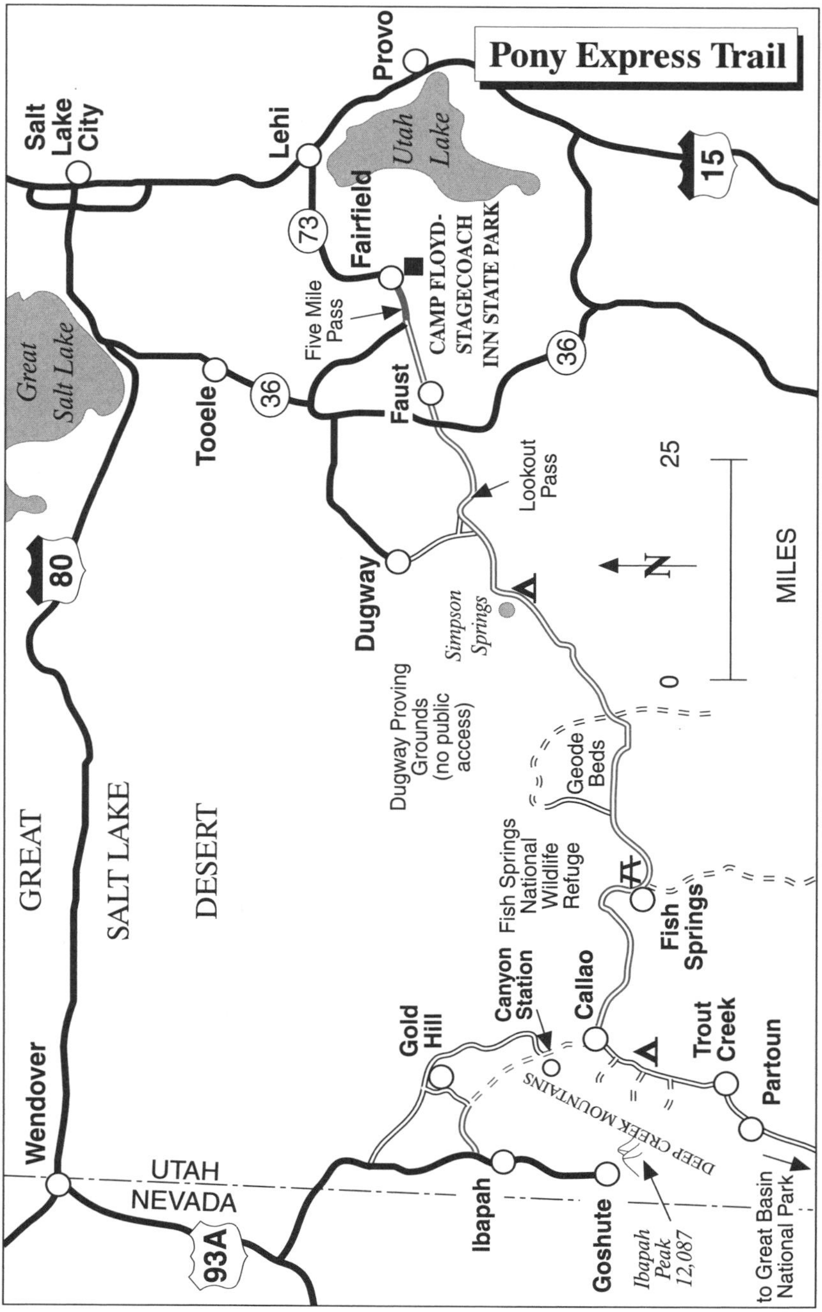
Pony Express Trail
Salt Lake City
Provo
Lehi
Utah Lake
Fairfield
73
CAMP FLOYD-STAGECOACH INN STATE PARK
Five Mile Pass
Great Salt Lake
Tooele
36
Faust
15
80
Lookout Pass
25
N
MILES
0
Dugway
Simpson Springs
Dugway Proving Grounds (no public access)
Geode Beds
Fish Springs National Wildlife Refuge
Fish Springs
GREAT
SALT LAKE
DESERT
Callao
Canyon Station
Gold Hill
Trout Creek
Partoun
DEEP CREEK MOUNTAINS
Wendover
UTAH
NEVADA
93A
Ibapah
Goshute
Ibapah Peak 12,087
to Great Basin National Park

Mayfield to Ferron

LOCATION: On the Wasatch Plateau between U.S. 89 and U-10. Manti-La Sal National Forest.

HIGHLIGHTS: Climbing a mile to Skyline Drive. Great vistas. The ramparts of Ferron Canyon. Ends at Millsite State Park, which has showers, campsites and a golf course.

DIFFICULTY: Easy. Watch for logging trucks.

TIME & DISTANCE: 2.5 hours; 47 miles to the park.

GETTING THERE: You start this east-west route at Mayfield or Ferron. I start at Mayfield, near Gunnison. From Main Street, turn east onto Canyon Road near the post office and City Hall, toward Skyline Drive. Reset your odometer.

THE DRIVE: Canyon Road goes through pinyon- and juniper-covered hills, and at mile 1.7 the pavement ends. At 3.6 you'll cross into the national forest, where the road becomes No. 022, and in a couple more miles you'll enter the Twelve-Mile Recreation Area. Here switchbacks climb steeply. Broad vistas of canyons, basins and mountains appear, with a particularly beautiful view at mile 11. You'll begin to see many exceptionally large aspens, and by about mile 15 you'll pass the Grove of the Aspen Giants Scenic Area, where the normally slight trees reach 30 inches in diameter. In another 3 miles or so you'll enter Twelve-Mile Flat, where there is a fine campground at 10,120 feet elevation. Turn left here onto road 150/22, part of superlative Skyline Drive III *(trip 20)*, and 1.7 miles farther road 022 resumes to the right, descending toward Ferron. If you've not been on this leg of Skyline Drive, go north a short distance to Hightop, at about 10,900 feet Skyline Drive's highest point. (Mayfield is at 5,660 ft.) Here you are on the divide between the Great Basin to the west and the Colorado River drainage to the east. Road 022 winds down through a basin, and passes Ferron Reservoir and Sky Haven Lodge. As you descend, trading forested mountains for desert, you'll have tremendous vistas of the badlands, sandstone cliffs and canyons of Plateau Country. At 36 you'll see the turnoff to Ferron Canyon Overlook, which gives you a preview of the spectacular canyon leading to Millsite State Park and Ferron.

REST STOPS: Camping at Twelve-Mile, Ferron Reservoir, Ferron Canyon & Millsite State Park. Cafe, gas, cabins at Sky Haven.

GETTING HOME: U-10 north to U.S. 6/191; south to I-70.

MAP: Manti-La Sal NF, Sanpete & Ferron Ranger Districts.

INFORMATION: Sanpete District, 283-4151; Ferron District, 384-2372.

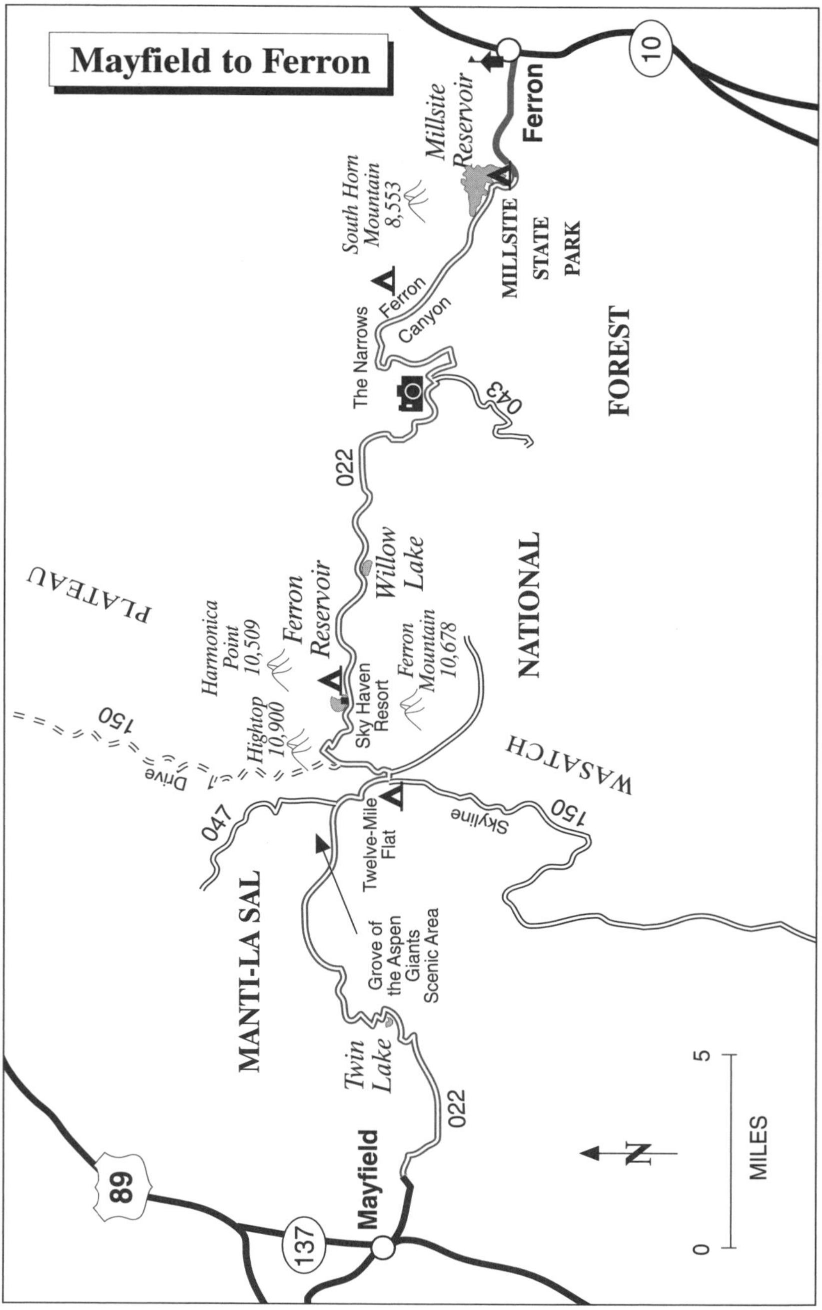

Mayfield to Ferron
Ferron
10
Millsite Reservoir
South Horn Mountain 8,553
MILLSITE STATE PARK
Ferron Canyon
The Narrows
043
FOREST
022
Willow Lake
NATIONAL
PLATEAU
Ferron Reservoir
Harmonica Point 10,509
Ferron Mountain 10,678
Sky Haven Resort
Hightop 10,900
150
Drive
WASATCH
047
Twelve-Mile Flat
Skyline
150
MANTI-LA SAL
Grove of the Aspen Giants Scenic Area
Twin Lake
022
Mayfield
89
137
N
0
5
MILES

Wedge Overlook/Buckhorn Draw

LOCATION: San Rafael Swell between U-10, I-70, U.S. 6/191.

HIGHLIGHTS: Little Grand Canyon. Rock art. High sandstone cliffs and deep canyons of the San Rafael Swell, a huge anticline. "Black boxes," very narrow "slot" canyons, of the San Rafael River.

DIFFICULTY: Easy. Mostly good dirt and gravel roads.

TIME & DISTANCE: 9.5 hours, 130 miles with spurs, including optional 15-mile (one-way) Mexican Mountain Road.

GETTING THERE: Take U-10 1.5 miles north from downtown Castle Dale. Turn east at the sign.

THE DRIVE: In the distance you'll see the canyons, knobs, domes and spires of the San Rafael Swell, an 80-mile by 30-mile uplift sculpted over millions of years by wind and water. Through it snakes the little San Rafael River. At mile 10.2 a road branches right. The 13-mile side trip passes a fascinating ravine (take the left two-track in 4.7 miles), and ends at lush Hamburg Bottoms, at the river. Back on the main road, in 2.8 miles take another right to the Wedge Overlook. You'll soon see the road to Fuller Bottoms, a riverside oasis. After passing through pinyon-juniper woodland, the road to the overlook abruptly ends at the brink of awesome Little Grand Canyon, with the river 1,200 feet below. 2.3 miles farther down the main road, turn right to go through beautiful Buckhorn Wash, which has stunning side canyons to explore. Stop at a developed site where the cliffs bear mysterious Barrier Canyon-style rock art 2,000 to 4,000 years old. 3.9 miles farther is scenic but dead-end Mexican Mountain Road. Explore spurs that go to the river. 0.2 mile before the locked gate a two-track crosses the bench to the right. It's a wilderness study area, so you must walk 300 yards or so across the bench to gaze into the so-called Black Boxes, where the river's already narrow gorge slims to a few yards wide. On the main road, cross the San Rafael Bridge and drive through pastoral hills and grasslands, and past a sink hole, to I-70.

REST STOPS: Primitive camping at Wedge Overlook; campground at San Rafael Bridge Recreation Site. Hike up side canyons you'll see along the way.

GETTING HOME: I-70 east or west. From Castle Dale, take U-10 north to Price or south to I-70.

MAPS: Recreation Map of the San Rafael Swell & San Rafael Desert; Recreational Map of Utah; also refer to the brochure, *Recreation Guide to the San Rafael Area.*

INFORMATION: BLM, Price Field Office, 636-3600.

Wedge Overlook/Buckhorn Draw

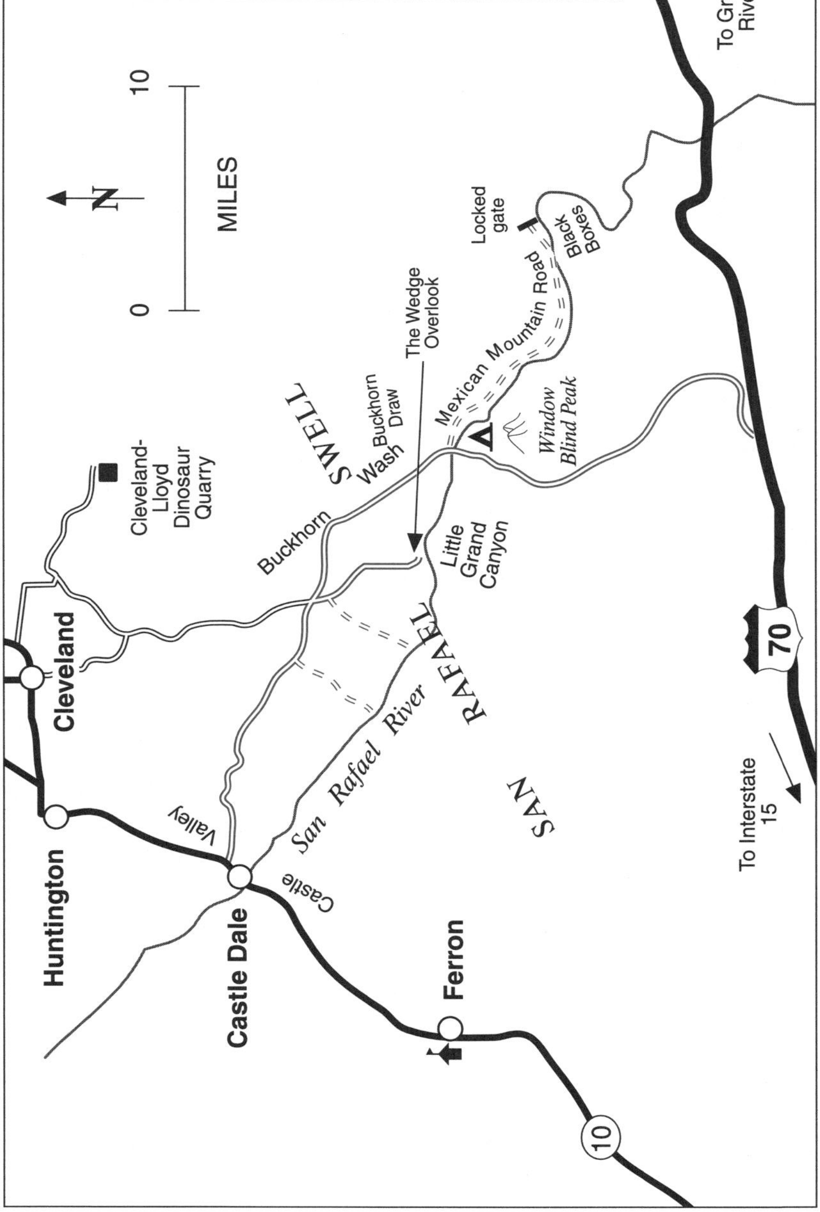

TRIP 24

Sego Ghost Town

LOCATION: North of Thompson Springs & I-70.

HIGHLIGHTS: Excellent roadside rock art panels. The ghost town of Sego. This is a short and convenient drive for anyone looking for a break from I-70.

DIFFICULTY: Easy. The county-maintained road is a public right of way, but Sego and adjacent lands are private property. Avoid trespassing. Do not take or disturb anything.

TIME & DISTANCE: 1.5-2 hours; 10 miles round-trip.

GETTING THERE: From I-70 about 5.3 miles east of Crescent Junction, drive into the hamlet of Thompson Springs. Continue through town, crossing the railroad tracks at the Amtrak station. Head directly toward the Book Cliffs.

THE DRIVE: Once an important shipping point for cattle, Thompson Springs is now a quiet little town of dusty memories. Sego, which had as many as 500-600 people, was named after Utah's state flower, the Sego lily, abundant on the nearby hills. But that was its third name. Its first was Ballard, Neslin its second. Drive north from Thompson Springs toward the Book Cliffs, a mix of sandstone, shale and coal at the base of the East Tavaputs Plateau. Where the pavement ends 3.4 miles from Thompson Springs, you'll see a developed rock art site with excellent interpretive signs. Rock art on the sandstone cliffs represents three separate cultures that lived in the area during the past several thousand years. (Never touch or in any way disturb rock art.) As you proceed up the canyon you'll see the remains of trestles for the railroad that hauled hard anthracite coal from mines around Sego. The town existed from the early 1900s to the early 1950s, when demand for coal to fuel railroad locomotives faded. About a half-mile from the rock art site turn right, and soon you'll see the old cemetery. The town site is a short distance ahead. There, you'll see the shells of the old American Fuel Co. store and a wood-frame boarding house. The hillsides are pocked by dugouts and other crude structures. The drive up the canyon is pretty, but the road is closed at the Uintah-Ouray Indian Reservation. On the return to Thompson Canyon go through a cut in a hill through which trains once passed.

REST STOPS: Toilets and tables at the rock art site.

GETTING HOME: Backtrack to I-70.

MAP: Recreational Map of Utah.

INFORMATION: Moab/Green River Visitor Information, 259-8825 or 1-800-635-6622; Grand County Roads Dept., 259-5308; BLM, Moab Field Office, 259-6111.

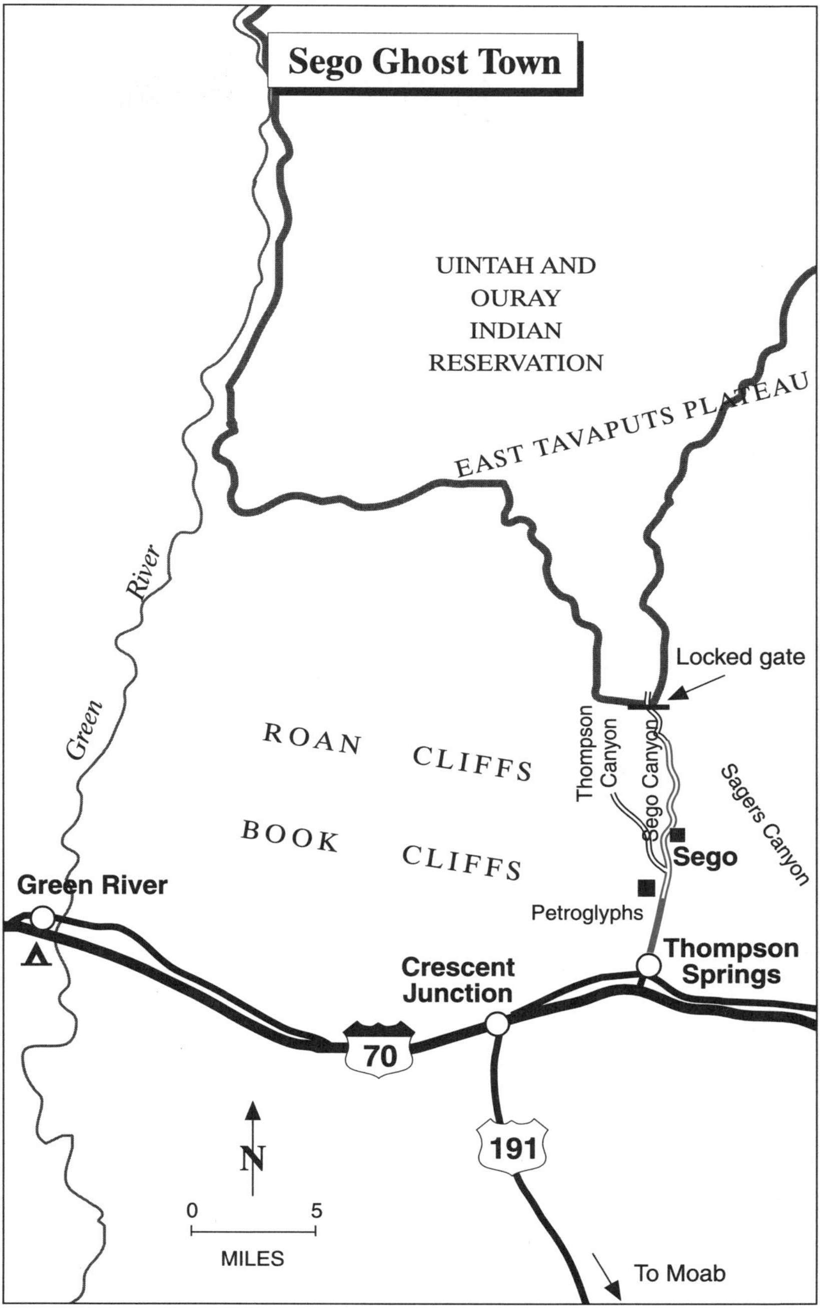
Sego Ghost Town
UINTAH AND
OURAY
INDIAN
RESERVATION
EAST TAVAPUTS PLATEAU
Green River
Locked gate
Thompson Canyon
Sego Canyon
Sagers Canyon
ROAN CLIFFS
BOOK CLIFFS
Sego
Petroglyphs
Green River
Thompson Springs
Crescent Junction
70
191
N
0
5
MILES
To Moab

TRIP 25

Pahvant Range Traverse

LOCATION: Pahvant (also spelled Pavant) Range between Fillmore and Richfield. Fishlake National Forest.

HIGHLIGHTS: Relentless beauty as you drive along the crest of a ridge between the Great Basin and Plateau Country. Stop at the old territorial statehouse in Fillmore. Completed in 1855, it is Utah's oldest governmental building.

DIFFICULTY: First 6.7 miles are easy. Remainder is moderate. Some real four-wheeling. Can be muddy. Closed in winter.

TIME & DISTANCE: 3.5 hours; 43 miles.

GETTING THERE: I start at Fillmore, on I-15, and end at Richfield, on I-70. From Main Street take 200 South Canyon Road east, following the U.S. Forest Service picnic area sign. 2.8 miles from Main Street you'll enter Fishlake National Forest, and the road turns to dirt. Set your odometer at 0 here.

THE DRIVE: The one-lane dirt road, No. 100, climbs up rugged Chalk Creek Canyon into mountains of ancient lakebed sediments. The views west across the Great Basin are excellent. Between 5.4 and 6.4 miles from the forest boundary you'll pass four pretty picnic areas. The road bends left at 6.7 miles, and becomes a 4x4 route as it winds up the side of the canyon. By mile 10 the serpentine track is a mere canyonside shelf. Soon it's quite rough; use 4wd. By mile 14.8 you're at about 9,200 feet, with endless vistas eastward across restless plateaus and, to the south, the Tushar Mountains. Reaching 12,169 feet, the Tushars are the highest range between the Rockies and the Sierra Nevada. At mile 17.8, over 9,000 feet high, road 100 reaches north-south road 096, the Richfield Pioneer Road, part of the popular Paiute ATV trail. Go right (south). You'll struggle to keep your eyes on this rough road instead of the awesome scenery. By about mile 10 you'll reach 9,500 feet elevation, where the panorama stretches from the Colorado Plateau to the east across the pale Great Basin to the west. Stay on 096 for another 7.9 miles, then follow it left toward Richfield where it meets road 500. The road improves some as you descend past rainbow-colored rock to Richfield.

REST STOPS: The picnic areas along Chalk Creek, which have toilets, tables and fishing (Forest Service has been allowing camping). Fillmore and Richfield have nice parks.

GETTING HOME: I-15 or I-70.

MAPS: Fishlake National Forest, Fillmore & Richfield Districts. Trails Illustrated's *Fishlake NF & BLM Sevier River Resource Area.*

INFORMATION: Fillmore Ranger District, 743-5721; Richfield Ranger District, 896-9233.

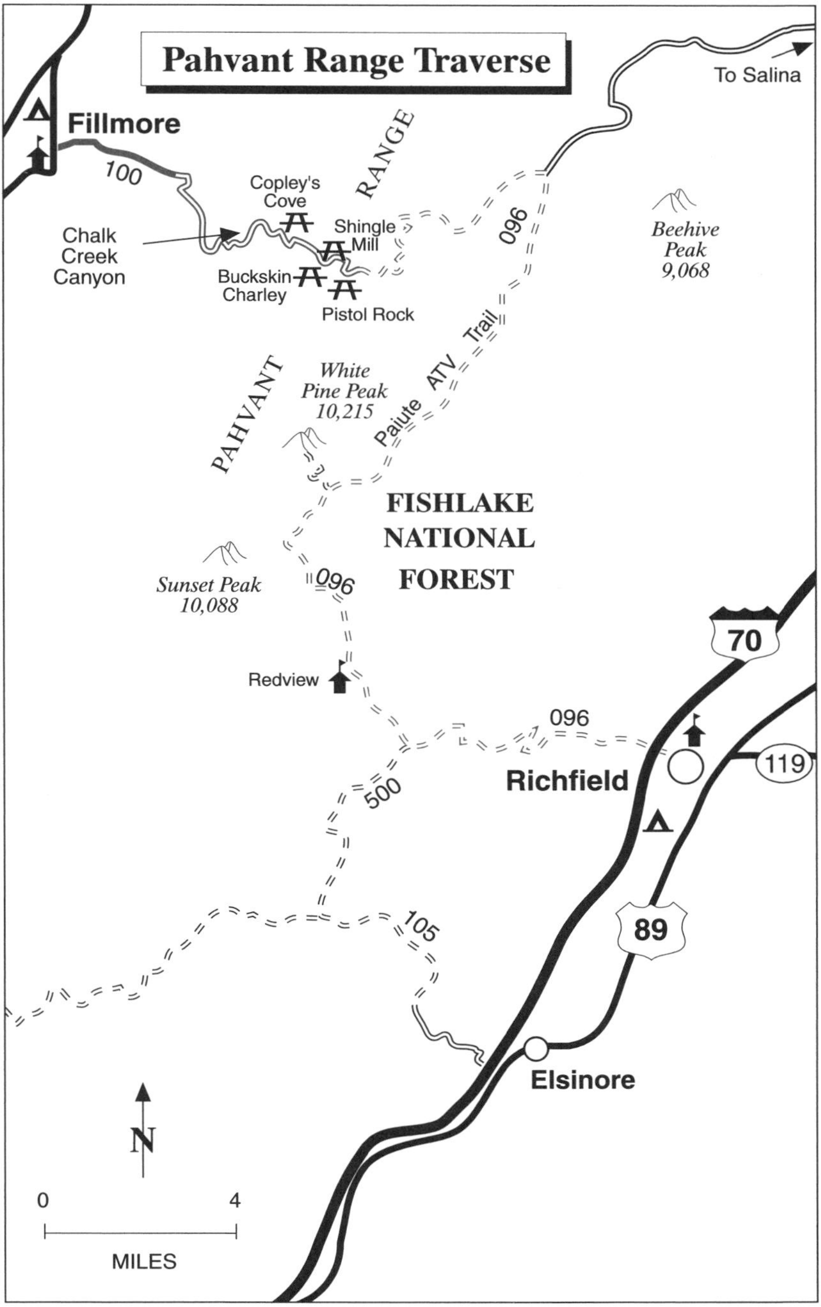

Pahvant Range Traverse
To Salina
Fillmore
100
Copley's Cove
RANGE
Shingle Mill
Chalk Creek Canyon
Buckskin Charley
Pistol Rock
096
Beehive Peak 9,068
Paiute ATV Trail
White Pine Peak 10,215
PAHVANT
FISHLAKE NATIONAL FOREST
Sunset Peak 10,088
096
70
Redview
096
Richfield
119
500
89
105
Elsinore
N
0
4
MILES

Kanosh Canyon

LOCATION: South of Kanosh, in the Pahvant (also Pavant) Range between I-70 & I-15. Fishlake National Forest.

HIGHLIGHTS: A pretty and relaxing cruise through pastoral hills; scenic Kanosh Canyon. Best in summer and fall.

DIFFICULTY: Easy. Closed in winter.

TIME & DISTANCE: 1.5 hour; 24 miles.

GETTING THERE: You can take this north-south drive in either direction. I go south, ending near I-70 between Cove Fort and Fremont Indian State Park. In Kanosh, take 300 South east off Main Street, toward Kanosh Canyon. Reset your odometer.

THE DRIVE: The pavement will end in less than a mile, and in less than 2 more miles you'll cross into Fishlake National Forest. Then you'll continue up narrow Kanosh Canyon, along Corn Creek, as you climb into the Pahvant Range. These mountains consist of lake deposits that are closely related to the brilliant pink deposits at Bryce Canyon National Park and Cedar Breaks National Monument. At mile 5.8 you'll pass Adelaide Campground. The hills are vegetated with grass, sagebrush, pinyon pines and junipers, scrub oak and creekside cottonwoods. By about mile 14.3 you'll go over a low summit, at about 7,000 feet, as you follow the course of an undulating valley. As you continue south, descending gradually through rolling hills and knobby mountaintops, you'll have fine views of the Tushar Mountains, which soar to 12,169 ft. at Delano Peak, making them the highest range between the Rockies and the Sierra Nevada. *(trips 31 & 36* take you through them.) By mile 24.3, after passing through a rocky flat called Devil's Dance Floor and then Mud Spring Hollow, you'll reach U-4. I-70 is about 2 miles to the right (west), but I recommend you go east to Fremont Indian State Park.

REST STOPS: Though it's beside the dirt road, Adelaide Campground is still very pretty. Visit Cove Fort, the best-preserved of Utah's 19th century forts; and Fremont Indian State Park, where you can picnic and see ancient rock art and artifacts. Camp at Castle Rock Campground, near the park.

GETTING HOME: I-15 or I-70.

MAPS: Fishlake National Forest; Fillmore, Richfield Ranger Districts; Trails Illustrated's *Paiute ATV Trail, Fishlake National Forest, BLM Sevier River Resource Area.*

INFORMATION: Fillmore Ranger District, 743-5721.

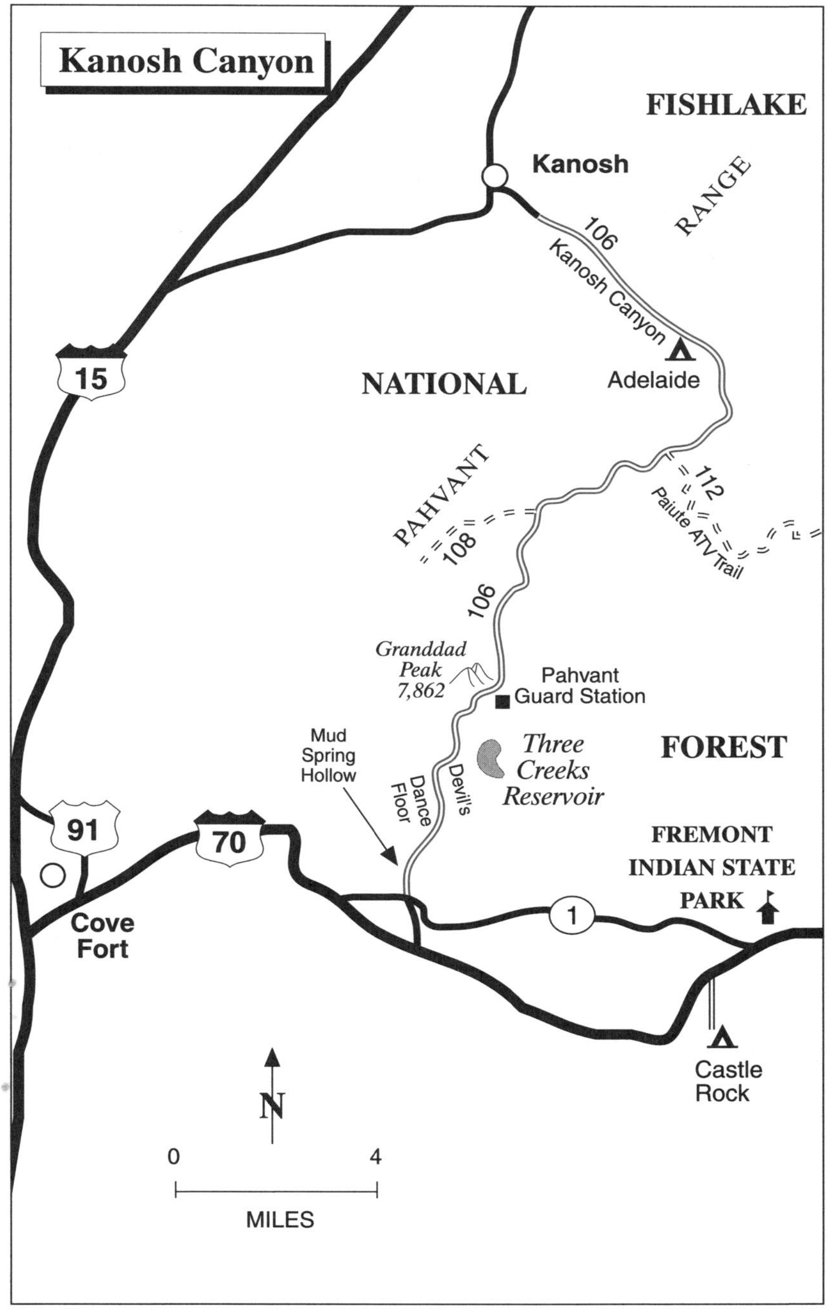
Kanosh Canyon
FISHLAKE
Kanosh
RANGE
106
Kanosh Canyon
Adelaide
NATIONAL
15
PAHVANT
112
Paiute ATV Trail
108
106
Granddad Peak 7,862
Pahvant Guard Station
Three Creeks Reservoir
FOREST
Mud Spring Hollow
Dance Floor
Devil's
91
70
FREMONT INDIAN STATE PARK
Cove Fort
1
Castle Rock
N
0
4
MILES

TRIP
27

Gooseberry-Fremont Road

LOCATION: Fishlake Plateau southeast of Salina, between I-70 and Johnson Valley Reservoir. Fishlake National Forest.

HIGHLIGHTS: The valley along Sevenmile Creek is one of the prettiest mountain valleys I know of. Wildflowers, wildlife, fine vistas. Soldier Canyon, at the north end, is beautiful.

DIFFICULTY: Easy on a graded road. Can be very dusty.

TIME & DISTANCE: 1.5 hours; 30 miles.

GETTING THERE: Take this north-south route in either direction. I start at Johnson Valley Reservoir and go north to I-70. About 4 miles north of Fremont, on U-72, turn north onto U-25 at the sign for Johnson Valley Reservoir and Fishlake NF. The highway, also designated road No. 036 on the Forest Service map, follows the Fremont River. 13.2 miles from U-72 turn north (right) onto dirt road No. 640. Set your odometer at 0.

THE DRIVE: You'll drive along Sevenmile Creek through meadows bordered by aspens and pines. As you continue north you'll pass verdant riparian (streamside) areas that have been fenced off to protect them from damage by cattle, and to study their recovery from the effects of grazing. This pastoral mountain valley lies at about 9,500 feet. The naturalness of its appearance — lush meadows and wetlands flanked by aspen forest — is striking. The road narrows to a single lane at the end of the valley, and soon you'll cruise beneath 11,547-ft. Mt. Terrell, on the right. You're climbing now, and at mile 10.2 you'll cross Niotche-Lost Creek Divide, at 10,550 ft. From here you'll descend down switchbacks toward another picturesque valley, passing Gooseberry Campground. In the distance far below lies the massive hump of the San Rafael Swell. Notice how the high-elevation vegetation is giving way to species common to drier climates. At mile 25.3, as you look out over Gooseberry Valley, you'll see road 037 going left to scenic Soldier Canyon. You can go straight 4 miles to I-70, but I recommend the pretty 7-mile drive on the small dirt road, No. 037, between the high, eroded cliffs of Soldier Canyon. Salina is 10 miles from this turnoff.

REST STOPS: Gooseberry Campground. On your way into Salina you'll pass wonderful Salina City Park.

GETTING HOME: From Salina, I-70 or U.S. 50 to I-15.

MAP: Fishlake National Forest, Richfield Ranger District.

INFORMATION: Richfield Ranger District, 896-9233.

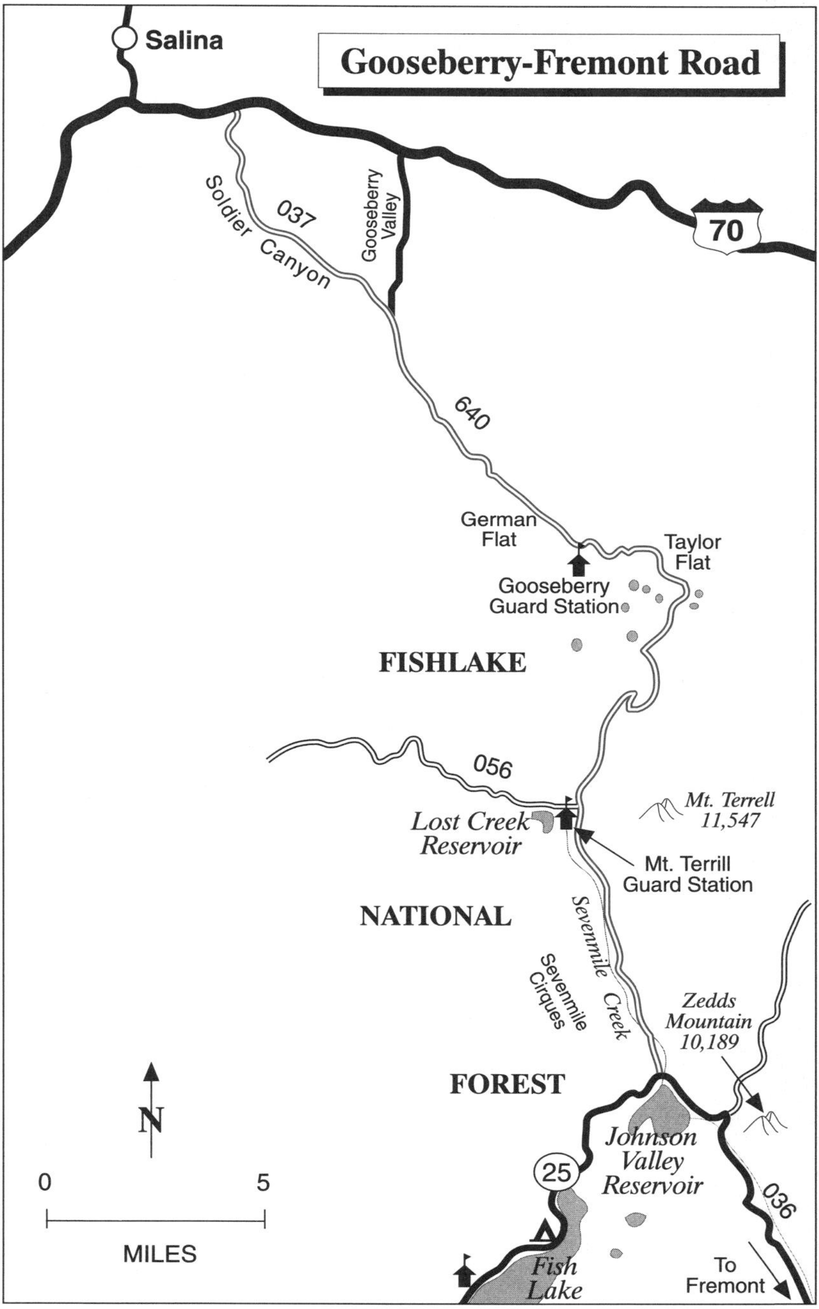
Gooseberry-Fremont Road
Salina
70
037
Soldier Canyon
Gooseberry Valley
640
German Flat
Taylor Flat
Gooseberry Guard Station
FISHLAKE
056
Lost Creek Reservoir
Mt. Terrell 11,547
Mt. Terrill Guard Station
NATIONAL
Sevenmile Creek
Sevenmile Cirques
Zedds Mountain 10,189
FOREST
N
0
5
MILES
Johnson Valley Reservoir
25
036
Fish Lake
To Fremont

TRIP 28

Reds Canyon/Hondoo Arch

LOCATION: South of I-70, west of Green River.

HIGHLIGHTS: The beautiful San Rafael Swell; awesome Reds Canyon; Hondoo Arch; Temple Mountain; bizarre Goblin Valley; historic Swasey Cabin; side canyons; pictographs.

DIFFICULTY: Easy-moderate; can be impassable if wet. Old mines in the area are dangerous.

TIME & DISTANCE: 6 hours & 90 miles with spurs.

GETTING THERE: You can begin near Goblin Valley State Park or I-70. I start at I-70. Take exit 129, 28 miles west of Green River. Watch for signs. Reset your odometer.

THE DRIVE: Drive across a grassland toward the buttes, cliffs and canyons of Sinbad Country, named for scenes in Arabian Knights. At mile 3.9 take the road on the right. At 4.1 go right again. A mile farther, as you drive among pinyon pines and junipers, go right again, through a fence. At 11 the main road continues straight; go right to Swasey Cabin, built by ranchers in 1921. On the main road, at mile 19 you'll reach a T at Taylor Flat. Go right for the exotic Reds Canyon loop. The adventure intensifies as you drive through a magnificent red rock gash in the Earth. By mile 33, as you approach Tomsich Butte, scan the skyline ahead for Hondoo Arch, named for its resemblance to a lariat's slip knot. The road will fork, right to the bottoms at Muddy Creek below Hondoo, left to climb out of Reds Canyon and continue the tour. In 5.2 miles you can go right on a spur that dead-ends in 11 miles where Muddy Creek passes beneath cliffs called Moroni Slopes. Beyond Reds Canyon return to Taylor Flat. Then it's on to Temple Mountain, said to resemble the Mormon temple at Manti, and Goblin Valley, with its odd sandstone figures. 0.2 mile after reaching pavement you'll see pictographs on cliffs to the left. Just beyond the Goblin Valley turnoff, a dirt road goes left (north) for a mile to a wash up a narrow canyon (on the left). It goes 3 miles to old uranium mines on Temple Mountain. (Good mountain biking.)

REST STOPS: Swasey Cabin. Goblin Valley State Park.

GETTING HOME: U-24 north back to I-70.

MAPS: Recreational Map of the San Rafael Swell & San Rafael Desert; Recreational Map of Utah; the flyers *Recreation Guide to the San Rafael Area* and, for another nearby drive, *San Rafael Desert Loop Auto Tour.*

INFORMATION: BLM, Price Field Office, 636-3600; Goblin Valley State Park, 564-3633; John Wesley Powell River History Museum in Green River, 564-3526.

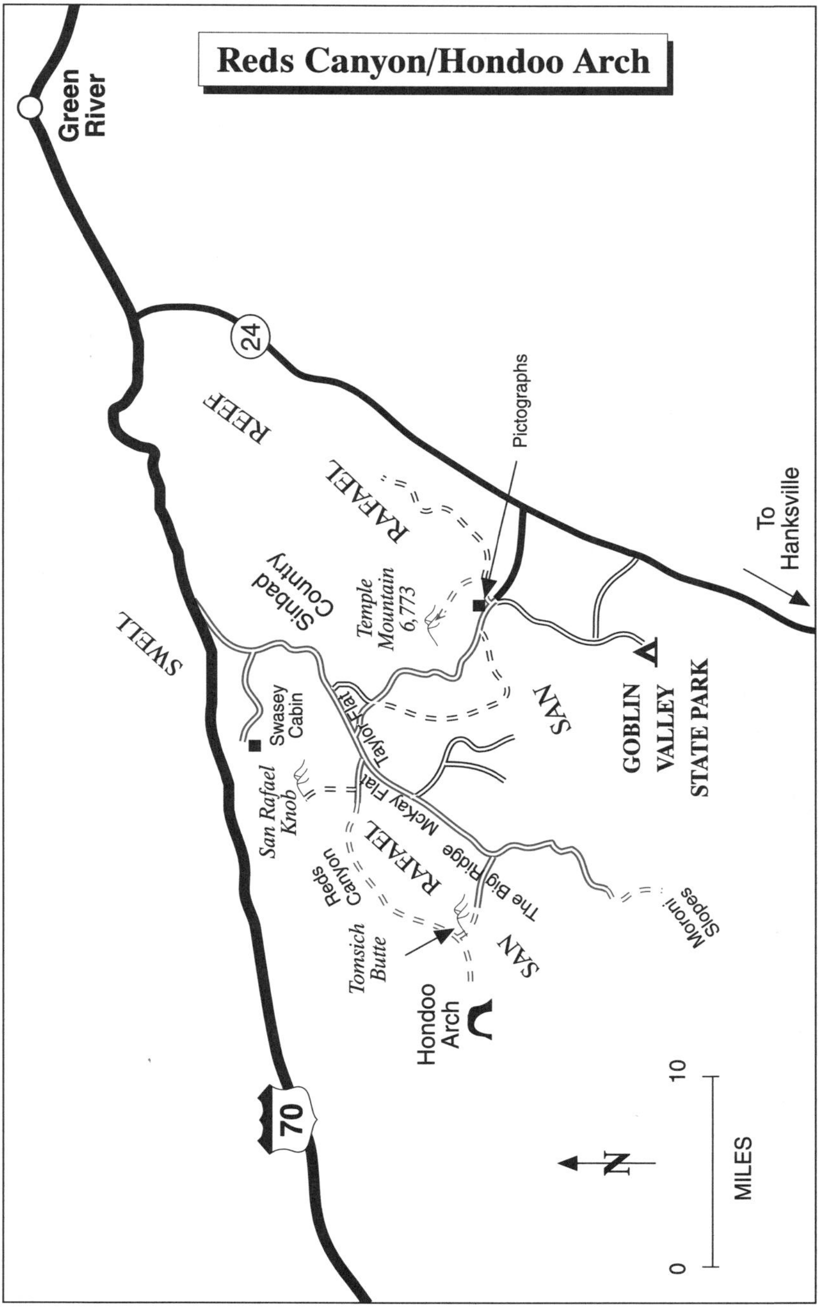
Reds Canyon/Hondoo Arch
Green River
24
REEF
RAFAEL
Pictographs
To Hanksville
Sinbad Country
Temple Mountain 6,773
SWELL
Swasey Cabin
Taylor Flat
SAN
GOBLIN VALLEY STATE PARK
San Rafael Knob
Mckay Flat
RAFAEL
Reds Canyon
The Big Ridge
Moroni Slopes
Tomsich Butte
SAN
Hondoo Arch
70
N
0
10
MILES

Tower Arch Loop

LOCATION: Arches National Park, near Moab.

HIGHLIGHTS: Klondike Bluffs, Marching Men, Tower and Eye of the Whale arches, views of the La Sal Mountains. Best spring and fall.

DIFFICULTY: Salt Valley Road is easy, but impassable when wet. The rest is moderate. Rocky spots, long sandy stretches (lower tire pressure), some slickrock. Hot in summer.

TIME & DISTANCE: 2 hours; 22.5 miles. Allow perhaps 2 hours more to visit Tower and Eye of the Whale arches.

GETTING THERE: From the park entrance follow the main park road 16.3 miles to the Salt Valley Road turnoff, past Fiery Furnace.

THE DRIVE: Below Salt Valley is a shifting salt bed thousands of feet thick, deposited by an evaporating sea 300 million years ago. Its movement has lifted and distorted the Jurassic (144-208 MYA) salmon-hued Entrada Sandstone and buff-colored Navajo Sandstone deposited on top of it by floods, winds and oceans. That movement and erosion created the park's arches. On the left at 7.1 miles is the 4x4 loop to Tower Arch, Herdina Park and Balanced Rock. The Klondike Bluffs/Tower Arch hiking trail is a mile ahead. Go left. The road is rocky and rough. To the southeast rise the La Sal Mountains, once magma that pushed up against overlying sedimentary rock, creating a dome. The magma cooled, and the sedimentary cap eroded away, exposing the mountains. Soon you'll see on the left the road south to Balanced Rock; you'll return to it. On the right are the humps of Klondike Bluffs and the fins and spires of Marching Men. Dip into the wash ahead and go up the hill on the other side. Angle north around the bluffs' west side. You'll soon reach a parking area from which you can hike to huge Tower Arch. The route to Balanced Rock follows sandy washes and crosses broad flats, with some slickrock to traverse. In the area called Herdina Park descend a sandy stretch. Look right for Eye of the Whale. Go left at Willow Flats Road to Balanced Rock.

REST STOPS: Tower Arch. Picnic at Balanced Rock. Devil's Garden Campground.

SPECIAL NOTES: Pets aren't advised. They must be kept on leashes and cannot leave the road corridor. No backcountry camping is permitted along the roads. If you explore on foot or bike, stick to slickrock and washes. Never step or ride on cryptobiotic crust, the fragile top soil you'll see everywhere. Vital to the ecology, it takes decades to recover.

MAPS: The park brochure, obtained at the entrance station, is adequate. Trails Illustrated's *Arches National Park* is best.

INFORMATION: Arches National Park, 259-8161; TTY (for the hearing-impaired), 259-5279.

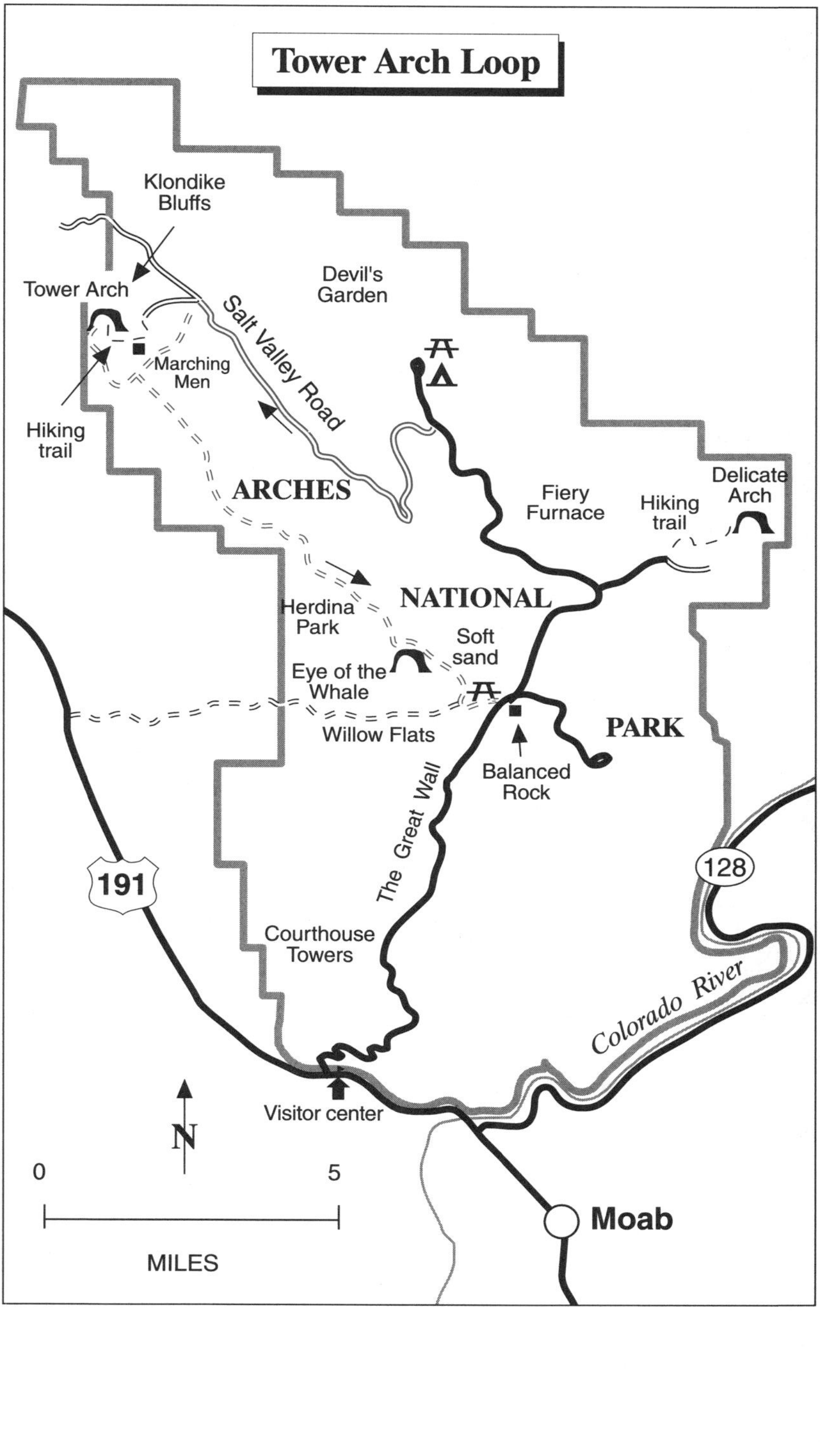
Tower Arch Loop
Klondike
Bluffs
Tower Arch
Devil's
Garden
Salt Valley Road
Marching
Men
Hiking
trail
ARCHES
Fiery
Furnace
Hiking
trail
Delicate
Arch
NATIONAL
Herdina
Park
Soft
sand
Eye of the
Whale
Willow Flats
PARK
Balanced
Rock
The Great Wall
191
128
Courthouse
Towers
Colorado River
Visitor center
N
0
5
MILES
Moab

TRIP 30

Cove Mountain Road

LOCATION: Southeast of Richfield, on the Sevier Plateau.

HIGHLIGHTS: Climbing almost 5,000 feet through high valleys and aspen forests that promise brilliant autumn color.

DIFFICULTY: Easy to moderate. Rocky, rutted in places.

TIME & DISTANCE: 2 hours; 36 miles.

GETTING THERE: In Richfield take 300 North (U-118) east off Main Street. You'll come to a Y where U-119 goes right toward Fishlake and Capitol Reef National Park. Take U-119 for about 4 miles; turn right at the sign for Cove Mountain and Glenwood. In Glenwood turn left at the stop sign at the town hall. You'll reach another Y at the Glenwood Fish Hatchery, where Cove Mountain Road is to the right. Set your odometer at 0.

THE DRIVE: The dirt and gravel road winds through hills of grass and sagebrush, boulders and rocks. At mile 2.8 you'll reach a T. Go left, on what will become road 068 in Fishlake National Forest. The climb from the T provides fine views to the north of the Wasatch Plateau and the valleys of the Sevier and San Pitch rivers, as well as the Great Basin to the west. At about mile 4.5 the road surface becomes quite rocky. In another half-mile the road crosses into the national forest, then runs along Bell Rock Ridge at about 7,400 feet. Continue climbing across broad Cove Mountain through gullies, ravines and hollows that separate slopes forested with aspens and pines. At 10.8, at over 8,000 feet, the road enters Hunter's Flat. Mile 13.2 will find you at Big Lake, in a basin at 9,000 feet. Continuing on 068, keep left at the next Y, where 080 branches right to Annabella Reservoir and Deep Lake. Soon you'll soar to 10,200 feet and cross Magleby Pass. Descending toward Koosharem (an Indian word for a red clover, or an edible tuber that grows in the valley), you'll have a view of the mountains and valleys to the east. At mile 27 is the right turn to Koosharem Guard Station, built in 1910. Two miles farther 068 meets 076. Take 076 to Koosharem, 7.4 miles farther.

REST STOPS: Primitive camping at Milo's Kitchen, 1.9 miles from the intersection of 068 and 076.

GETTING HOME: U-62 north to U-24 & I-70. Or U-62 south to U.S. 89.

MAPS: Fishlake National Forest, Fillmore & Richfield Districts; Trails Illustrated's *Fishlake NF & BLM Sevier River Area.*

INFORMATION: Richfield Ranger District, 896-9233.

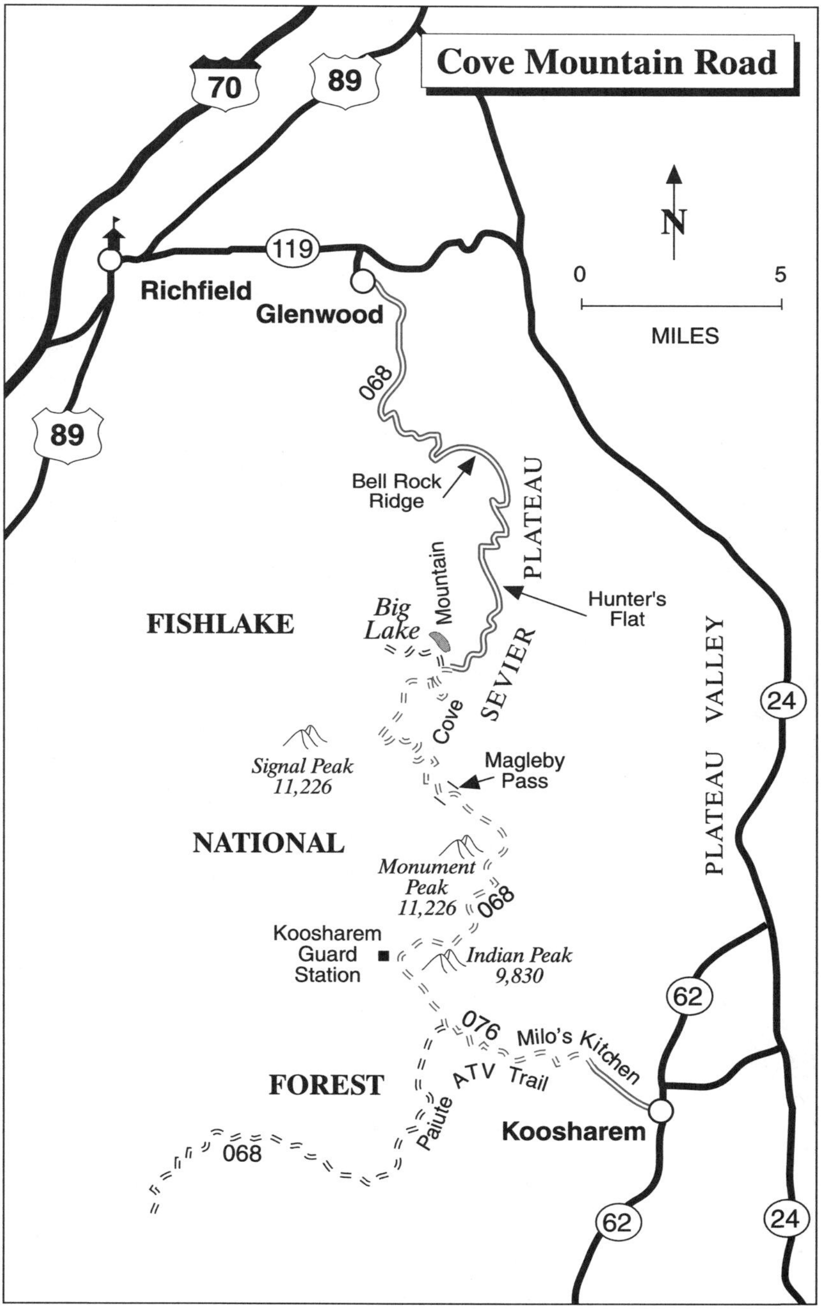
Cove Mountain Road
70
89
119
Richfield
Glenwood
89
N
0
5
MILES
068
Bell Rock Ridge
PLATEAU
Mountain
Big Lake
Hunter's Flat
FISHLAKE
SEVIER
Cove
PLATEAU VALLEY
24
Signal Peak 11,226
Magleby Pass
NATIONAL
Monument Peak 11,226
068
Koosharem Guard Station
Indian Peak 9,830
62
076
Milo's Kitchen
FOREST
Paiute ATV Trail
Koosharem
068
62
24

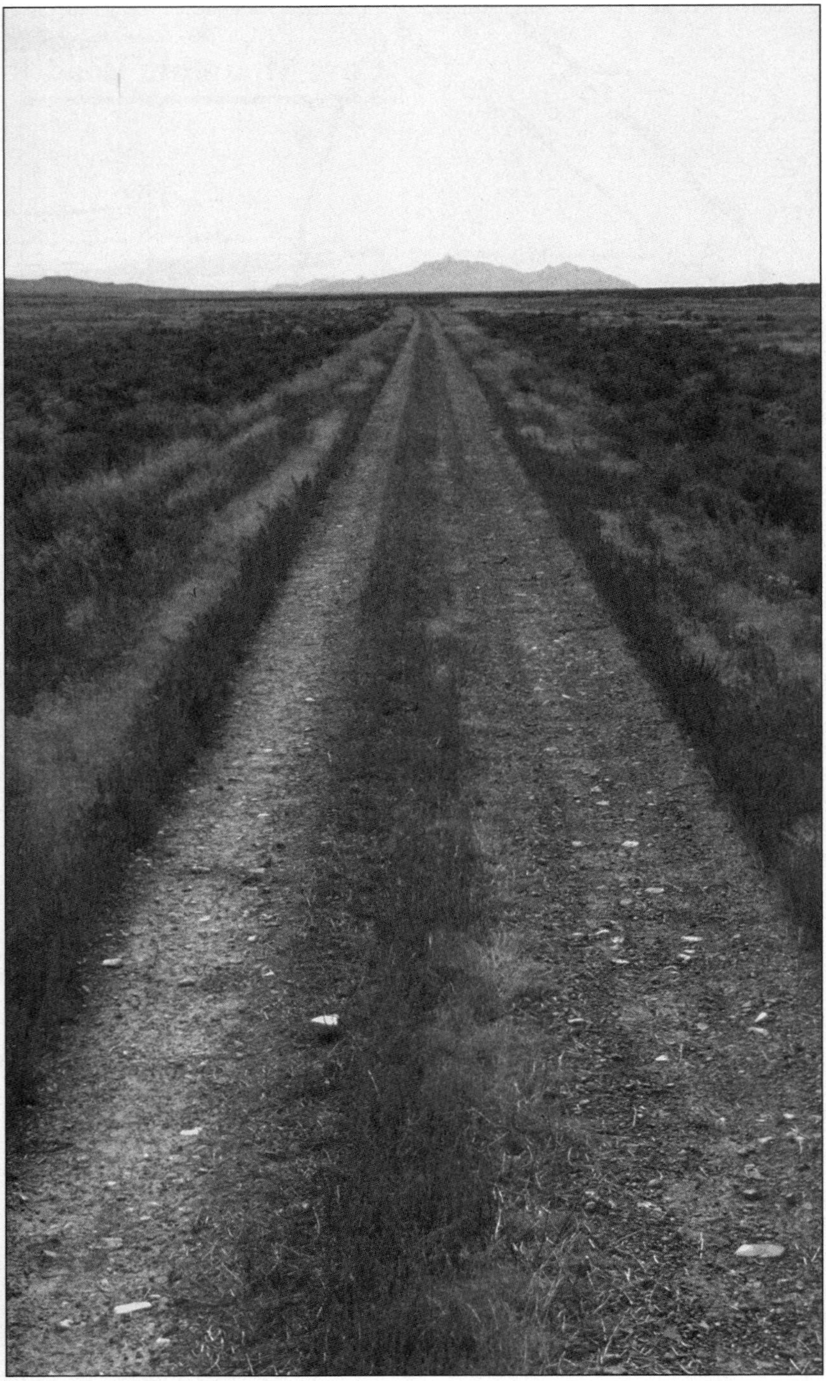

Transcontinental Railroad

Kelton Cemetery, Transcontinental Railroad

Skyline Drive III

Kimberly-Big John Road

Pony Express Trail and Stagecoach Route

Hurrah Pass

Pictographs, Canyonlands National Park

Petroglyphs, Nine-Mile Canyon

Lockhart Basin Road

White Rim Road, Canyonlands National Park

Paul Bunyan's Potty, Horse Canyon, Canyonlands National Park

Tower Ruins, Horse Canyon, Canyonlands National Park

TRIP
31

Kimberly-Big John Road

LOCATION: In the volcanic Tushar Mountains (highest range between the Rockies and the Sierra Nevada), northeast of Beaver and south of I-70. Fishlake National Forest.

HIGHLIGHTS: A thrilling drive to over 11,400 feet. Alpine meadows, lofty peaks. Summer wildflowers. Autumn colors. Wildlife. Fremont Indian State Park rock art.

DIFFICULTY: Moderate. Much of the land along the way is privately owned; avoid trespassing.

TIME & DISTANCE: 2.5 hours; 30 miles.

GETTING THERE: At Beaver, along I-15, take U-153 east for about 16 miles. Turn left (north) on road No. 123 about 2.8 miles before Elk Meadows Ski Area. This is the way I go. From I-70, take road 113 off U-4 a mile west of the state park visitor center. It goes under I-70. Another access is on U-153's beautiful, unpaved eastern leg from Junction, on U.S. 89.

THE DRIVE: You're about 8,600 feet high where you turn onto road 123. Follow the sign for Big John Flat. The somewhat rough road climbs gradually at first, through pines and aspens and open grassy areas. At Big John Flat (el. 9,954), a meadow ringed by high peaks, you'll see a trailhead for the Skyline National Recreation Trail. Be sure you're in 4wd from here. The rough one-lane road switchbacks to a gap at mile 8.1, providing an inspiring view of Mt. Baldy (12,122 ft.) and Mt. Belknap (12,137 ft.) ahead, and Delano Peak (12,169) to the southeast. You're above 11,400 feet here. The road soon edges along a hair-raising ledge at the base of exposed peaks. (More ledges are to come.) At 16.1 the road splits and becomes No. 113. Go left, descending toward I-70. The road, still on a ledge high above a deep canyon, improves some as you pass beneath forest canopies. At about 20.7 you'll pass Winkler Point, which offers another great vista. In a couple of miles you'll begin seeing mine ruins as you pass through the sites of Upper and Lower Kimberly, turn-of-the-century camps where gold, silver, lead and copper were mined. Eventually you'll see the cliffs of Red Narrows down below. Before long you'll pass through them, and then beneath I-70 and into the state park.

REST STOPS: Many primitive campsites. Pit toilets at Big John Flat. Castle Rock Campground, picnic sites and outstanding rock art at Fremont Indian State Park off I-70.

GETTING HOME: I-70.

MAPS: Fishlake National Forest, Beaver District; Trails Illustrated's *Paiute ATV Trail, Fishlake National Forest, BLM Sevier River Area.*

INFORMATION: Beaver Ranger District, 438-2436.

SAM WELLER'S

05/22/98 12:38 F 20 14706
1@ 8.99 MAPS 20%$ 7.19
1@ 15.95 0963656082 20%$ 13.56
UTAH BYWAYS
1@ 14.95 156044486X 20%$ 11.96
SCENIC DRIVING U
SUBTOTAL $ 32.71
SALES TAX @ 6.350% $ 2.08
TOTAL $ 34.79
TENDER Check $ 34.79

254 SOUTH MAIN STREET 328-2586
MERCHANDISE CREDIT ONLY

SAM WELLER'S

05/22/98	12:38	F	20	14706
1@	8.99	MAPS	20%$	7.19
1@	16.95	0963656082 UTAH BYWAYS	20%$	13.56
1@	14.95	156044486X SCENIC DRIVING U	20%$	11.96
SUBTOTAL			$	32.71
SALES TAX @ 6.350%			$	2.08
TOTAL			$	34.79
TENDER Check			$	34.79

254 SOUTH MAIN STREET 328-2586

MERCHANDISE CREDIT ONLY

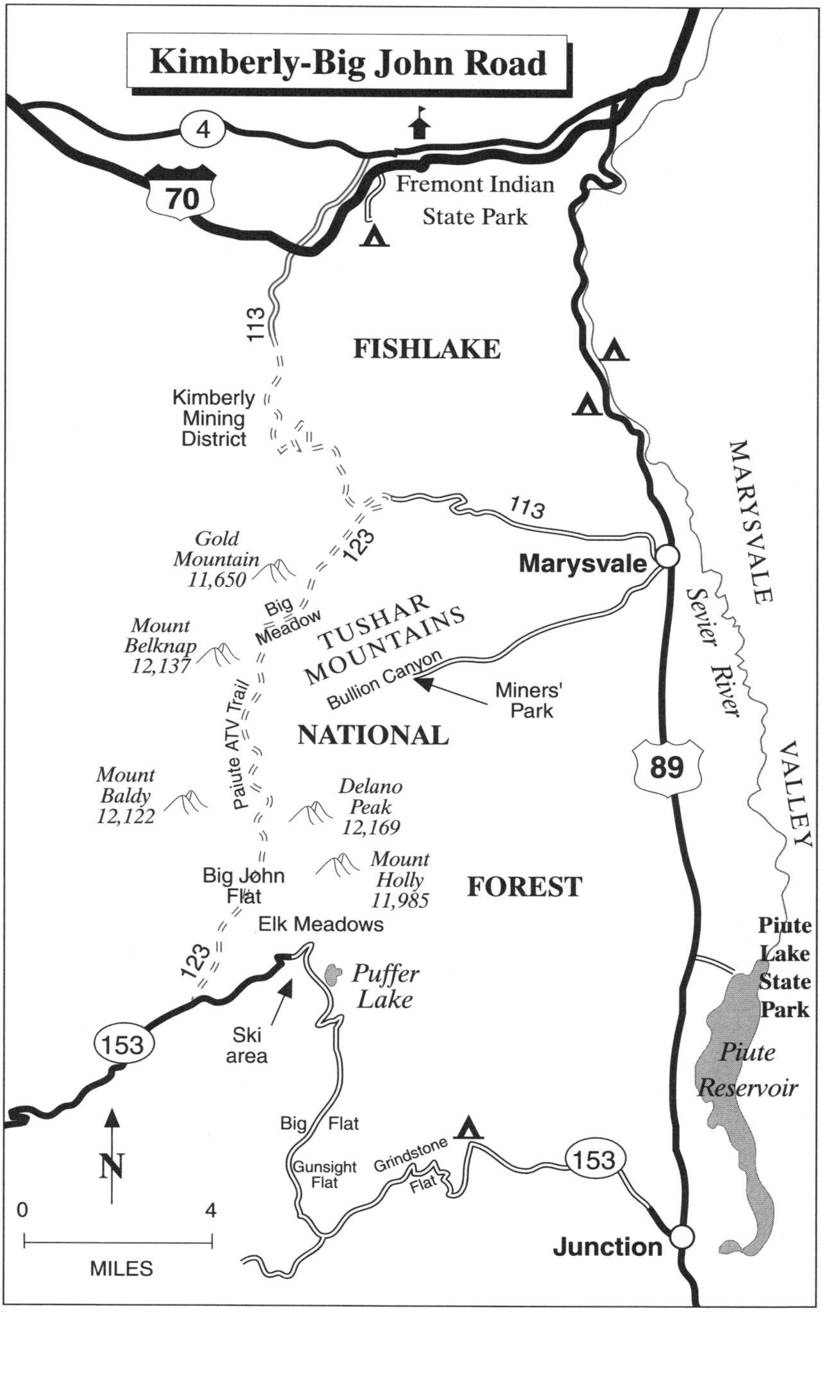

Kimberly-Big John Road
4
70
Fremont Indian
State Park
113
FISHLAKE
Kimberly
Mining
District
113
123
Gold
Mountain
11,650
Marysvale
MARYSVALE
Big
Meadow
TUSHAR
MOUNTAINS
Mount
Belknap
12,137
Bullion Canyon
Miners'
Park
Sevier
River
Paiute ATV Trail
NATIONAL
89
VALLEY
Mount
Baldy
12,122
Delano
Peak
12,169
Mount
Holly
11,985
Big John
Flat
FOREST
Elk Meadows
Piute
Lake
State
Park
123
Puffer
Lake
Ski
area
153
Piute
Reservoir
N
Big
Flat
Gunsight
Flat
Grindstone
Flat
153
0
4
MILES
Junction

TRIP
32

Thousand Lake Mt. to Cathedral Valley

LOCATION: Northeast of Fremont, in Fishlake National Forest and the northern end of Capitol Reef National Park.

HIGHLIGHTS: A loop that plunges 3,000 feet from forested Thousand Lake Mountain into the desert of spectacular Upper Cathedral Valley and Waterpocket Fold.

DIFFICULTY: Easy to moderate. Some rocky stretches. Lower desert areas are hot in summer; flash-flood danger then, too.

TIME & DISTANCE: 2.5 hours; 39 miles.

GETTING THERE: About 5.5 miles north of Fremont on U-72 turn east onto road 206. Reset your odometer.

THE DRIVE: There are a few small lakes on Thousand Lake Mt., but it's possible someone mistook it for the Aquarius Plateau and Boulder Mt. to the south, where there are many lakes. At a Y at mile 4.5, at Heart Lake, go right toward Cathedral Valley. (The road to the left, 020, will be your return route.) Here you're at about 9,500 feet. Turn left onto road 022 at mile 5, and soon you'll begin the descent to Cathedral Valley. Note the contrast of aspen forest in the foreground and the great expanse of restless desert rolling into the distance. At 5.5 pass road 211 on the left. You'll enter the park at mile 10.8; in another mile you'll reach Hartnet Junction. You'll go left here, past Cathedral Valley CG and down switchbacks to Upper Cathedral Valley. But for now continue ahead to Upper Cathedral Valley Overlook and Upper South Desert Overlook. In Cathedral Valley you'll pass high, intricately fluted walls, cliffs, spires and monoliths of relatively soft Entrada Sandstone capped by harder, protective Curtis Sandstone, both from Jurassic time (135-190 MYA). Go left at Cathedral Valley Junction, along vertical slabs of upthrusting volcanic rock and up to a bench. At 21.7, after leaving the park, go left at the Y toward Thousand Lake Mt., which looms beyond the oasis of rustic Baker Ranch. Soon you'll re-enter the national forest, ascending the mountain on road 020, which will return you to road 206 and the highway.

REST STOPS: Elkhorn CG on Thousand Lake Mt.; Waterless Cathedral Valley Campground, near Hartnet Junction. The overlooks.

SPECIAL NOTES: In the park pets must be kept on leashes and are restricted to road corridors. Bring a portable toilet.

MAPS: Fishlake National Forest, Loa District; at the park get *The Valley of Cathedrals*; Recreational Map of Utah.

INFORMATION: Fishlake National Forest, Loa District, 836-2811; Capitol Reef National Park, 425-3791.

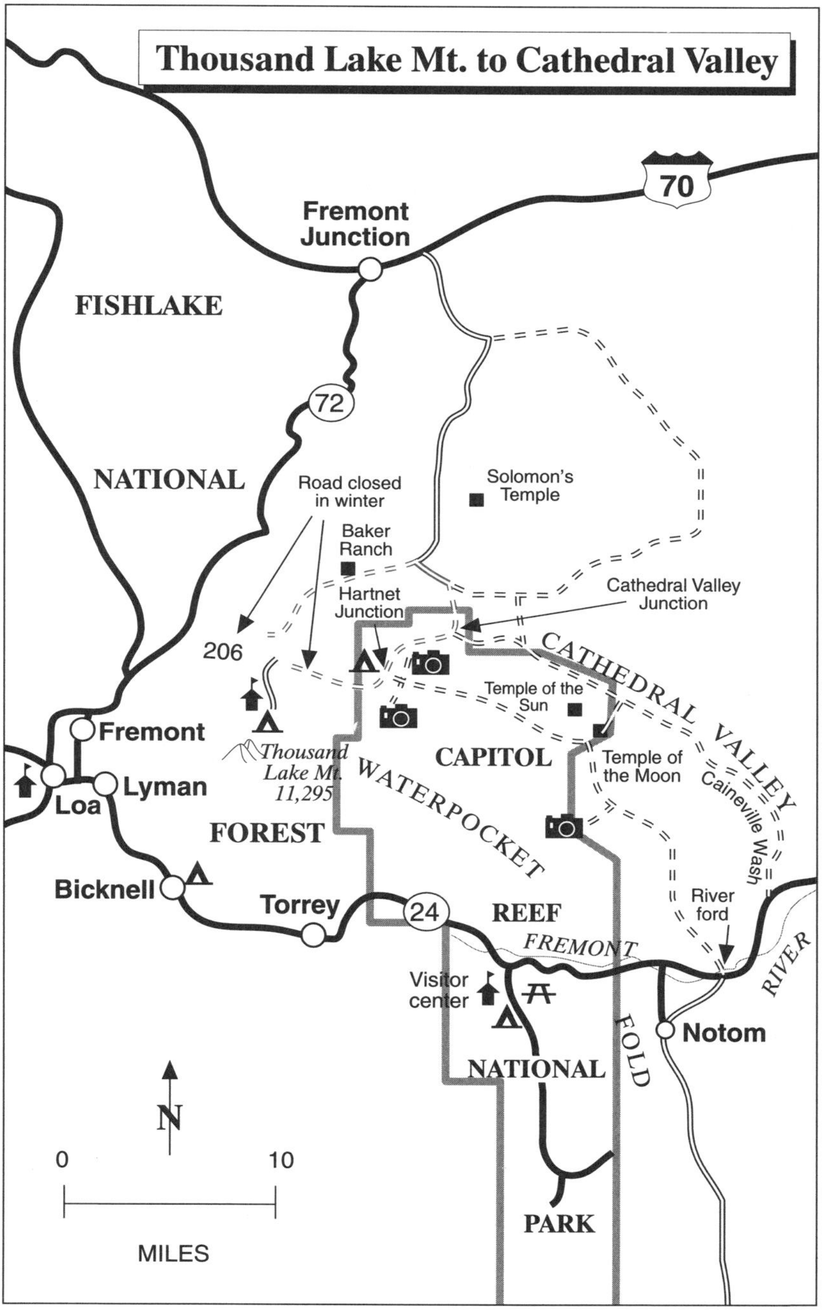
Thousand Lake Mt. to Cathedral Valley
70
Fremont Junction
FISHLAKE
72
NATIONAL
Road closed in winter
Solomon's Temple
Baker Ranch
Hartnet Junction
Cathedral Valley Junction
206
CATHEDRAL VALLEY
Temple of the Sun
Fremont
Thousand Lake Mt. 11,295
CAPITOL
Temple of the Moon
Caineville Wash
Loa
Lyman
WATERPOCKET
FOREST
Bicknell
Torrey
24
REEF
River ford
FREMONT
RIVER
Visitor center
Notom
FOLD
NATIONAL
N
0
10
MILES
PARK

TRIP
33

Caineville Wash to I-70

LOCATION: Goes north from U-24 near Caineville through Cathedral Valley to I-70 near Fremont Junction.

HIGHLIGHTS: Rainbow-colored hills; fascinating sandstone formations; Cathedral Valley's imposing cliffs, fins and monoliths; remote Last Chance Desert; North Caineville Reef. Best spring and fall.

DIFFICULTY: Easy. Many washes. Impassable when wet. Hot in summer; flash-flood danger then, too.

TIME & DISTANCE: 3 hours; 51 miles.

GETTING THERE: Take U-24 about 0.2 miles west of the Caineville city limit, or 18.7 miles east of the park visitor center. Go north at the sign; reset your odometer.

THE DRIVE: Driving up Caineville Wash you'll be surprised by the array of rock textures and pastel colors: pink hues of the wash, saffron cliffs, beige ravines. On the right you'll see the dramatically upthrusting sawtooth exposures of North Caineville Reef. At mile 5.2 you're confronted by haughty Queen of the Wash, a hill of colored bentonite, a soft rock of volcanic ash, mud, silt sand deposited about 140 MYA. By mile 11, in the Middle Desert, Cathedral Valley presents its fluted cliffs, spires, fins and isolated monoliths of Entrada Sandstone, relatively soft rock capped by harder, more erosion-resistant Curtis Sandstone. Temple of the Moon and Temple of the Sun preside like royal siblings near a knob of gypsum with an exaggerated name, Glass Mountain. (Don't take a piece.) At 24.8 is Cathedral Junction. Turn right (north) here at a sharp, vertical volcanic rock exposure. Climb to a bench. From here, the eastern slopes of Thousand Lake Mountain and the rest of Utah's high spine melt into the eastward repose of the Last Chance Desert. Beyond Solomon's Temple, a butte east of the road some 7 miles north of Cathedral Junction, the Earth's surface rises gradually toward the San Rafael Swell. High cliffs form an abrupt escarpment to the west. Go right at a Y at 29.4; follow the cliffs northward. A long cruise (watch for washed out spots) toward bluffs, through a broad expanse, ends at a climb up dramatic Last Chance Anticline. You'll cross flats strewn with volcanic boulders washed down from high lava fields by the waters of melting ice-age glaciers. Soon you're in pinyon-juniper woodland. At 51.5 you're at I-70.

REST STOPS: Primitive camping on BLM land. Park's dry Cathedral Valley Campground. Picnic sites along Caineville Wash.

SPECIAL NOTES: In the park pets must be kept on leashes and are restricted to road corridors. No water, facilities. Bring a portable toilet.

MAPS: At the park visitor center get *The Valley of Cathedrals*, a detailed guide to the route; Recreational Map of Utah.

INFORMATION: BLM in Hanksville, 542-3461; in Price, 636-3600. Capitol Reef National Park, 425-3791.

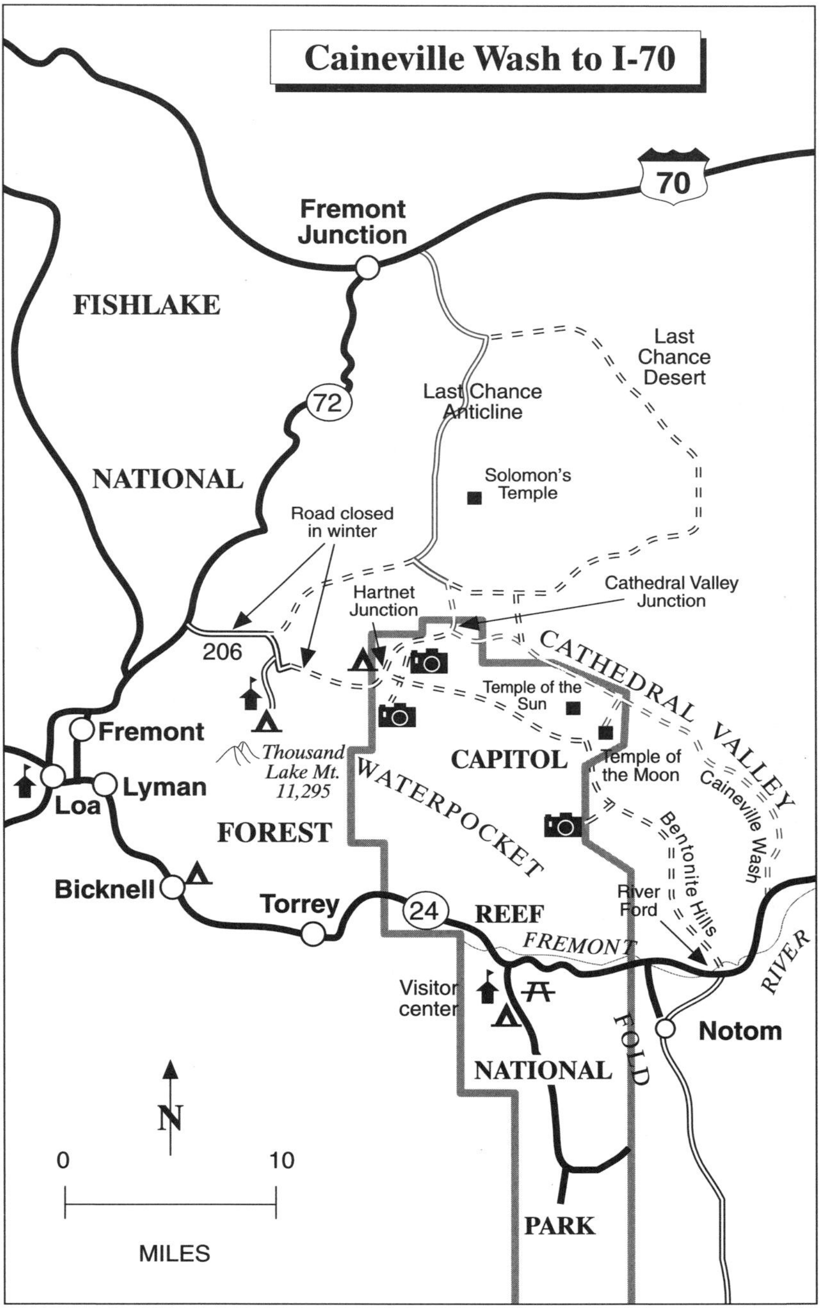
Caineville Wash to I-70
70
Fremont Junction
FISHLAKE
NATIONAL
FOREST
72
Last Chance Desert
Last Chance Anticline
Solomon's Temple
Road closed in winter
Hartnet Junction
Cathedral Valley Junction
CATHEDRAL VALLEY
206
Temple of the Sun
Temple of the Moon
Caineville Wash
Bentonite Hills
Fremont
Lyman
Loa
Thousand Lake Mt. 11,295
CAPITOL
WATERPOCKET
REEF
FOLD
Bicknell
Torrey
24
River Ford
FREMONT
RIVER
Notom
Visitor center
NATIONAL
PARK
N
0
10
MILES

Potash Road

LOCATION: Southwest of Moab.

HIGHLIGHTS: Dinosaur tracks, Indian rock art on the way to the starting point. Outstanding scenery from terraces above the river. The thrilling Shafer Switchbacks.

DIFFICULTY: Easy. Shafer Switchbacks are exciting, but not difficult. Watch for mountain bikers. Best spring and fall.

TIME & DISTANCE: 2 hours; 24 miles.

GETTING THERE: 1.3 miles north of the Colorado River bridge north of Moab, turn west off U.S. 191 toward Potash, on U-279. Follow the Colorado River canyon, watching for petroglyphs. There's a pullout where you can look through a pipe aimed at dinosaur tracks. The pavement ends, and the drive begins, in 16.9 miles. Set your odometer at 0.

THE DRIVE: The road climbs above the river onto a bench below towering sandstone cliffs, hills and mesas. Ahead is 5,715-ft. Pyramid Butte. At mile 3.1 follow a fence line at Moab Salt Production & Packaging's evaporation ponds. At 5.3 go through a fence. In a half-mile you'll see a spur going left to Pyramid Butte. It goes around the butte to a bench above the river. 2.7 miles beyond this spur the road angles right, around a rock outcrop. Here you can walk to a point with a head-spinning view. Other vista points will provide similar opportunities to watch the Colorado River loop around a meander called the Goose Neck. 0.9 mile from the point the road edges between red cliffs of the Permian (245-286 MYA) Cutler Formation and the river canyon. 2 miles farther, as you continue across a limestone bed of the Elephant Canyon Formation, the road enters the park and climbs through the Middle Fork of Shafer Canyon to the junction with the White Rim Road *(trip 38)*. Here you'll get a close-up view of red-brown stream deposits, and then the defining layer of White Rim Sandstone. At the junction, go right toward the head of Shafer Canyon. Yes, there's a road up the face of the cliff, narrow and steep with tight switchbacks. You'll soon be atop Island in the Sky, a broad mesa, at U-313. The park visitor center is left.

REST STOPS: Campground at Shafer Canyon (national park permit required); toilet at the White Rim Road junction.

GETTING HOME: U-313 to U.S. 191 and Moab.

MAP: Trails Illustrated's *Canyonlands National Park, Needles & Island in the Sky.*

INFORMATION: Canyonlands National Park, 259-7164; BLM, Moab Field Office, 259-6111.

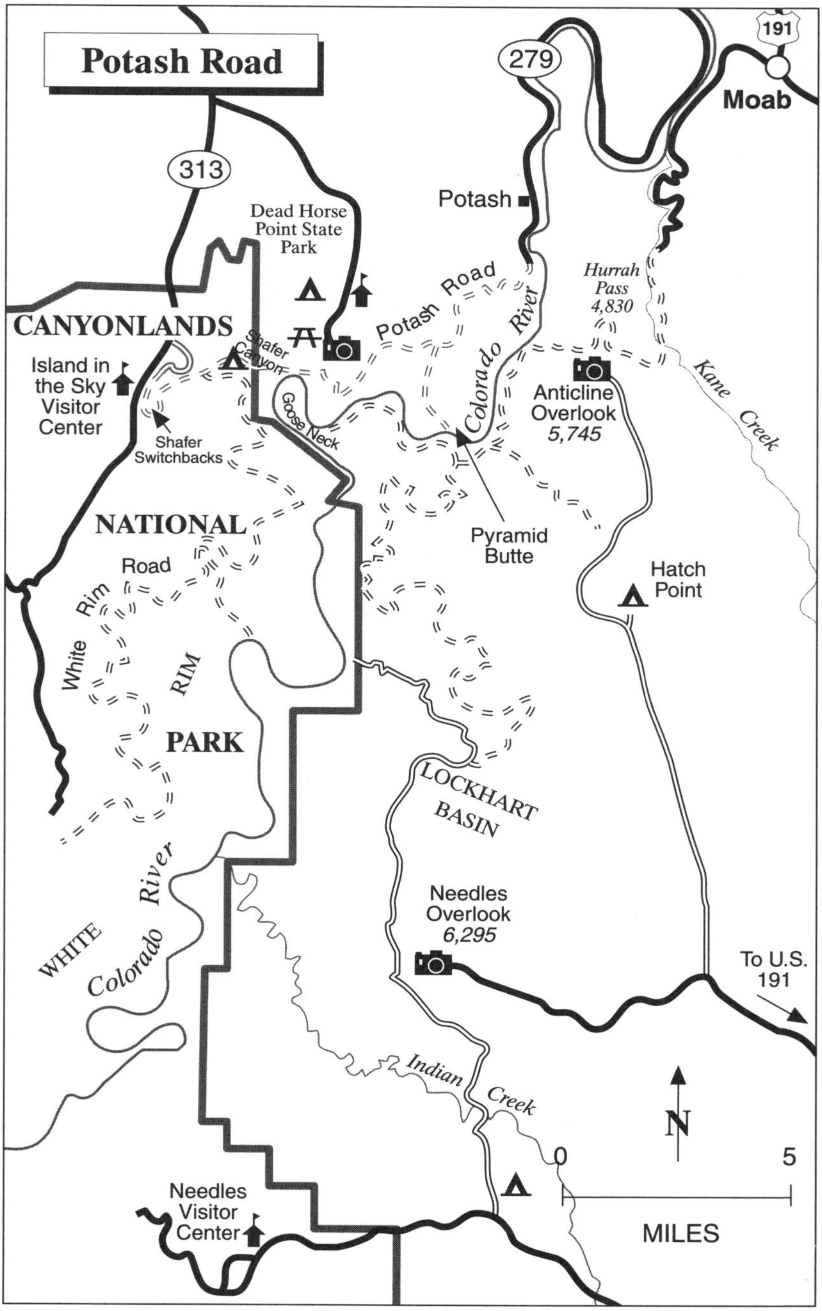

Potash Road
313
279
191
Moab
Potash
Dead Horse Point State Park
Hurrah Pass 4,830
Potash Road
Colorado River
CANYONLANDS
Shafer Canyon
Island in the Sky Visitor Center
Goose Neck
Anticline Overlook 5,745
Kane Creek
Shafer Switchbacks
Pyramid Butte
NATIONAL
Road
Hatch Point
White Rim
RIM
PARK
LOCKHART BASIN
Colorado River
WHITE
Needles Overlook 6,295
To U.S. 191
Indian Creek
N
0
5
MILES
Needles Visitor Center

TRIP
35

La Sal Mountains

LOCATION: East of Moab. Crosses Manti-La Sal National Forest, La Sal Mountains State Forest and private land.

HIGHLIGHTS: Vistas of Canyonlands and the Colorado Rockies as you reach 10,700 feet in the lofty La Sal Mountains.

DIFFICULTY: Easy.

TIME & DISTANCE: 4 hours; 106 miles (54 on dirt).

GETTING THERE: I start at the Colorado River bridge north of Moab, on U-128. Set your odometer at 0.

THE DRIVE: Take the highway along the Colorado River for 15.5 miles, then turn off to Castle Valley at the sign. Besides the La Sals, the valley is dominated by the sandstone cliffs of Porcupine Rim and Castle Rock, which rises 2,000 feet above the valley floor. At 26.2 continue ahead toward Gateway Road. 0.6 mile farther you'll enter the national forest, where the road becomes No. 207. Bid asphalt adieu by mile 32. Go east above Fisher Valley and Bull Canyon into stands of Ponderosa pine. At 33.9, at the turnoff to Gateway, Colo., stay on 207. The road bends south through dense scrub oak. Go right at 38.6 toward Sally's Hollow. 9.8 miles later, after crossing Taylor Flat, go right again. The road climbs gently here through grassy hills, sage-brush and scrub oak. At the next Y keep left on a rocky single-lane road. Look east to see Colorado's snowy San Juan Mountains. Go right at the turnoff for Buckeye Reservoir, and 3.9 miles later pass through Canopy Gap. When you re-enter the national forest the road is 208; 1.5 miles later turn north on 129 toward Geyser Pass. La Sal peaks dominate now. The highest, 12,721-ft. Mt. Peale, looms ahead. They began as magma rising against the overlying sedimentary layers, creating a dome. The magma cooled before breaking through. Erosion peeled the sedimentary layers away, exposing the mountains we see. 4 miles from where you turned onto 129 keep right at the Y. 4.7 miles farther a two-track, 723, goes a half-mile to a beautiful basin. From here the main road becomes a shelf with vistas to the east. In another half-mile you'll reach 10,700 feet, and 3.5 miles later you'll cross Geyser Pass, 100 feet lower. Here the road, 071, becomes two-lane dirt and gravel. When you reach semi-paved La Sal Loop Road you can go left toward Moab, about 20 miles. Better yet, go right to take in the spectacular view from Castle Valley Overlook, and complete a loop by returning via Castle Valley (15 miles).

REST STOPS: Big Bend Recreation Area, 7 miles from Moab on U-128.

GETTING HOME: U.S. 191 north to I-70.

MAP: Manti-La Sal NF, Moab/Monticello Ranger Districts.

INFORMATION: Moab/Monticello Districts, 587-2041.

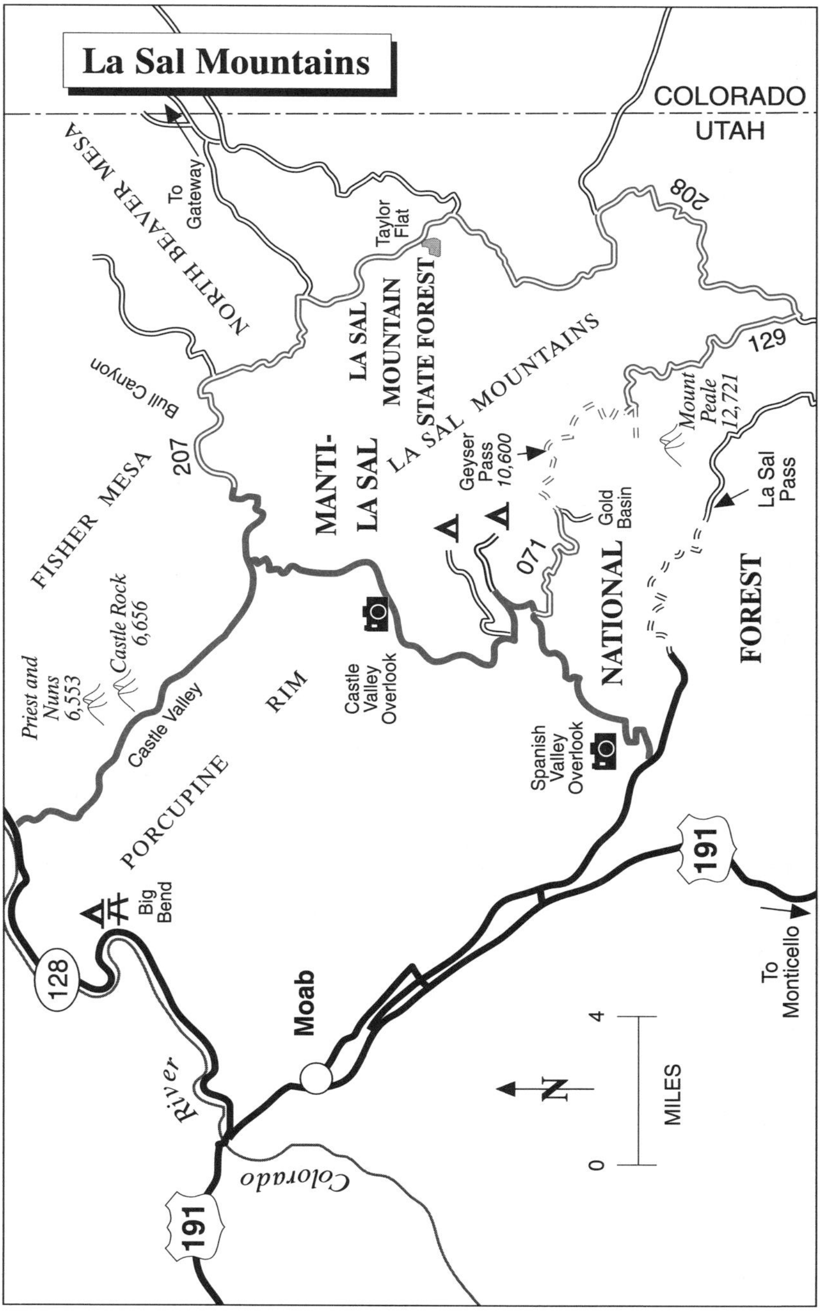
La Sal Mountains
COLORADO
UTAH
To Gateway
NORTH BEAVER MESA
Taylor Flat
208
MANTI-LA SAL
LA SAL MOUNTAIN STATE FOREST
LA SAL MOUNTAINS
Bull Canyon
207
FISHER MESA
Geyser Pass 10,600
Mount Peale 12,721
129
La Sal Pass
Gold Basin
071
NATIONAL
FOREST
Castle Rock 6,656
Priest and Nuns 6,553
Castle Valley
Castle Valley Overlook
RIM
PORCUPINE
Spanish Valley Overlook
Big Bend
128
191
Moab
To Monticello
River
Colorado
N
MILES
0
4

TRIP 36

Canyon of Gold

LOCATION: Tushar Mountains (highest range between the Rockies and the Sierra Nevada); southwest of Marysvale.

HIGHLIGHTS: Climbing to 11,000 feet on a loop that has history, scenery, high-elevation thrills and convenience. You'll enjoy the *Canyon of Gold Driving Tour* in Bullion Canyon, and Miners' Park historic site. Fall colors. Bullion Falls.

DIFFICULTY: Easy to Miner's Park; Cottonwood Canyon is moderate, especially if you go in the opposite direction.

TIME & DISTANCE: 23 miles; 3 hours.

GETTING THERE: In Marysvale, turn west off U.S. 89 onto Bullion Ave., a.k.a. Center Street. Reset your odometer.

THE DRIVE: Follow the signs for Bullion Canyon, a historic gold mining area. Soon you'll see the cleft in the mountains. About 4.1 miles from town you'll enter Fishlake National Forest, on road No. 126. Then you'll see a decorated ore car on the right that announces the "Canyon of Gold" tour. Take a guide booklet from the box and put a buck in the pipe. The booklet explains sites along the 2.5-mile drive up Pine Creek to Miner's Park. I'll let the booklet describe what you'll see, which will include a streamside *arrastra,* or grinding stone possibly used by early Spaniards to mill gold-bearing rock. At the site of Bullion City you'll see the left turn (road 126) to Cottonwood Canyon. Bullion City once had some 1,600 people and was, for a time, the Piute County seat. At tour's end is a wonderful historical park. The single-lane road to Cottonwood Canyon is good, with turnouts that provide excellent views across Marysvale Valley to the Sevier Plateau. (It's 16 miles to U-89.) About 4.5 miles from the turnoff the road narrows and becomes rougher with steeper switchbacks. In another mile you'll cross a saddle beneath 11,650-ft. Edna (also Aetna) Peak. Soon you'll reach about 10,950 feet on a ledge, with vistas across waves of mountains and valleys. You'll see some mine trash as you approach a fork in the road, where you'll make a hard left. Descend along Cottonwood Canyon on a rough road that would be a long climb in the opposite direction. The road improves as you near the highway.

REST STOPS: Picnic at Miners' Park. Hike to Bullion Falls, a mile (one-way) from the Bullion City site. Much of the land along the drive is privately owned; avoid trespassing.

GETTING HOME: North or south on U.S. 89.

MAPS: Fishlake National Forest, Beaver District; Trails Illustrated's *Paiute ATV Trail, Fishlake National Forest, BLM Sevier River Area.*

INFORMATION: Beaver Ranger District, 438-2436.

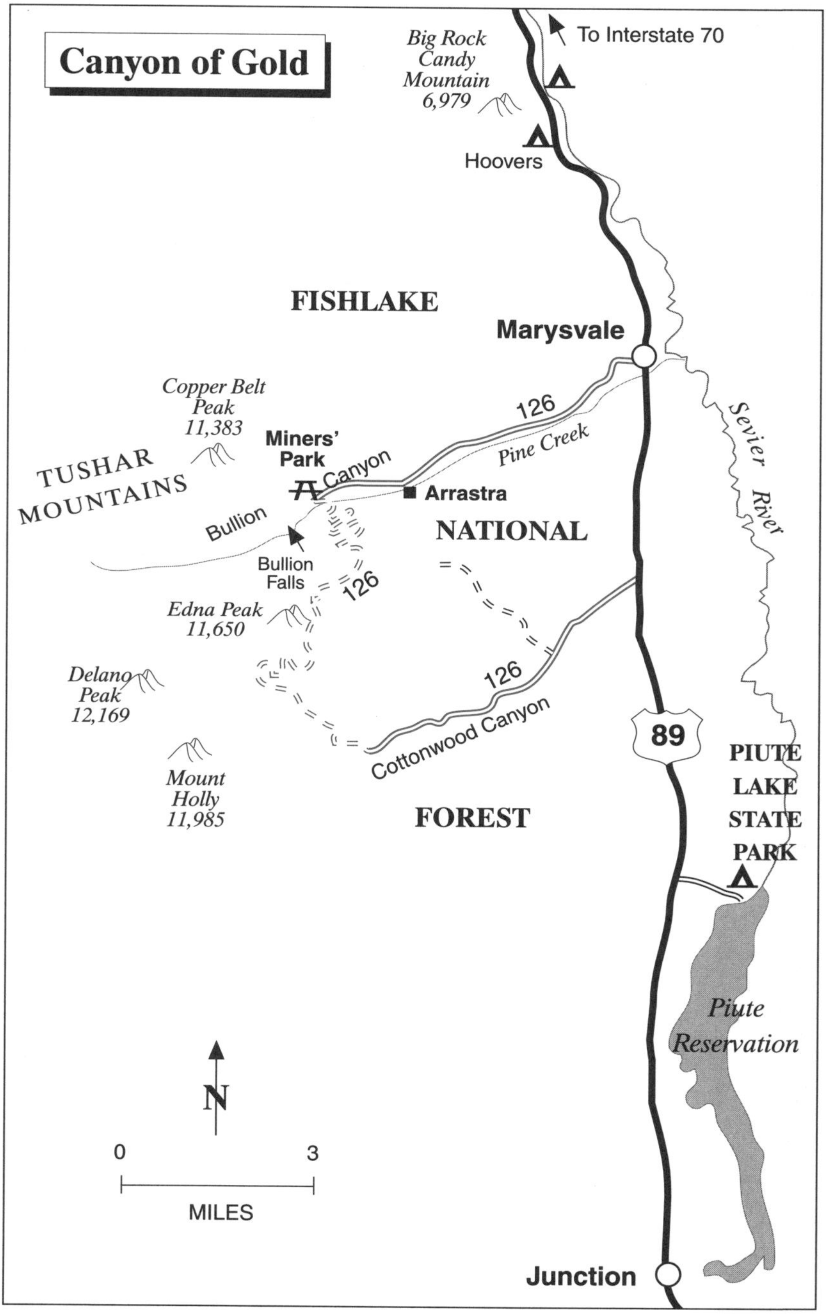
Canyon of Gold
To Interstate 70
Big Rock Candy Mountain 6,979
Hoovers
FISHLAKE
Marysvale
Copper Belt Peak 11,383
Miners' Park
Canyon
126
Pine Creek
Sevier River
TUSHAR MOUNTAINS
Arrastra
Bullion
NATIONAL
Bullion Falls
126
Edna Peak 11,650
Delano Peak 12,169
126
Cottonwood Canyon
89
PIUTE LAKE STATE PARK
Mount Holly 11,985
FOREST
Piute Reservation
N
0
3
MILES
Junction

TRIP
37

River Ford to Cathedral Valley

LOCATION: North of U-24, partially in Capitol Reef National Park.

HIGHLIGHTS: Fording Fremont River; crossing Bentonite Hills; overlooks; Cathedral Valley; Caineville Wash.

DIFFICULTY: Easy to moderate. River may be high in spring and after summer storms. Bentonite Hills are slippery when wet, and should be avoided then. Hot in summer; flash-flood danger then, too.

TIME & DISTANCE: 5-6 hours; 68 miles. Retraces part of Caineville Wash to I-70 (*trip 33*).

GETTING THERE: Start at River Ford so you can check the river's level at the outset. Take U-24 east 11.7 miles from the park visitor center, or 7 miles west of Caineville. Turn north at the sign for Hartnet Road. Reset your odometer and follow the road to the fording site.

THE DRIVE: Beyond the river the road climbs past colorful hills and Dry Wash Dropoff (look for nests small animals make in the rock). As you cross North Blue Flats, you'll see areas strewn with volcanic rocks. By mile 9 you're in the moonscape of the Morrison Formation Bentonite Hills, deposited in the Jurassic Period about 140 MYA. The soft, color-banded rock is composed of volcanic ash, mud, silt and sand. Cross them to enter The Hartnet's low cliffs and sandy flats. At mile 14.1 is the turnoff to Lower South Desert Overlook. In 13 miles turn to Upper South Desert Overlook for the sight of a red trough paralleling the Waterpocket Fold. Go on to Upper Cathedral Valley Overlook and Hartnet Junction. Turn right. Take the switchbacks to the upper valley's great walls, fins, spires and monoliths of relatively soft Entrada Sandstone capped by a protective layer of younger, harder Curtis Sandstone, both from Jurassic time (135-190 MYA). Detour to Gypsum Sink Hole, then follow the cliffs down Middle Desert past Layercake Wall's thin laminations. Pay homage at Temples of the Sun and Moon, isolated sandstone siblings. Stop at Glass Mountain, an incongruous knob of gypsum (don't take a piece) in a sandstone Hall of Fame. Cruise the widening desert guarded by Wood Bench and brightened by the rounded Queen of the Wash's showy bentonite hues, then end in Caineville Wash.

REST STOPS: The overlooks. Waterless Cathedral Valley Campground, near Hartnet Junction. Primitive picnic areas along Caineville Wash.

SPECIAL NOTES: In the park pets must be kept on leashes and are restricted to road corridors. Bring a portable toilet.

MAPS: Get *The Valley of Cathedrals* and the park brochure at the visitor center; Trails Illustrated's *Fishlake National Forest & Capitol Reef National Park.*

INFORMATION: BLM, Henry Mountains Field Station, 542-3461. Capitol Reef National Park, 425-3791.

River Ford to Cathedral Valley

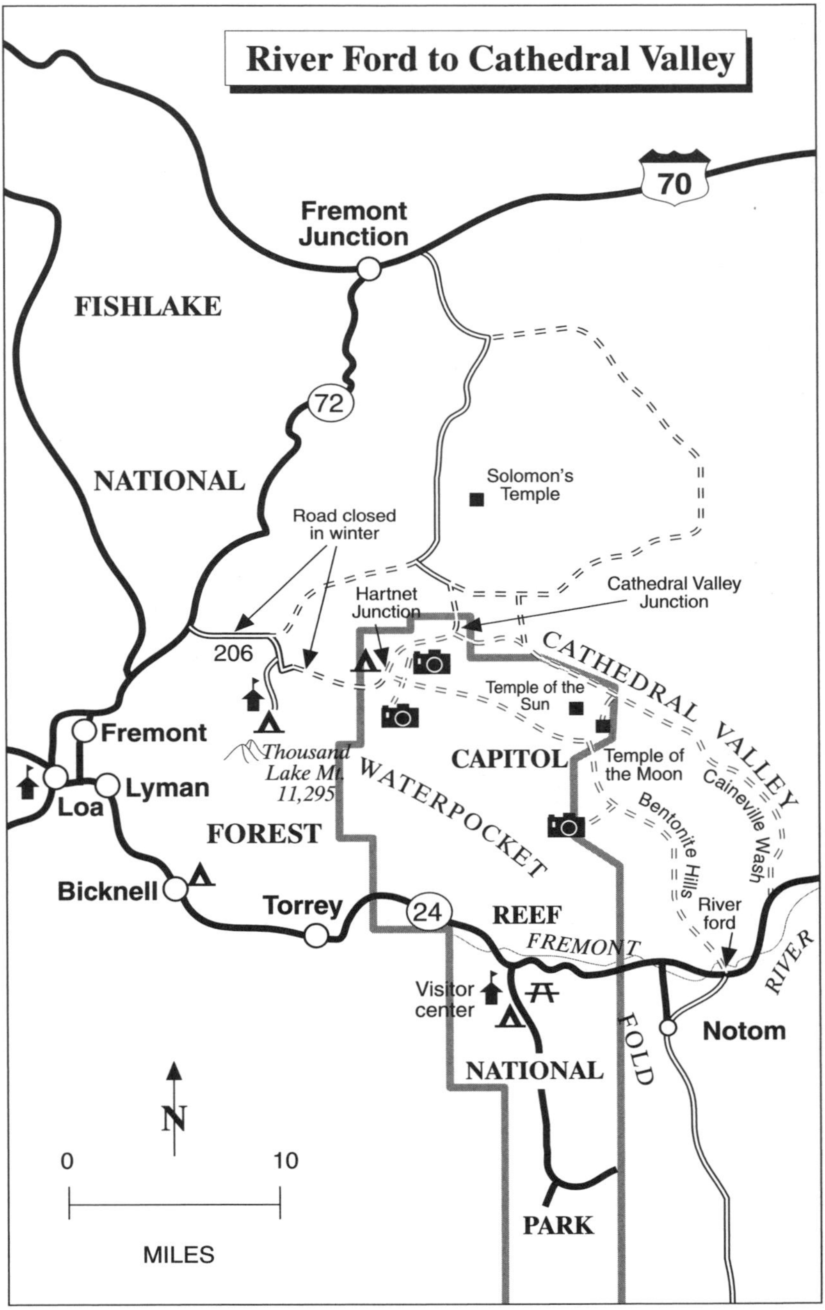

TRIP
38

White Rim Road

LOCATION: Canyonlands NP, Island in the Sky District.

HIGHLIGHTS: Towering cliffs and buttes. Canyons of the Colorado & Green rivers. Steep switchbacks, Monument Basin, Musselman Arch, desert bighorn sheep. Very pleasant in spring and fall.

DIFFICULTY: Moderate. Rocky stretches, narrow ledges, steep climbs. Watch for mountain bikers. No water or fuel. Hot in summer.

TIME & DISTANCE: 2 1/2 days; 110 miles with spurs. Or just take day trips. Camping permit required.

GETTING THERE: From U.S. 191 north of Moab take U-313 to the park entrance. Go left 0.2 miles beyond it.

THE DRIVE: From Island in the Sky Mesa you'll plunge 1,400 feet in 4.5 thrilling miles on the Shafer Road. The old Indian and stock trail was improved by prospectors and the Atomic Energy Commission during the 1950s uranium boom. You can see the White Rim Road, another boom relic, threading along a rim of white coastal sandstone (Permian Period, 245-286 MYA). Above the trail loom an ancient sea's brown tidal mud flats (Moenkopi Formation, 240-245 MYA). Far below, the Colorado River meanders through its gorge. By mile 5.2 you're at Potash Road *(trip 34)*, on the White Rim. At 6.5 walk to a view of the river snaking around the Goose Neck. The cryptobiotic crust on the ground is vital to stabilizing the desert soil; stay off it. You'll also see "potholes," depressions in the rock that teem with life after rains. Leave them alone, too. Soon you're walled in by imposing red-brown cliffs of Wingate Sandstone from a Jurassic-Triassic desert's sands. At 8.6 is Musselman Arch. 8 miles farther go 3.7 miles down Lathrop Canyon to an oasis with tables and river access. 15 miles farther are the pillars of Monument Basin, where caps of White Rim Sandstone are perched atop eroding pedestals of softer brown Organ Shale Rock. Beyond White Crack veer north at Junction Butte, above the Green River & Stillwater Canyon. (The Green & Colorado meet south of here.) Climb up Murphy Hogback, then drop into Soda Springs Basin. Beyond Potato Bottom are more switchbacks, then a viewpoint overlooking Fort Bottom. There you can hike up the point to an ancient Puebloan (Anasazi) structure. In 4.5 miles take the 5-mile spur up Taylor Canyon to the monoliths Zeus & Moses. About 2.5 miles farther you'll leave the park. Mineral Bottom switchbacks take you up to Horsethief Point. Drive 13 miles through pinyon-juniper woodlands to U-313.

REST STOPS: 10 camping areas along the way ($25 reservation fee; reserve sites 6 months in advance). Picnic in Lathrop Canyon.

SPECIAL NOTES: Camp only in designated campsites. No pets in the backcountry. No wood fires.

MAP: Trails Illustrated's *Canyonlands-Island Recreation Map.*

INFORMATION: Canyonlands National Park, Island in the Sky District, 259-4712; for park information, 259-7164; for backcountry campsite reservations, 259-4351.

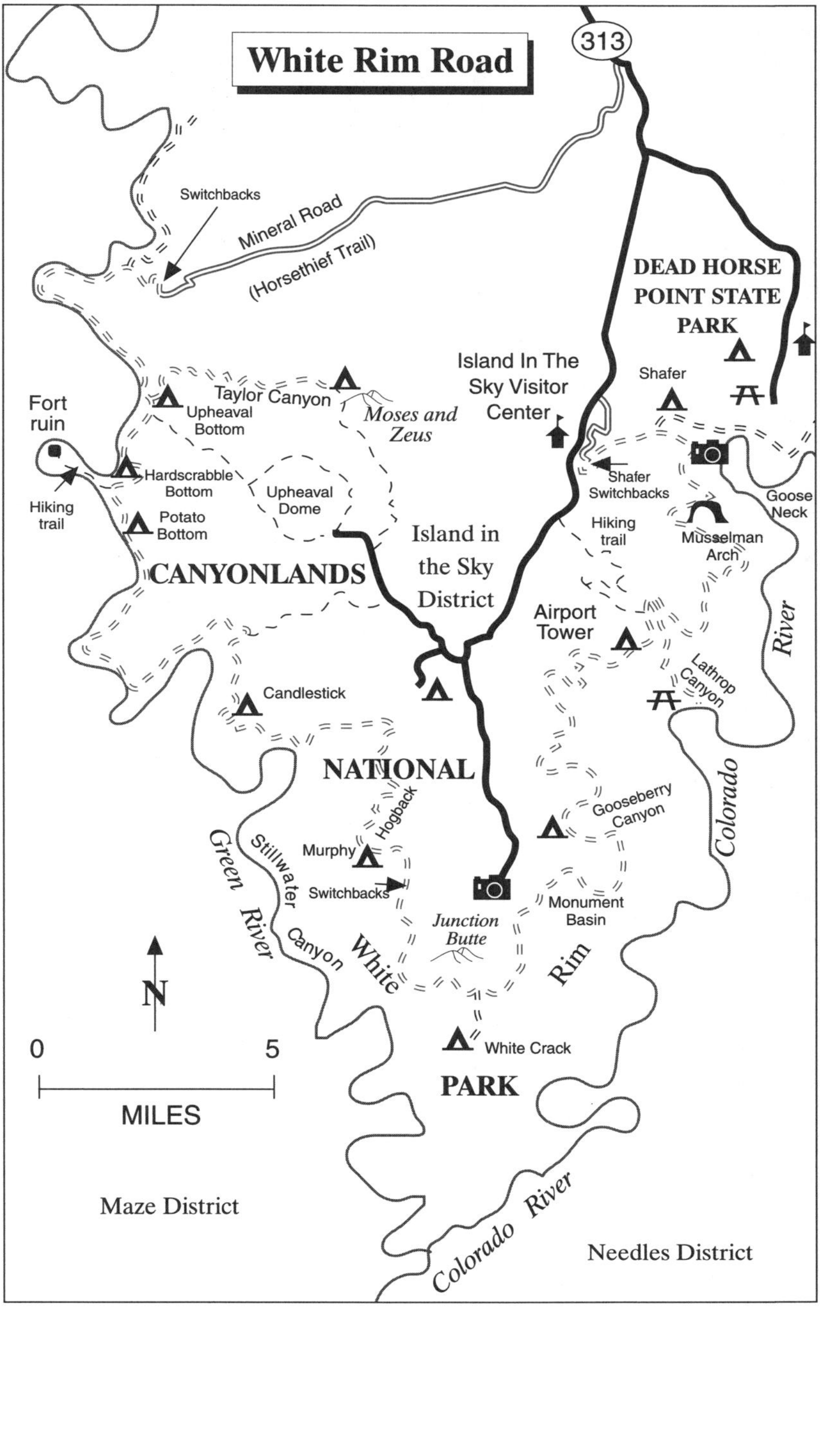
White Rim Road
313
Switchbacks
Mineral Road
(Horsethief Trail)
DEAD HORSE POINT STATE PARK
Island In The Sky Visitor Center
Shafer
Fort ruin
Taylor Canyon
Upheaval Bottom
Moses and Zeus
Hardscrabble Bottom
Upheaval Dome
Shafer Switchbacks
Goose Neck
Hiking trail
Potato Bottom
Island in the Sky District
Hiking trail
Musselman Arch
CANYONLANDS
Airport Tower
River
Lathrop Canyon
Candlestick
NATIONAL
Hogback
Gooseberry Canyon
Colorado
Green River
Stillwater Canyon
Murphy
Switchbacks
Junction Butte
Monument Basin
White Rim
N
0
5
MILES
White Crack
PARK
Maze District
Colorado River
Needles District

Hurrah Pass to Chicken Corners

LOCATION: Southwest of Moab.

HIGHLIGHTS: Spectacular views of the Colorado River gorge and the La Sal Mountains. Petroglyphs. Hair-raising Chicken Corners.

DIFFICULTY: Easy to moderate. The first 4.7 miles are paved, then easy dirt and gravel to Kane Creek, which can run high in spring and after storms. There's a short but nasty pitch just below Hurrah Pass on the west side of the anticline. No water, toilets or services of any kind. Bring a portable toilet. Hot in summer. Best in spring and fall.

TIME & DISTANCE: 2 hours & 24.6 miles one-way from Moab.

GETTING THERE: I start in downtown Moab, at Kane Creek Road and Main Street (at the McDonald's restaurant). Reset your odometer.

THE DRIVE: Take Kane Creek Road along the Colorado River through its magnificent high-walled canyon. The pavement ends at mile 4.7, then veers away from the river to wind up Kane Creek Canyon. At mile 6 walk down to a large boulder below the road to the right. It bears terrific petroglyphs. (Never touch or disturb rock art.) At mile 11 ford Kane Creek, then curve right and drive up the anticline to Hurrah Pass, at 4,830 feet. The high bluff to the south is Anticline Overlook. Far below are benches overlooking the river. In the distance you'll see Moab Salt Production & Packaging's evaporation ponds. You'll immediately encounter a bad spot in the road as you descend toward the benches. In a ravine at 17.4 the road angles sharply right. Beyond the ravine the road becomes smooth, packed sediments as it angles south on the bench among reddish-brown Wingate Sandstone cliffs and side canyons. At 18.9 continue south toward Lockhart Basin Road. *(trip 40)*, which you'll see at 21.4. You'll pass outstanding vista points high above the river that are great picnic spots. As you continue along the bench, cliffs gradually force the road closer to the brink of the river gorge. Soon it's squeezed between boulders and cliffs on the left and the long, sheer dropoff to the river on the right. This is Chicken Corners. Just beyond the ledge is a turnaround area where you can enjoy the outstanding scenery directly below Dead Horse Point, at the start of the river's much-photographed meander around a hook of land called the Goose Neck. The road narrows to a trail in a little more than a mile; turn back here.

REST STOPS: Camping in the canyon along the Colorado River, a designated recreation area where restrictions apply, such as use of portable toilets. Picnic on the benchlands overlooking the river.

GETTING HOME: Return to Moab and U.S. 191.

MAPS: F.A. Barnes' *Canyon Rims & Needles Areas*; Trails Illustrated's *Canyonlands NP, Needles & Island in the Sky.*

INFORMATION: BLM, Moab Field Office, 259-6111.

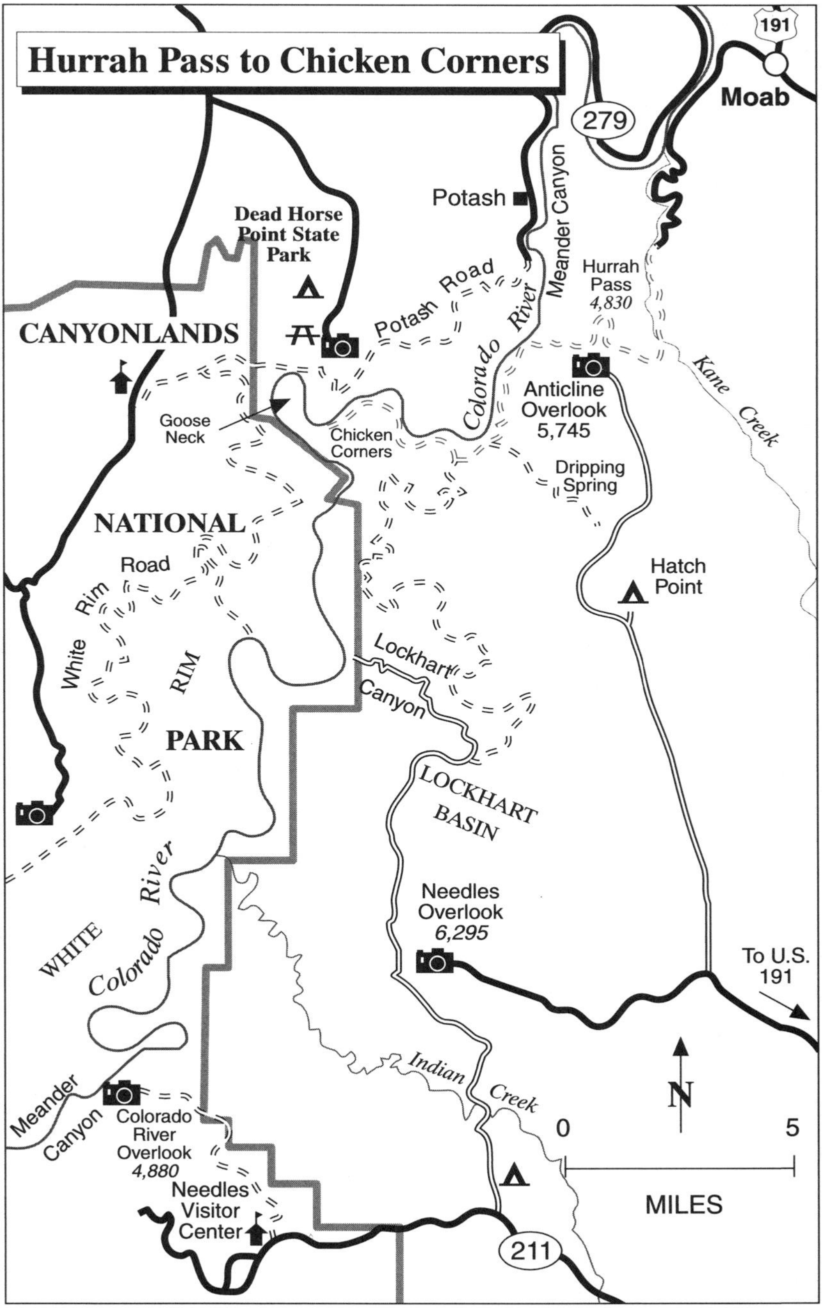

Hurrah Pass to Chicken Corners
191
Moab
279
Potash
Meander Canyon
Dead Horse Point State Park
Potash Road
Hurrah Pass
4,830
Colorado River
CANYONLANDS
Anticline Overlook
5,745
Kane Creek
Goose Neck
Chicken Corners
Dripping Spring
NATIONAL
Road
Hatch Point
White Rim
RIM
Lockhart Canyon
PARK
LOCKHART BASIN
River
WHITE
Colorado
Needles Overlook
6,295
To U.S. 191
Indian Creek
Meander Canyon
Colorado River Overlook
4,880
Needles Visitor Center
N
0
5
MILES
211

TRIP
40

Lockhart Basin Road

LOCATION: Just east of Canyonlands National Park.

HIGHLIGHTS: Immersion in a remote, rugged and beautiful red rock world. Some real four-wheeling. Best in spring and fall.

DIFFICULTY: The first mile off the Hurrah Pass-Chicken Corners road *(trip 39)* involves a difficult climb up a rocky ravine. With my wife and daughter as spotters, I maneuvered a new, full-size Toyota Land Cruiser through without a scratch. I rate the slow 20-mile journey from the ravine to Lockhart Basin moderate because of the rocky roadbed and numerous small washes. The graded road beyond Lockhart Basin is easy. Indian Creek, which you'll ford at the south end, can be high in spring or after storms. No water or services of any kind. No toilets until beyond Indian Creek; you must bring your own.

TIME & DISTANCE: 8 hours; about 37 miles from the Hurrah Pass-Chicken Corners road to U-211. Add 10.8 miles for Lockhart Canyon.

GETTING THERE: Go south to decide if you want to attempt the ravine. Take the Hurrah Pass-Chicken Corners route 21.4 miles from Main Street in Moab; go left up the ravine. (There's a sign for Lockhart Basin.) If you only want to go to Lockhart Basin, take the easy road segment north from U-211 near the Needles District.

THE DRIVE: Plan your course up the ravine carefully. Beyond it you'll have views across the Colorado River canyon to the White Rim *(trip 38)*, Dead Horse Point and countless other features. About 3.6 miles beyond the ravine you'll reach a divide with a sweeping view of the sandstone remains of great deserts, seas and rivers. To the west is Island in the Sky Mesa; to the south, the pinnacles of the Needles District; to the east, the La Sal Mts. Ahead lie miles of rocky roadbed and small washes as you drive below Hatch Point. About 14 long, tedious miles farther the amphitheater of boulder-strewn Lockhart Basin, where the road improves, appears below. In another 3.3 miles you'll reach the right turn for the 5.4-mile spur down Lockhart Canyon to the river (access is poor). It ends at a nice spot just inside Canyonlands NP where cliffs are etched with petroglyphs. South of the basin, you'll see the glint of the kiosk at Needles Overlook high atop Wingate Sandstone cliffs formed of an ancient desert's dunes. In the distance to the south rise North and South Six Shooter Peaks. U-211 is about miles beyond the Lockhart Canyon spur.

REST STOPS: Indian Creek is a pleasant place to rest. (Scan the cliffs on the north side for a tiny ruin.) Only barren and primitive campsites until you get beyond Indian Creek. The BLM maintains picnic tables and pit toilets in the Hamburger Rock area 1.5 miles north of U-211. There are primitive campsites in the area as well.

GETTING HOME: U-211 to U.S. 191.

MAPS: F.A. Barnes' *Canyon Rims & Needles Areas*; Trails Illustrated's *Canyonlands NP, Needles & Island in the Sky.*

INFORMATION: BLM, Moab Field Office, 259-6111.

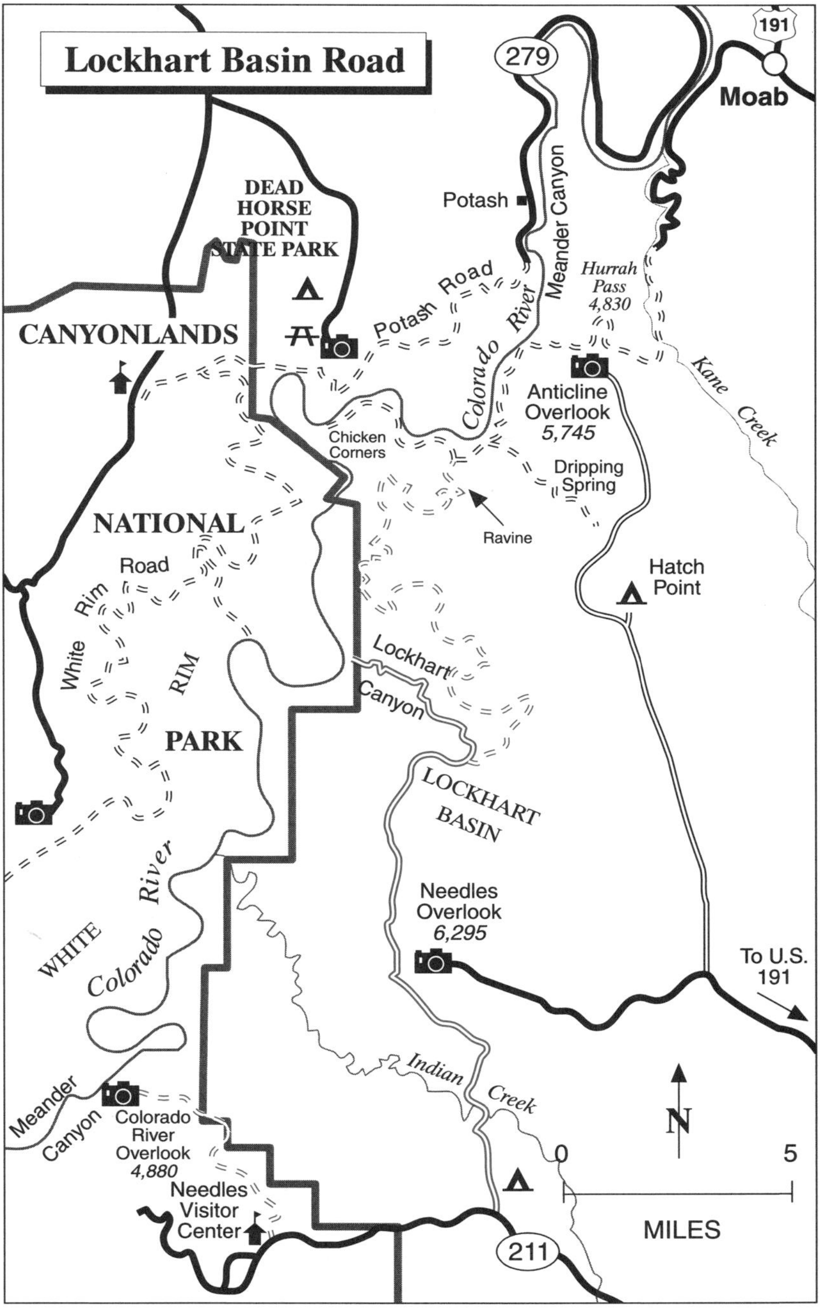
Lockhart Basin Road
279
191
Moab
DEAD
HORSE
POINT
STATE PARK
Potash
Meander Canyon
Hurrah
Pass
4,830
Potash Road
CANYONLANDS
Colorado River
Kane Creek
Anticline
Overlook
5,745
Chicken
Corners
Dripping
Spring
Ravine
NATIONAL
Road
Rim
White
RIM
Hatch
Point
Lockhart
Canyon
PARK
LOCKHART
BASIN
River
WHITE
Colorado
Needles
Overlook
6,295
To U.S.
191
Indian
Creek
N
Meander
Canyon
Colorado
River
Overlook
4,880
Needles
Visitor
Center
0
5
MILES
211

TRIP
41

Posey Lake Road

LOCATION: Crosses the Aquarius Plateau between Bicknell and Escalante. Dixie National Forest.

HIGHLIGHTS: An enchanting cruise across a high plateau with countless lakes to almost 10,000 feet, followed by the 4,000-foot descent into the red desert of the Escalante region. Best in late afternoon or early evening. Closed in winter.

DIFFICULTY: Easy on a maintained dirt and gravel road.

TIME & DISTANCE: 2 hours; 50 miles.

GETTING THERE: Take this north-south route either way. I go south from Bicknell, on U-24. Turn south off the highway at the Utah Scenic Backway sign. The road is 154 in Dixie National Forest. Reset your odometer.

THE DRIVE: The pavement ends soon as you roll through undulating farmlands and barren foothills, climbing toward forested mountains on a good dirt and gravel road across the sparsely vegetated, rolling Awapa Plateau. When you reach mile 15 you'll see a two track up Smooth Knoll, on the right. It provides a panorama from about 9,350 ft. of pink cliffs to the north, mountain ridges to the west and the volcanic plateau below. At 18.1 (with the spur to the knoll) you enter the national forest, passing alternately through woodlands and open areas, with expansive, inspiring vistas. You'll pass a number of verdant wetlands. At 29.1 you'll see the right turn for Griffin Top Road *(trip 46, Escalante Mountains)*, and 4 miles farther you'll see grassy Cyclone Lake, pretty when autumn sets the aspens around it alight. The road ahead provides glimpses of the sandstone cliffs and canyons of Capitol Reef and Escalante country. Then comes the turnoff to Posey Lake, where you can picnic, camp and fish. 1.7 miles farther pass Hell's Backbone Road, a good dirt and gravel road above craggy Box-Death Hollow Wilderness. As you descend from the plateau, pines largely give way to pinyon-juniper woodlands. But huge Ponderosa pines grow in cracks in the Triassic-Jurassic Period Navajo Sandstone (144-208 MYA) of the spectacular Antone Bench, the high ridge to the east (left) along Pine Creek Road. Pavement is at mile 48.1. U-12 is a couple of miles farther.

REST STOPS: Posey Lake. Escalante Petrified Forest State Park.

GETTING HOME: U-12 west to U.S. 89 or north to U-24.

MAPS: Dixie National Forest, Escalante, Teasdale ranger districts; ACSC's Indian Country.

INFORMATION: Escalante Ranger District, 826-5400; Teasdale Ranger District, 425-3702; Escalante Interagency Visitor Center, 826-5499, on U-12 at Escalante's west end.

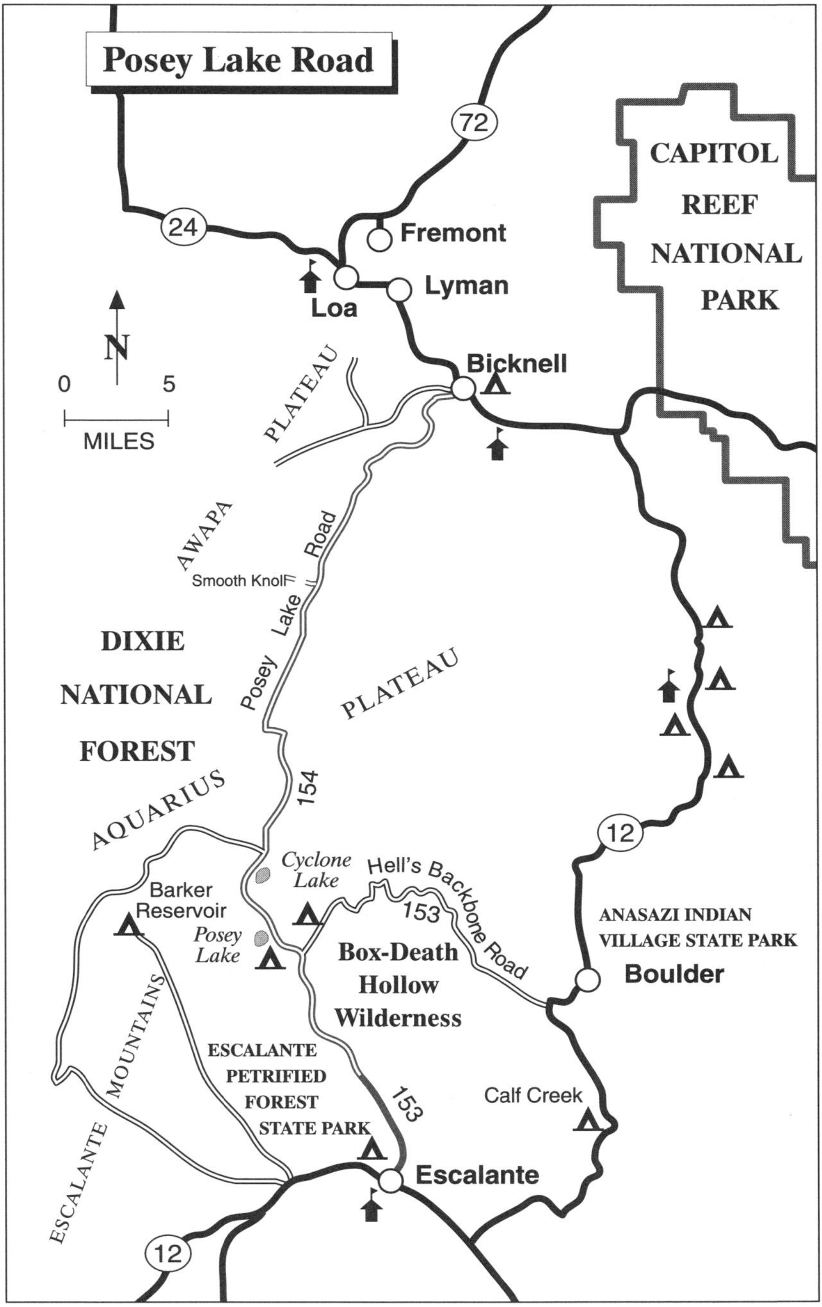
Posey Lake Road
72
24
CAPITOL
REEF
NATIONAL
PARK
Fremont
Lyman
Loa
N
0
5
MILES
Bicknell
PLATEAU
AWAPA
Road
Smooth Knoll
Lake
Posey
DIXIE
NATIONAL
FOREST
PLATEAU
154
AQUARIUS
12
Cyclone
Lake
Hell's Backbone Road
153
Barker
Reservoir
Posey
Lake
Box-Death
Hollow
Wilderness
ANASAZI INDIAN
VILLAGE STATE PARK
Boulder
MOUNTAINS
ESCALANTE
PETRIFIED
FOREST
STATE PARK
153
Calf Creek
Escalante
ESCALANTE
12

TRIP
42

Notom Road

LOCATION: South of U-24, west of the Henry Mountains. Much of the road is in Capitol Reef National Park.

HIGHLIGHTS: Waterpocket Fold, a geologic phenomenon that includes the park's namesake, Capitol Reef. Henry Mountains, Burr Trail, Upper Muley Twist Canyon.

DIFFICULTY: Easy; a very good dirt and gravel road. It can be washed out in places and impassable when wet. Avoid washes during summer storms. The first 4.9 miles are paved.

TIME & DISTANCE: 1.5 hours & 32.7 miles from U-24 to the Burr Trail junction.

GETTING THERE: 9 miles east of the Capitol Reef National Park visitor center, turn south from U-24 onto Notom Road.

THE DRIVE: The north-south road runs along a trough between the Henry Mountains, a granitic "island" range that soars to 11,522 feet; Boulder Mountain, which presides over the Aquarius Plateau from 11,330 ft.; and the awesome Waterpocket Fold, a 100-mile crease in the Earth's crust named after depressions in the sandstone that collect water. The road has many spots to stop and explore or just enjoy the view. 65 MYA, when geologic forces lifted the Colorado Plateau, sediments laid down over hundreds of millions of years by ancient seas, tidal flats, deserts and rivers were lifted and folded (tilted and curved). The upper layers, which lay high above the scene you see now, were eroded away. Today, the Fold's domes, cliffs, spires and dramatically tilted sawtooth exposures, which continue to be eroded by wind and water, only hint at the Fold's original size. The scenery is dominated by the Fold's crest of gray-white peaks and domes of Navajo Sandstone, then the Kayenta Formation's ledges of river and stream deposits, and finally the massive cliffs of reddish Wingate Sandstone. Navajo and Wingate are the cemented sands of Triassic-Jurassic (144-208 MYA) deserts. Beyond the Burr Trail junction the road continues south, becoming paved as it passes the dead-end Halls Creek (Grand Gulch) Overlook spur and Big Thompson Mesa. It reaches U-276 north of Bullfrog, on Lake Powell.

REST STOPS: Waterless Cedar Mesa CG, 21.4 miles south of U-24. For the humbling view of the region from Strike Valley Overlook, leave the Burr Trail at Upper Muley Twist Canyon, drive up the wash to the trailhead (note the arches on the way), park at the end of the road and hike to the crest of the Fold, following the cairns.

GETTING HOME: Go to Bullfrog, 36 miles south at Lake Powell. Or take scenic Burr Trail west 36 miles to Boulder, on U-12. You could even make the spectacular and rugged traverse over the Henry Mountains to Hanksville, almost 44 miles.

MAPS: At the park visitor center get *The Waterpocket Fold*, a guide to a 125-mile loop; BLM's *General Recreation Map, The Henry Mountains & Surrounding Deserts* is excellent; ACSC's *Indian Country*.

INFORMATION: BLM, Henry Mountains Field Station, 542-3461; Capitol Reef National Park, 425-3791.

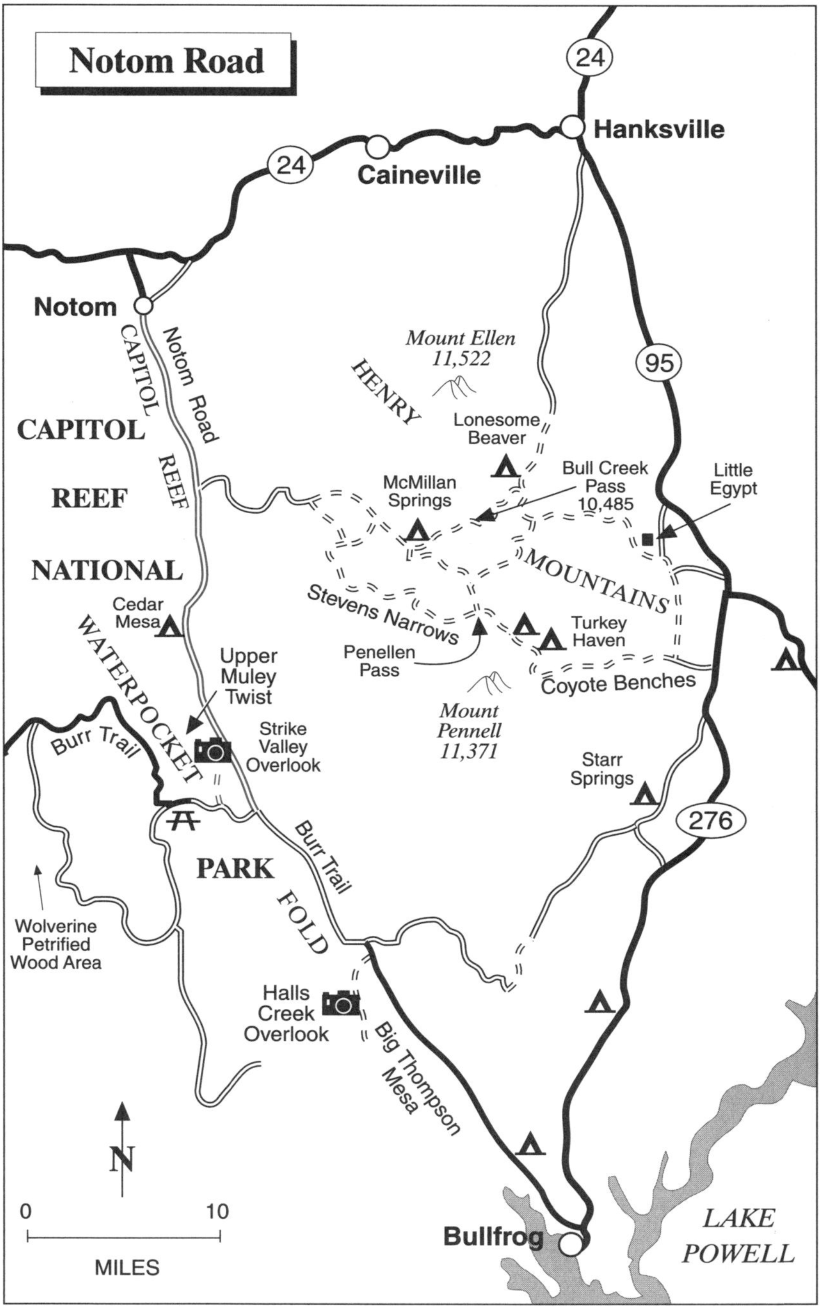
Notom Road
24
Hanksville
24
Caineville
Notom
CAPITOL
Notom Road
Mount Ellen
11,522
HENRY
95
CAPITOL
Lonesome
Beaver
REEF
Bull Creek
Pass
10,485
Little
Egypt
McMillan
Springs
REEF
NATIONAL
MOUNTAINS
Stevens Narrows
Cedar
Mesa
Turkey
Haven
WATERPOCKET
Upper
Muley
Twist
Penellen
Pass
Coyote Benches
Mount
Pennell
11,371
Burr Trail
Strike
Valley
Overlook
Starr
Springs
276
PARK
Burr Trail
FOLD
Wolverine
Petrified
Wood Area
Halls
Creek
Overlook
Big Thompson
Mesa
N
0
10
MILES
LAKE
POWELL
Bullfrog

TRIP
43

Henry Mountains

LOCATION: A National Back Country Byway south of Hanksville; east of Capitol Reef National Park, west of U-95.

HIGHLIGHTS: Views of the Colorado Plateau from granitic mountains that rose through layers of sedimentary rock to loom 6,500 feet above the desert. The last range in the Lower 48 to be explored and named. 10,485-ft. Bull Creek Pass, Little Egypt Geologic Site. Free-roaming buffalo herd descended from 18 transplanted from Yellowstone National Park in 1941.

DIFFICULTY: Moderate. Rocky roads; prepare for flats. Bull Creek Pass is generally snow-free July through October.

TIME & DISTANCE: A 5-hour, 68-mile loop.

GETTING THERE: Take U-95 south from Hanksville for 21 miles. Turn right (west) onto a dirt road. Look for signs.

THE DRIVE: You have more than a mile to climb. At mile 1.4 you'll pass Little Egypt, with sandstone figures like those at Goblin Valley. Go right at mile 3.7 to climb through hills dotted with pinyons and junipers. By 12 you're among scrub oak, aspens and pines. Pass through the site of Eagle City, marked by a collapsed wooden building; make a hard right at 13.2. Edge along the mountainside toward Wickiup Pass. By about mile 16 you're at an intersection; go left toward Notom. In 2.6 miles you're on Bull Creek Pass, looking across the Waterpocket Fold. This is the trailhead for a 5-mile (round-trip) hike north up 11,522-ft. Mt. Ellen. Descend on a narrow road with switchbacks to McMillan Springs. At 26.8 there's an optional turnoff to the left that goes 8.1 miles along Salt Creek Ridge to Penellen Pass. I recommend continuing ahead, down the mountains. At 33.6, at the T at Sweetwater Creek, go left toward King Ranch. (Going right will take you on a gorgeous drive past sandstone monoliths to Notom Road, *trip 42*.) In 1.9 miles go right at the Y, toward Stevens Narrows. Now you're in a raw, colorful landscape of sandstone monoliths that are presided over by the Henry Mountains' five peaks. Go through Stevens Narrows. At a Y at 45.4 turn left. The road climbs 3.8 miles to Penellen Pass and the Horn. Keep right. At Straight Creek Junction go left, descending to Coyote Benches, Trachyte Ranch and U-95.

REST STOPS: Developed campgrounds at Lonesome Beaver, McMillan Springs. Undeveloped campgrounds at Penellen Pass, Turkey Haven. Dandelion Flat Picnic Area 0.5 mile before Lonesome Beaver on the road from Hanksville.

GETTING HOME: U-95 north to U-24.

MAPS: BLM's *General Recreation Map, The Henry Mountains & Surrounding Deserts* is excellent; BLM's *Bull Creek Pass Byway* brochure has lots of information; ACSC's *Indian Country.*

INFORMATION: BLM, Hanksville, 542-3461.

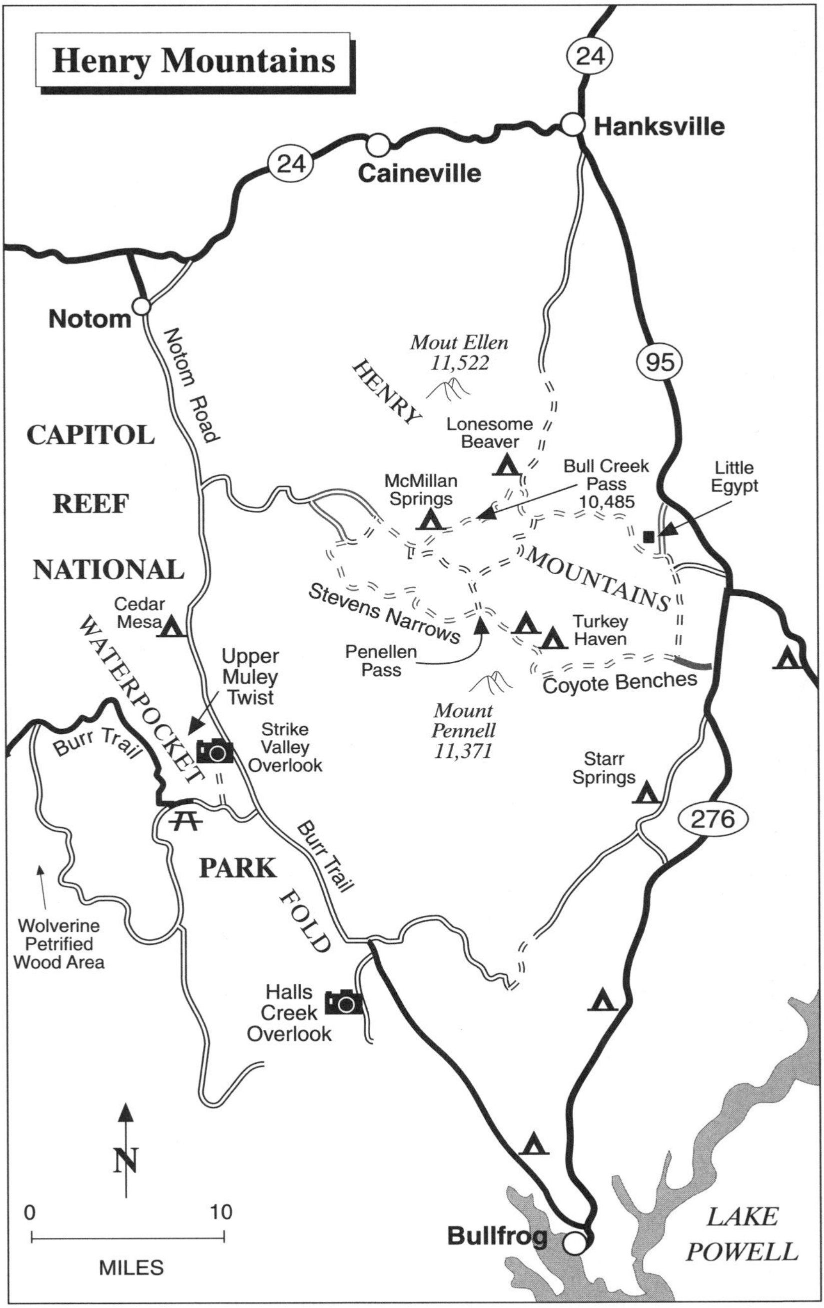
Henry Mountains
24
Hanksville
Caineville
Notom
Notom Road
Mout Ellen
11,522
HENRY
95
CAPITOL
REEF
NATIONAL
Lonesome
Beaver
McMillan
Springs
Bull Creek
Pass
10,485
Little
Egypt
MOUNTAINS
Stevens Narrows
Cedar
Mesa
Turkey
Haven
Penellen
Pass
WATERPOCKET
Upper
Muley
Twist
Coyote Benches
Mount
Pennell
11,371
Burr Trail
Strike
Valley
Overlook
Starr
Springs
276
PARK
Burr Trail
FOLD
Wolverine
Petrified
Wood Area
Halls
Creek
Overlook
N
0
10
MILES
Bullfrog
LAKE
POWELL

Salt Creek Canyon

LOCATION: Canyonlands National Park, The Needles District.

HIGHLIGHTS: Marbled sandstone labyrinth rich in ancient Indian structures and rock art that are difficult but fun to spot. Explore side canyons on foot; carefully scan cliffs and rock faces. Climb to Angel Arch. Inquire about the Colorado River Overlook route.

DIFFICULTY: Moderate to difficult, depending on weather and conditions. Several deep water fordings. Sandy and rocky in places. Flash floods and quicksand possible. Cancel if storms are in the area. Permit required. Best in spring and fall.

TIME & DISTANCE: 8 hrs; longer if you explore, climb to Angel Arch, etc. 24 miles round-trip from the locked gate.

GETTING THERE: Take U-211 to Needles Visitor Center for the $5 vehicle day-use permit and lock combination. Just past the center go left. Turn left again at the sign for Salt Creek/Cave Springs. In 0.8 mile turn right, onto the road to Salt Creek/Horse Canyon. Reset your odometer. Lock the gate behind you.

THE DRIVE: With its reliable water, good soil and abundant plants and wild game, Archaic and ancestral Puebloan (Anasazi) Indians found this a habitable area for at least 7,600 years. In 1975 the Salt Creek Archaeological District was placed on the National Register of Historic Places. At mile 2.3 the road splits, left to Horse Canyon *(trip 45)*, right to Salt Creek Canyon. At 2.8 slowly ford the first deep water, at Peekaboo Spring. Do the same at the pools to come. At 3.3 is Peekaboo Camp. A cliff above the camp bears pictographs painted 700-1,000 years ago. Some are painted over Barrier Canyon-style figures possibly as old as 3,000-7,000 years. Ford more deep water as you wind through a system of narrow, tortuous canyons of pink and white Cedar Mesa Sandstone, dune and sandbar deposits from the Permian Period 245-286 MYA, and layers of reddish river deposits. Pass a small parking area (for hikers) with a toilet. At 12.2 is the parking area below 150-ft.-tall Angel Arch, the symbol of Canyonlands, and a precariously perched, toothlike rock dubbed The Molar. Walk a short distance to a viewpoint and you'll see more arches on the opposite side of the canyon. Scramble up a sometimes difficult trail, marked by cairns, to Angel Arch.

REST STOPS: Peekaboo Camp (2 sites, pit toilet; $25 reservation fee).

SPECIAL NOTES: Only 10 vehicle day-use permits are issued daily. Reservations are recommended for spring and holiday weekends. Don't touch rock art or ruins. Do not enter ruins, disturb or remove artifacts. Walking near ruins can cause damage. Artifacts, archaeological sites & rock art are protected by law. Camp only at Peekaboo. No pets or wood fires are permitted.

MAP: Trails Illustrated's *Canyonlands NP, Needles District.*

INFORMATION: Canyonlands National Park, the Needles District, 259-4711; day-use and backcountry campsite reservations, 259-4351; general park information, 259-7164.

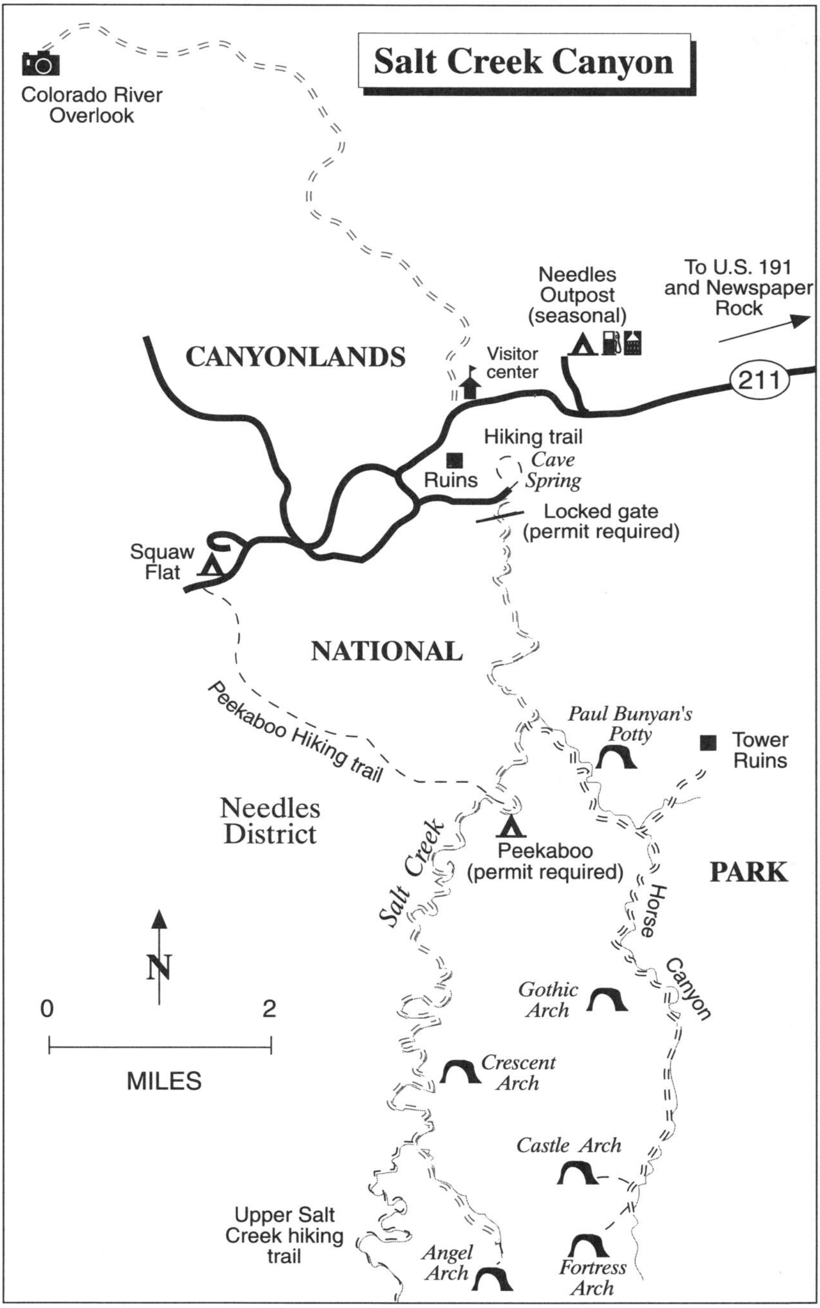
Salt Creek Canyon
Colorado River Overlook
CANYONLANDS
Visitor center
Needles Outpost (seasonal)
To U.S. 191 and Newspaper Rock
211
Hiking trail
Cave Spring
Ruins
Locked gate (permit required)
Squaw Flat
NATIONAL
Peekaboo Hiking trail
Needles District
Paul Bunyan's Potty
Tower Ruins
Salt Creek
Peekaboo (permit required)
PARK
Horse Canyon
N
0
2
MILES
Gothic Arch
Crescent Arch
Castle Arch
Upper Salt Creek hiking trail
Angel Arch
Fortress Arch

TRIP 45

Horse Canyon

LOCATION: Canyonlands National Park, The Needles District.

HIGHLIGHTS: Tower Ruins; Paul Bunyan's Potty; Fortress & Castle arches. Many ancient structures and rock art sites in an archaeological district listed on the National Register of Historic Places. Drive slowly and stop often to carefully scan the cliffs (binoculars help). Explore side canyons on foot. Inquire about the Colorado River Overlook route, near the Needles visitor center. Best spring and fall.

DIFFICULTY: Moderate to difficult depending on weather and route conditions. Deep sand (air down). Very rocky for the last 200 yards. Flood, quicksand danger. Cancel if storms are in the area.

TIME & DISTANCE: 4-5 hours; 15 miles round-trip.

GETTING THERE: Take U-211 to the Needles Visitor Center to get the required $5 vehicle day-use permit and the combination to the locked gate. Turn left just past the visitor center. Follow the paved road a short distance, then go left at the sign for Salt Creek & Cave Springs. In 0.8 mile go right onto the road to Salt Creek & Horse canyons. Unlock the gate, then lock it behind you. In 2.3 miles the road splits. Horse Canyon is left, Salt Creek Canyon *(trip 44)* right. Reset your odometer.

THE DRIVE: Archaic and ancestral Puebloan (Anasazi) Indians inhabited this area for at least 7,600 years, leaving silent buildings and mysterious rock art panels. You'll be fascinated by the color-banded and complex canyons, amphitheaters and arches eroded into the Cedar Mesa Sandstone, dune and sandbar deposits from the Permian Period (245-286 MYA). You'll see reddish riverbed deposits as well. The verdant canyon starts out wide, but its marbled cliffs gradually close in. Soon you'll see Paul Bunyan's Potty, a cave-pothole-type arch. A mile farther is the turnoff to Tower Ruins, ancient Puebloan buildings tucked in a cave (don't climb up to them). At mile 7.6 pass below a cliff overhang, where your vehicle will squeeze between the overhang and a boulder. The washbottom road becomes rocky by 8.2. Watch on the right for the short trail to a view of Castle Arch. The road ends soon at the start of the half-mile trail to Fortress Arch, visible ahead.

REST STOPS: 2 campsites at Peekaboo ($25 reservation fee). Toilet at Paul Bunyan's Potty.

SPECIAL NOTES: Vehicle day-use permit is $5; only 10 are issued daily. Reservations recommended for spring and holiday weekends. Don't touch rock art or ruins. Do not enter ruins, disturb or remove artifacts. Walking near ruins can cause damage. Artifacts, archaeological sites & rock art are protected by law. Camp only at Peekaboo. No pets or wood fires.

MAP: Trails Illustrated's Canyonlands NP, Needles District.

INFORMATION: Canyonlands National Park, the Needles District, 259-4711; day-use and campsite reservations, 259-4351; general park information, 259-7164.

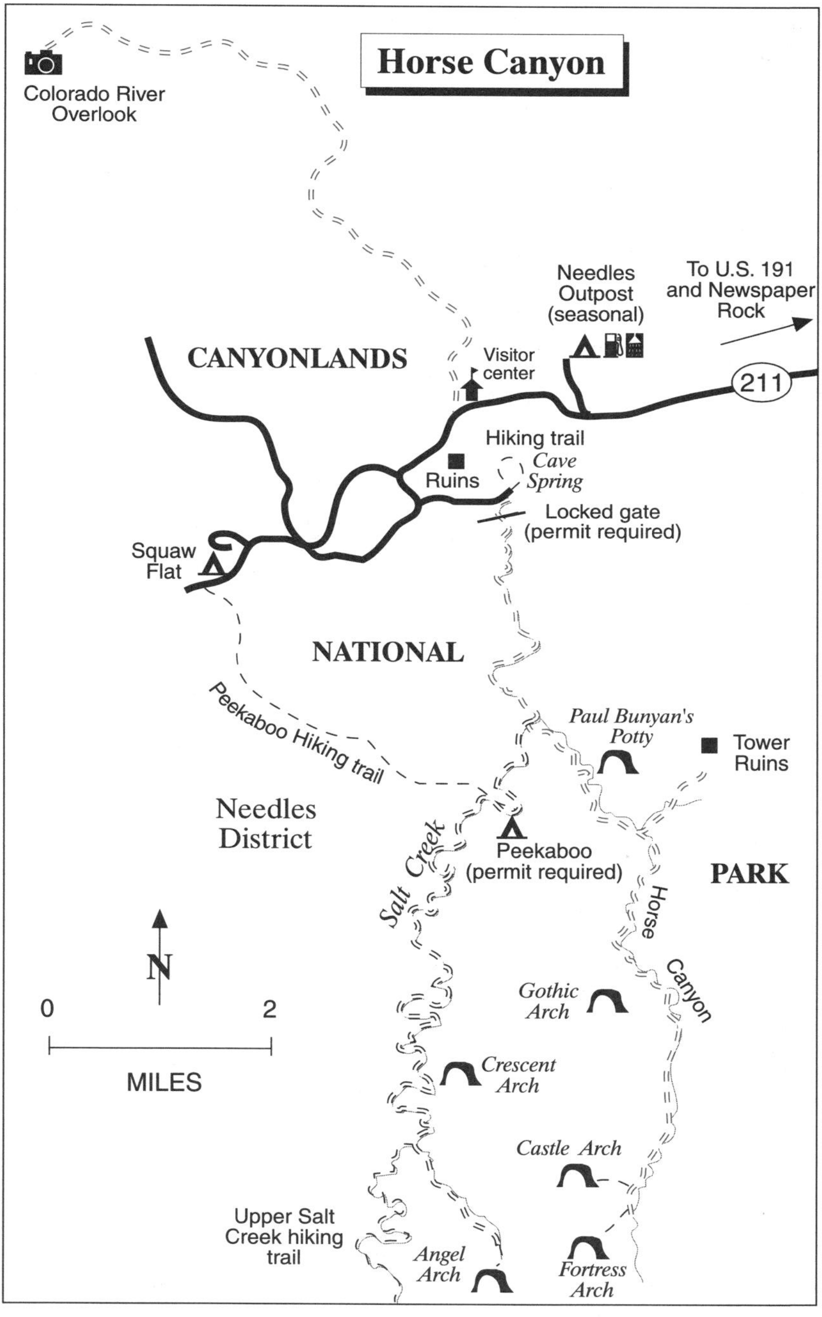
Horse Canyon
Colorado River Overlook
Needles Outpost (seasonal)
To U.S. 191 and Newspaper Rock
CANYONLANDS
Visitor center
211
Hiking trail
Cave Spring
Ruins
Locked gate (permit required)
Squaw Flat
NATIONAL
Peekaboo Hiking trail
Paul Bunyan's Potty
Tower Ruins
Needles District
Salt Creek
Peekaboo (permit required)
PARK
Horse Canyon
N
0
2
MILES
Gothic Arch
Crescent Arch
Castle Arch
Upper Salt Creek hiking trail
Angel Arch
Fortress Arch

Escalante Mountains

LOCATION: Dixie National Forest, northwest of Escalante.

HIGHLIGHTS: High meadows and forest as you climb to 10,500 feet. Vistas take in the Escalante River Basin, Capitol Reef, Glen Canyon. Antelope, deer, elk, waterfowl.

DIFFICULTY: Easy loop; maintained dirt and gravel road.

TIME & DISTANCE: 2.5-3 hours; 58 miles.

GETTING THERE: In Escalante, turn north off U-12 onto Pine Creek Road/Hell's Backbone Road. It becomes road 153 when it enters the national forest, then 154 as it climbs toward Posey Lake and Bicknell. Reset your odometer.

THE DRIVE: For the first 21.6 miles follow the southern leg of the Posey Lake route *(trip 41)*. To the east (right) rise the Antone Bench's gray-orange Navajo Sandstone cliffs, capped by rock of the Jurassic (144-208 MYA) Carmel Formation. The bench separates The Box and Death Hollow areas of Box-Death Hollow Wilderness. The road climbs about 3,700 ft. onto the volcanic Aquarius Plateau, through a forest of spruce, fir and aspen. At mile 21.6, past Cyclone Lake, turn left (west) onto road 140, the Griffin Top Road. The mountain it traverses is named for sheep rancher Charles Griffin. Climb gradually through long, open meadows bordered by pine and aspen forest. At 28.3 pass through an area where large boulders have been left in fields to keep people from driving across them. Through the trees you'll glimpse Escalante country's expanses of deeply carved Navajo Sandstone. At mile 35 you've peaked at about 10,500 feet on Griffin Top. In another 5 miles the views change from rolling meadows and hilltops to rugged, mountainous terrain. At 42 you'll have vistas to the south and east of Capitol Reef, Glen Canyon and the Henry Mountains. Eventually you'll reach a T at road 17, at 9,200-ft. Escalante Summit. From there you can go right to John's Valley, past the remains of the old farm town of Widtsoe. I think it's more scenic to go left down Main Canyon, along Birch Creek past terraced white and yellow cliffs whiskered with pinyons-junipers to reach U-12 at 58.5.

REST STOPS: Posey Lake. Box-Death Hollow Wilderness offers outstanding hiking in deep, high-walled canyons.

GETTING HOME: U-12 west to U.S. 89, north to I-70.

MAPS: Dixie National Forest, Teasdale, Escalante districts; ACSC's Indian Country.

INFORMATION: Escalante Ranger District, 826-5400; Escalante Interagency Visitor Center, 826-5499, on U-12 (Main Street) at Escalante's west end.

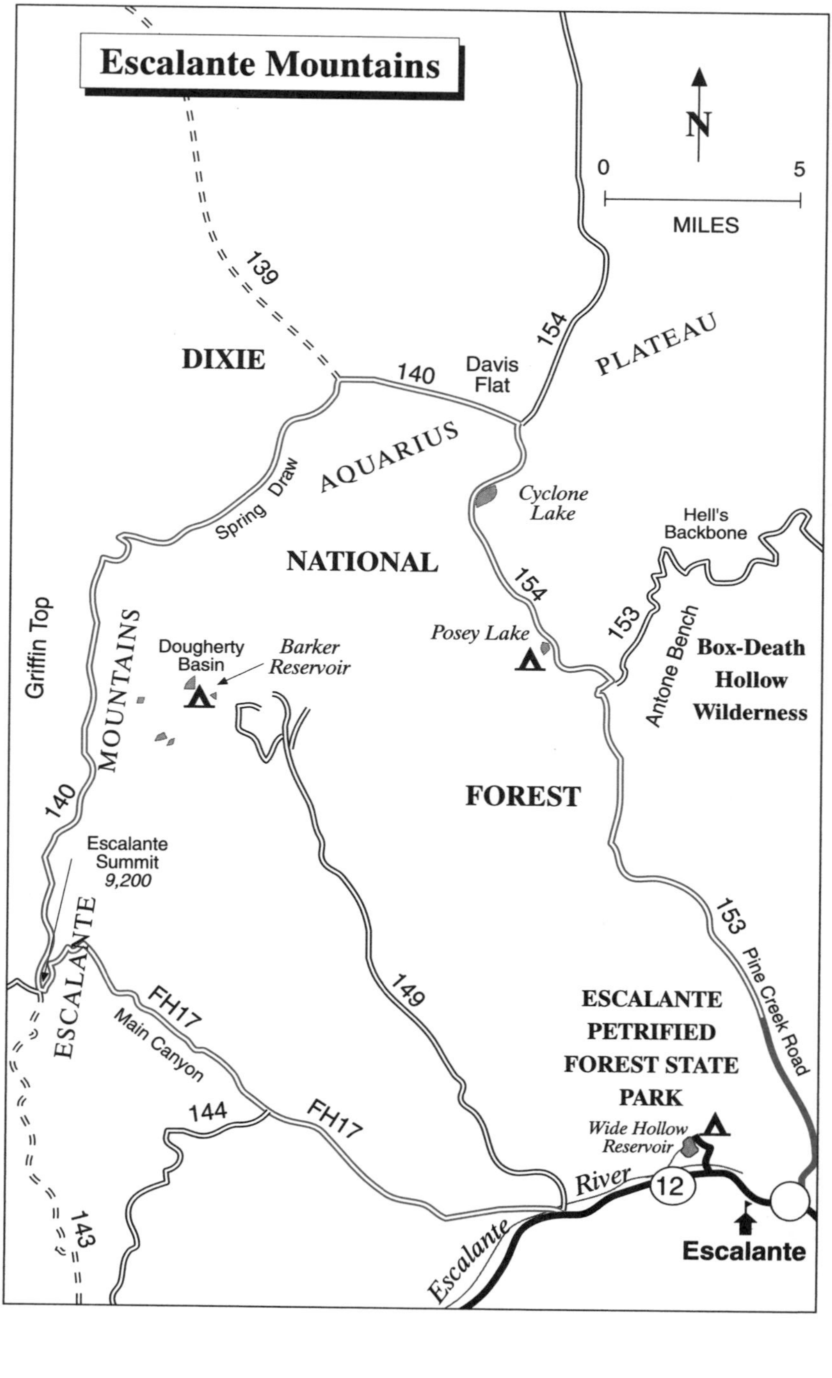
Escalante Mountains
N
0
5
MILES
139
DIXIE
140
Davis
Flat
154
PLATEAU
AQUARIUS
Spring Draw
Cyclone
Lake
Hell's
Backbone
NATIONAL
154
153
Posey Lake
Griffin Top
MOUNTAINS
Dougherty
Basin
Barker
Reservoir
Antone Bench
Box-Death
Hollow
Wilderness
FOREST
140
Escalante
Summit
9,200
153
Pine Creek Road
ESCALANTE
FH17
Main Canyon
149
ESCALANTE
PETRIFIED
FOREST STATE
PARK
144
FH17
Wide Hollow
Reservoir
River
12
143
Escalante
Escalante

TRIP
47

Wolverine Road-Burr Trail

LOCATION: S.E. of Boulder, west of Capitol Reef National Park.

HIGHLIGHTS: A spur off the once-wild Burr Trail, a.k.a. Boulder to Bullfrog Road, tamed by asphalt in 1990 to the park boundary. The Circle Cliffs; Horse Canyon; trailheads to canyons of the Escalante River; Wolverine Petrified Wood Natural Area; Upper Muley Twist Canyon; Strike Valley Overlook; the descent to Capitol Reef NP.

DIFFICULTY: Easy. Horse and Upper Muley Twist canyons are moderate. Hot in summer. Best spring and fall.

TIME & DISTANCE: 3 hrs.; 44 mi. with Horse Canyon and Upper Muley Twist. Longer for the petrified wood hike.

GETTING THERE: From Boulder, on U-12, take the Burr Trail (a.k.a. Boulder to Bullfrog Road) 18.4 miles through awesome Long Canyon. Go right onto Wolverine Loop Road.

THE DRIVE: Asphalt is to backcountry roads what dams are to wild rivers. Like dammed rivers, paved roads can have tributaries that recall the main stem's wild past. So it is with Wolverine Road, and the leg of the Burr Trail that switchbacks down a 100-mile wrinkle in the Earth's crust, Waterpocket Fold. Wolverine Road courses beneath the soaring Wingate Sandstone Circle Cliffs, once the dunes of a Triassic-Jurassic (144-208 MYA) desert, then crosses a grassy valley. 4 miles from the Burr Trail, walls on either side close in as the road becomes sandy. About 1.2 miles farther a wash on the right goes several miles down intriguing Horse Canyon, ending at a gate. 4.5 miles farther the Wolverine Petrified Wood Natural Area is on the right. There, hike a mile or so up Wolverine Wash to an area in the Chinle Formation with large petrified stumps and logs. (No collecting is allowed. The area has already experienced substantial losses.) Eventually the main road reaches a T. Go left for 8.1 miles to the paved Burr Trail. The asphalt ends in 1.7 miles at the park boundary. 2.2 miles from the boundary go left to Upper Muley Twist Canyon. Drive 2.7 miles up a wash flanked by cliffs and arches. At the end of the road hike up to Strike Valley Overlook for a top-of-the-world view of Waterpocket Fold and beyond. From the turnoff a spectacular remnant of old Burr Trail plunges to Notom Road (*trip 42*).

REST STOPS: Camp at waterless Deer Creek Recreation Site, on the Burr Trail. There's a picnic table at the park boundary. Anasazi Indian Village State Park in Boulder. Inquire at the Escalante Interagency Visitor Center about recreational rock collecting in the area.

GETTING HOME: Beautiful Notom Road north to U-24.

MAPS: BLM's *Escalante Resource Area*; Trails Illustrated's *Canyons of the Escalante*; ACSC's *Indian Country*.

INFORMATION: BLM, Escalante Area, 826-4291; Escalante Interagency Visitor Center, 826-5499; Capitol Reef NP, 425-3791. There's an information booth in Boulder at the start of the Burr Trail.

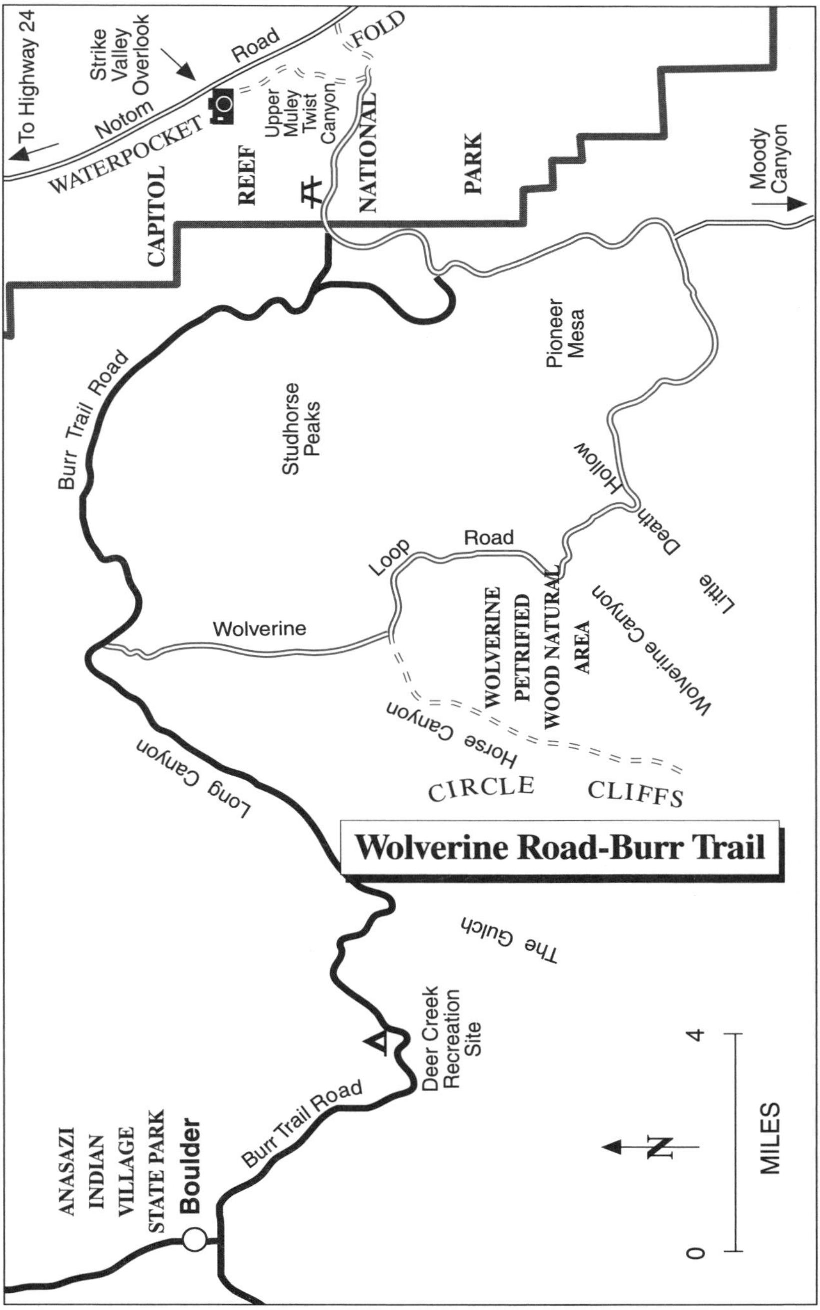
Wolverine Road-Burr Trail
To Highway 24
Strike Valley Overlook
Notom Road
WATERPOCKET FOLD
Upper Muley Twist Canyon
CAPITOL REEF NATIONAL PARK
Moody Canyon
Pioneer Mesa
Studhorse Peaks
Burr Trail Road
Death Hollow
Little
Loop Road
Wolverine
WOLVERINE PETRIFIED WOOD NATURAL AREA
Wolverine Canyon
Horse Canyon
Long Canyon
CIRCLE CLIFFS
The Gulch
Deer Creek Recreation Site
Burr Trail Road
ANASAZI INDIAN VILLAGE STATE PARK
Boulder
N
0
4
MILES

TRIP
48

Peavine Corridor

LOCATION: N.E. of Natural Bridges National Monument, in Manti-La Sal National Forest and Dark Canyon Wilderness.

HIGHLIGHTS: A deep, beautiful and forested sandstone canyon reached on a legal trail through a designated wilderness area. Arch, high cliffs. Best June-October.

DIFFICULTY: Easy to Little Notch; moderate to difficult in the Peavine Corridor. Many wash crossings. Paint-scratching trailside brush between Peavine and Dark canyons, especially beyond my stopping point. In the wilderness area mechanized travel is restricted to the 66-ft.-wide road corridor.

TIME & DISTANCE: 6 hours & 62.5 miles round-trip from U-95; or 2.5-3 hours & 17 miles round-trip from Elk Ridge *(trip 50)*. I stop at Dark Canyon, where road 089 splits.

GETTING THERE: Follow the Elk Ridge Road directions to Little Notch. Or, from U-95 6.3 miles west of the U-95/U.S. 191 junction, take county road 268 to forest road 092, then Elk Ridge Road, No. 088, to Little Notch. I start at U-95.

THE DRIVE: Keep right at a Y at 0.9 mile, where road 268 becomes dirt and gravel. You'll see Elk Ridge to the west and north. At mile 11.3, in the national forest, the road narrows and becomes rougher. As you make the 3,000-ft. climb to Elk Ridge, trading pinyon-juniper woodland for pine forest, you'll see the Colorado Rockies to the east. Keep right at the Y at mile 19.8, taking road 088/225 toward Big Notch, a.k.a. The Notch. 2 miles farther, at Little Notch, road 089 branches left. Take it. You'll soon see a sign-in box. Descend 1,300 feet in 2 miles along Kigalia Canyon on a narrow, rocky road to Peavine Canyon, in Dark Canyon Wilderness' mix of ponderosa pines, oak, cottonwoods, and white and pink sandstone cliffs dotted with pinyons and junipers. At canyon bottom the route crosses the wash often. At 30.6, the route splits at Dark Canyon. Stop and scan the cliffs ahead for a large arch. I stop here. Left goes to Rig Canyon, to a late-1920s oil drilling site. The right, very narrow and brushy with a badly eroded spot, goes to Scorup Cabin, a historic cowboy cabin that was moved from Rig Canyon when drilling for oil there ended in 1930. From here use a mountain bike, or hike.

REST STOPS: Primitive campsites. Hiking. Natural Bridges National Monument has camping, facilities.

GETTING HOME: Take Elk Ridge Road south to U-275, or north toward U-211 (see *trip 50, Elk Ridge Road*).

MAPS: Manti-La Sal National Forest, Moab/Monticello districts; Trails Illustrated's *Dark Canyon & Natural Bridges NM*; *Dark Canyon Trail Guide* (Canyonlands Natural History Association).

INFORMATION: Monticello Ranger District, 587-2041.

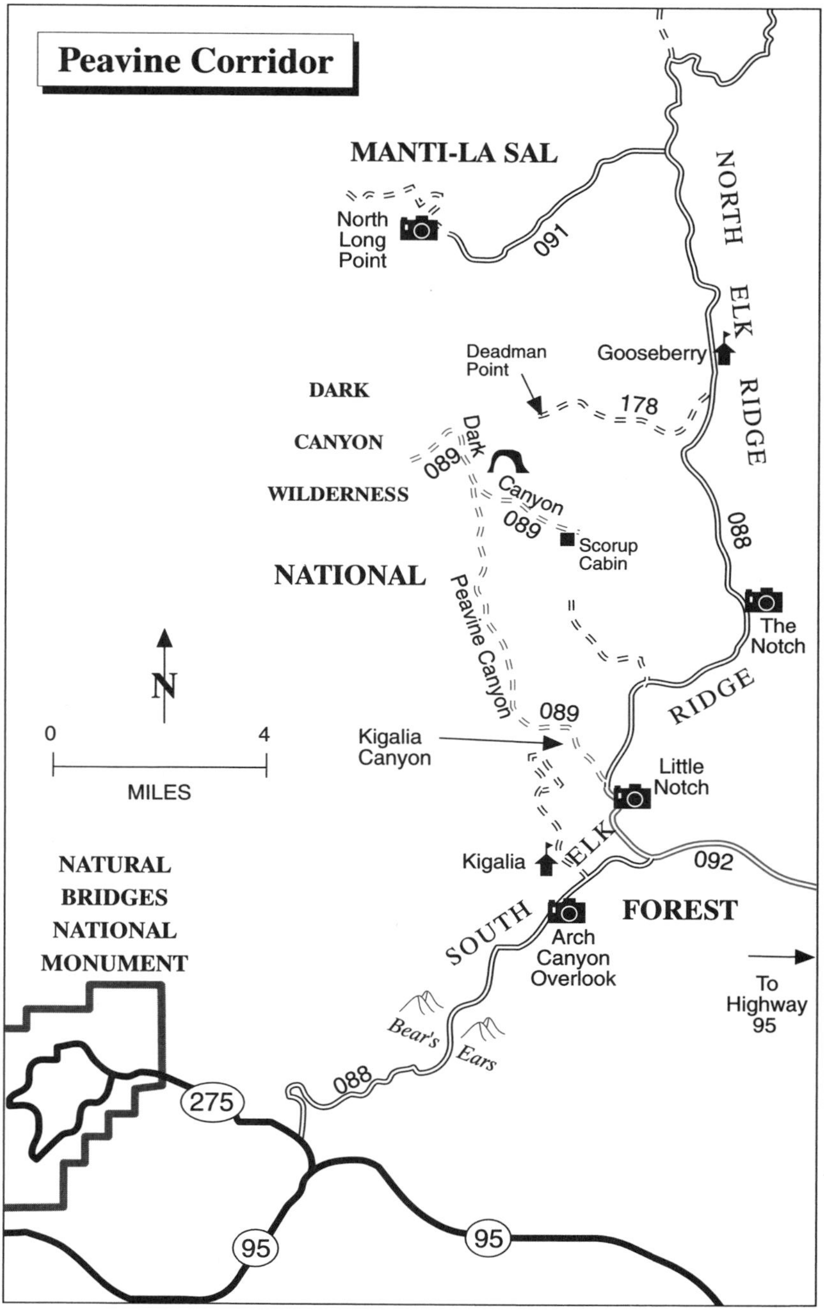
Peavine Corridor
MANTI-LA SAL
North Long Point
091
NORTH ELK RIDGE
Deadman Point
Gooseberry
178
DARK CANYON WILDERNESS
Dark Canyon
089
Scorup Cabin
088
NATIONAL
Peavine Canyon
The Notch
N
0
4
MILES
Kigalia Canyon
RIDGE
Little Notch
Kigalia
092
SOUTH ELK
FOREST
Arch Canyon Overlook
To Highway 95
NATURAL BRIDGES NATIONAL MONUMENT
Bear's Ears
275
95

TRIP
49

Abajo Mountains

LOCATION: West of Monticello; Manti-La Sal National Forest.

HIGHLIGHTS: A beautiful mountain trip off U.S. 191 that returns you to the highway after climbing to about 10,500 feet. You'll go through pine forest, grassy slopes and dramatic mountains on a road that at times runs along a mountainside ledge. Fine view of the desert of southern Utah.

DIFFICULTY: Easy. Impassable after heavy rains. Rocky and steep in places, some switchbacks. Narrow ledges.

TIME & DISTANCE: 1 hour; 21.4 miles from where the asphalt ends to where it resumes.

GETTING THERE: In Monticello go west off U.S. 191 on 2nd South toward Hart's Draw Loop Road. In 5.3 miles turn left (south) onto dirt road No. 079, toward Blanding.

THE DRIVE: Like the La Sal Mountains, the Abajos (a.k.a. Blue Mountains) are "island" mountains that tower above sandstone canyon country. They began as magma (molten rock) pushing up through faults and layers of sedimentary rock. The upper sedimentary layers formed a dome as the magma rose, but the magma cooled before breaking through. The sedimentary layers eroded away, exposing the igneous rock. Abajo is Spanish for down, below or underneath. The road immediately climbs through pines and grassy slopes as you drive up North Creek Canyon to North Creek Pass, at almost 10,500 feet the high point of the route 3.9 miles from the start. Around you are peaks that exceed 11,000 ft., including 11,360-ft. Abajo Peak to the southeast. You'll wind along a ledge high above a forested canyon, then descend along a mountainside into the canyon. By mile 7.3 you'll reach Indian Creek at the bottom of the canyon. The roadbed is loose and rocky as you climb out. After another 3 miles you can gaze across the vast desert expanse to the south as you drive through ponderosa pines. At mile 16 the serpentine road begins to straighten, and at 17.2 you'll see the Elk Ridge turnoff on the right. Asphalt resumes in 4.2 miles. Blanding is 7.8 miles.

REST STOPS: Buckboard & Dalton Springs campgrounds near the start. Dinosaur Museum and Edge of the Cedars State Park (museum and Anasazi ruins) in Blanding.

MAPS: Manti-La Sal National Forest, Moab & Monticello districts; Trails Illustrated's *Manti-La Sal National Forest*. ACSC's *Indian Country*.

INFORMATION: Monticello District, 587-2041.

ALSO TRY: Road 087 up Abajo Peak for a spectacular vista. About 17 miles round-trip. Easy to moderate.

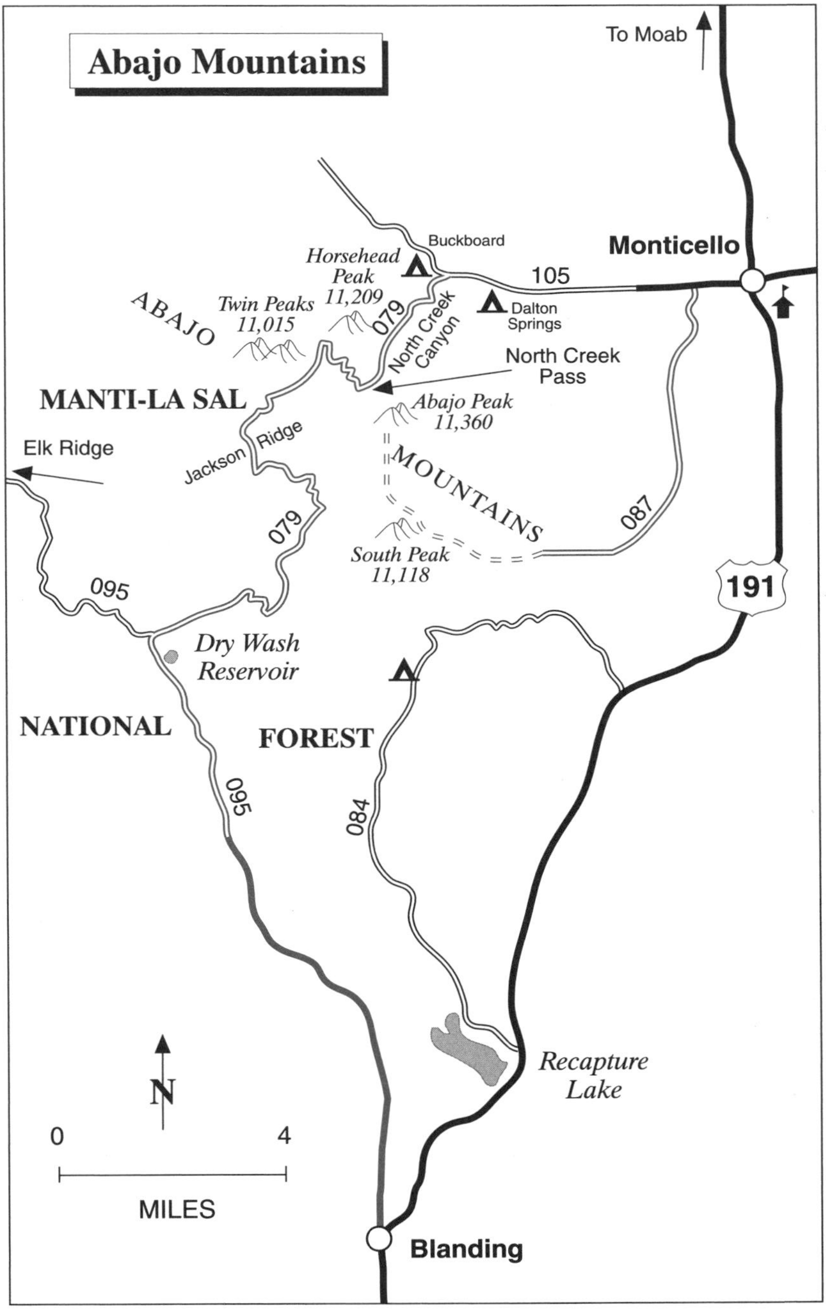
Abajo Mountains
To Moab
Monticello
Buckboard
Horsehead Peak 11,209
105
Twin Peaks 11,015
079
North Creek Canyon
Dalton Springs
ABAJO
North Creek Pass
MANTI-LA SAL
Abajo Peak 11,360
Elk Ridge
Jackson Ridge
MOUNTAINS
079
087
South Peak 11,118
095
191
Dry Wash Reservoir
NATIONAL
FOREST
095
084
N
0
4
MILES
Recapture Lake
Blanding

TRIP
50

Elk Ridge Road

LOCATION: North of Natural Bridges National Monument, south of Canyonlands National Park. Manti-La Sal National Forest.

HIGHLIGHTS: A ridge with views of Canyonlands, Dark Canyon Wilderness, Arch & Salt Creek canyons, the Abajo, La Sal and Henry mountains. Natural Bridges. Best May-Oct.

DIFFICULTY: Easy. Can be impassable after heavy rains.

TIME & DISTANCE: 3-4 hours; 58 miles.

GETTING THERE: I go north to end at U-211. Take U-275 northwest from U-95 toward Natural Bridges. 0.7 mile from U-95 go north onto South Elk Ridge Road (forest road 088/San Juan County Road 228).

THE DRIVE: The graded road climbs up Maverick Point through pinyon-juniper woodland, passing between two peaks called the Bear's Ears. Rising from the desert to the west are the Henry Mountains, igneous "islands" in a sandstone world. You'll pass Ponderosa pines, scrub oak and aspen, and meadows. Keep right at 7.9. At 9.6 gaze down into Arch and Texas canyons. At 11.8 go left to North Elk Ridge. When you reach the head of Hammond Canyon, at Little Notch, you'll have views of the Abajo Mountains to the east. The 4x4 road down Peavine Corridor *(trip 48)* into Dark Canyon Wilderness branches left here. As you continue on 088 you'll have excellent views of the wilderness area's sandstone terraces. Elk Ridge Road narrows to a ledge, and at 19.4 you'll reach The Notch, a.k.a. Big Notch. Look down into Dark Canyon to the west and Notch Canyon to the east. At 26.7, at Sego Flat, go left at the Y, toward Beef Basin. 3.3 miles farther you can take easy 091 west to North Long Point (about 6 miles one-way) for a terrific view of Dark Canyon and Canyonlands. Road 088 continues to the right, providing views of North and South Six Shooter Peaks in the distance. At 32.8 is the left to Beef Basin, famous for Anasazi ruins. As you descend you'll have vistas across the expanse of sandstone canyons, buttes and mesas. In 2 miles you're on Salt Creek Mesa at the head of Salt Creek Canyon *(trip 44)*. Soon you'll pass the marbled mass of Cathedral Butte, then the cliffs of Bridger Jack Mesa. You'll reach U-211 at mile 57.8.

REST STOPS: Lots of primitive camping. Campgrounds at Natural Bridges, Canyonlands and Newspaper Rock.

GETTING HOME: Take U-211 east to U.S. 191.

MAPS: Manti-La Sal National Forest, Monticello Ranger District; ACSC's *Indian Country*.

INFORMATION: Monticello Ranger District, 587-2041.

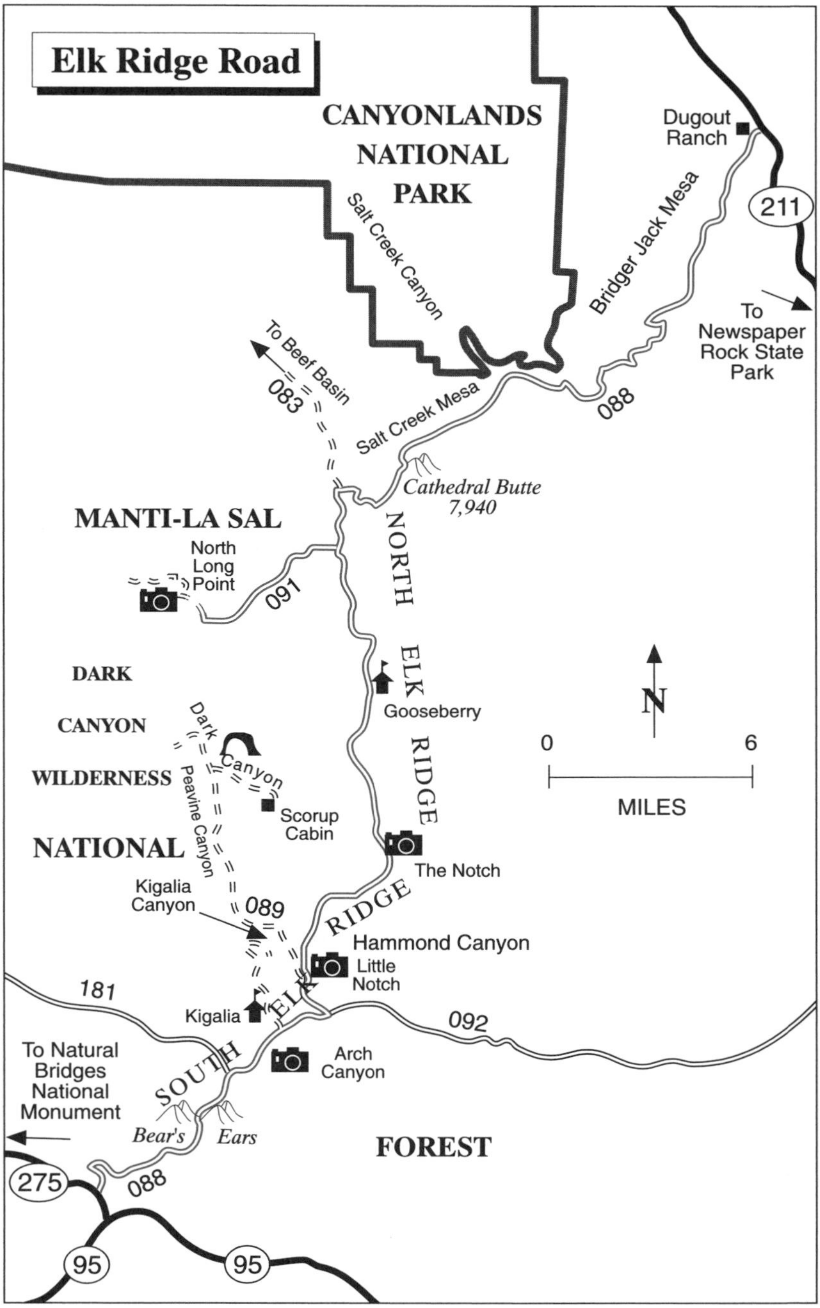

Elk Ridge Road
CANYONLANDS NATIONAL PARK
Dugout Ranch
211
Salt Creek Canyon
Bridger Jack Mesa
To Newspaper Rock State Park
To Beef Basin
083
Salt Creek Mesa
088
Cathedral Butte 7,940
MANTI-LA SAL
North Long Point
091
NORTH ELK RIDGE
Gooseberry
N
0
6
MILES
DARK CANYON WILDERNESS
Dark Canyon
Peavine Canyon
Scorup Cabin
NATIONAL
The Notch
Kigalia Canyon
089
RIDGE
Hammond Canyon
Little Notch
181
Kigalia
ELK
092
SOUTH
Arch Canyon
To Natural Bridges National Monument
Bear's Ears
FOREST
275
088
95
95

TRIP
51

Dry Lakes/Summit Canyon

LOCATION: East of Cedar City and I-15.

HIGHLIGHTS: An idyllic autumn drive with outstanding views of the Great Basin and the pink cliffs of Cedar Breaks National Monument. Pretty stretches through picturesque aspen and pine forests. You'll climb more than 3,000 feet. Lots of deer.

DIFFICULTY: Easy. Steep and somewhat rocky in places. Closed in winter. Watch for logging trucks.

TIME & DISTANCE: 1 hour; 20.6 miles.

GETTING THERE: On I-15 exit at Summit, north of Cedar City. A half-mile north of Summit go east on the dirt and gravel road toward Hurricane Cliffs. Reset your odometer.

THE DRIVE: As you drive east toward the escarpment of the Hurricane Cliffs, which rise from the Hurricane Fault, you're crossing a geologic frontier. Behind you, the Great Basin spreads westward. Directly ahead, to the east, the Hurricane Cliffs welcome you to the great Colorado Plateau and the many smaller plateaus that comprise Utah's spectacular plateau country. Beyond the cliffs rise the Markagunt (Piute for highland of trees) Plateau and the Paunsaugunt (Piute for home of the beavers) Plateau. The road climbs steadily up Summit Canyon, then steeply as it angles south through mostly private land. You'll be amazed by the view west across the checkerboard fields of the Parowan and Cedar valleys and the Escalante Desert, where the southernmost evidence of ice age Lake Bonneville is found. At 5.3 you'll pass Summit Mt. At 10.8 you'll enter Dixie National Forest, where the road is No. 265. (You'll leave and enter the national forest several times.) By mile 12.3 the road climbs above 9,700 feet elevation as it crosses Sugarloaf Mountain At 12.4 there's a pullout where you can gaze at the ancient lakebed deposits that are brilliant Cedar Breaks. Descend along Dry Lakes Creek to reach U-143 at 20.6. Brian Head Ski Area is 4 miles south.

REST STOPS: Brian Head Ski Area, Cedar Breaks.

GETTING HOME: U-143 north to I-15 or south to U-14.

MAPS: The 1982 edition of Dixie National Forest's map for the Pine Valley & Cedar City Ranger Districts more clearly and accurately depicts the road than the 1995 edition. ACSC's *Indian Country* is good as well.

INFORMATION: Iron County, 586-8652; Cedar City Ranger District, 865-3200.

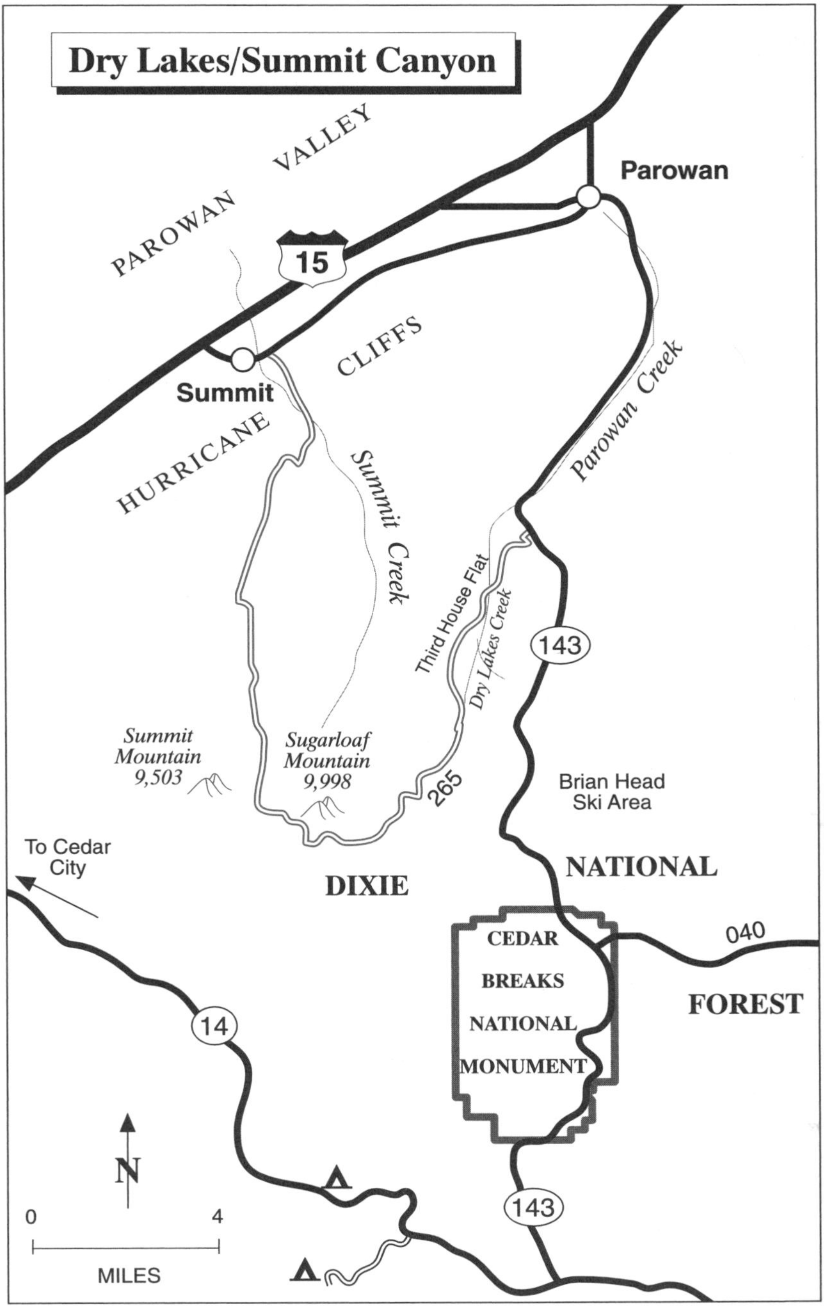
Dry Lakes/Summit Canyon
PAROWAN VALLEY
Parowan
15
CLIFFS
Summit
HURRICANE
Summit Creek
Parowan Creek
Third House Flat
Dry Lakes Creek
143
Summit Mountain 9,503
Sugarloaf Mountain 9,998
265
Brian Head Ski Area
To Cedar City
DIXIE
NATIONAL
CEDAR BREAKS NATIONAL MONUMENT
040
FOREST
14
N
0
4
MILES
143

TRIP
52

Pink Cliffs

LOCATION: West of Bryce Canyon National Park, along the East Fork of the Sevier River.

HIGHLIGHTS: Brilliant pink cliffs like those in the park, but smaller and without the crowds. Spur to a historic viewpoint. A pretty cruise along Podunk Creek.

DIFFICULTY: Easy to moderate.

TIME & DISTANCE: 3 hours; 56 miles.

GETTING THERE: Take U-12 10.8 miles east from U.S. 89. Turn south onto a wide gravel road (a Utah Scenic Backway) that becomes No. 087 in Dixie National Forest.

THE DRIVE: For miles the road resembles an unpaved highway as it parallels the East Fork of the Sevier River, the longest river entirely in Utah. It goes up a valley on the Paunsaugunt (Piute for home of the beaver) Plateau. Here and there you'll see eroded pink and white rock, Tertiary (1.6-66.4 MYA) lakebed deposits suggestive of the sights in Bryce Canyon. Pass Tropic Reservoir. At mile 15.2 pass road 099, which branches left up Podunk Creek to the park boundary (a locked gate blocks access). Soon you'll see the Podunk Guard Station. At Dairy Hollow, mile 17.7, go left toward Crawford Creek on road 092. Climb 2.2 miles to 8,511-foot Crawford Pass. Turn right here onto a rougher road, No. 203. It climbs 3.6 miles to the rim of dramatically eroded pink cliffs. Just beyond them is a Y. The route goes left, following 203 down Pipeline Canyon. Road 215 goes right; take it 0.5 mile, then go left on a spur. About a mile from 215 the road ends at a flat with a panorama, from almost 9,400 feet, of more brilliant cliffs, Bryce Canyon and much of canyon and plateau country. Watch for a faint trail that branches left to the brink of Pink Cliff, el. 9,394 ft., a triangulation point used by the expedition led by explorer John Wesley Powell. Descend Pipeline Canyon for views of the pink cliffs you looked down on earlier. In 4.3 miles 203 reaches rough 092 at Meadow Canyon. Go left to Crawford Pass. There, turn right on road 098 (there might be a sign saying it's 1211) and follow it down to Podunk Creek. Go left there to return to road 087.

REST STOPS: Camp at Tropic Reservoir. Many picnic spots.

GETTING HOME: Return to U-12.

MAPS: Dixie National Forest, Powell Ranger District; Trails Illustrated's *Paunsaugunt Plateau, Mt. Dutton, Bryce Canyon.*

INFORMATION: Powell Ranger District, 676-8815.

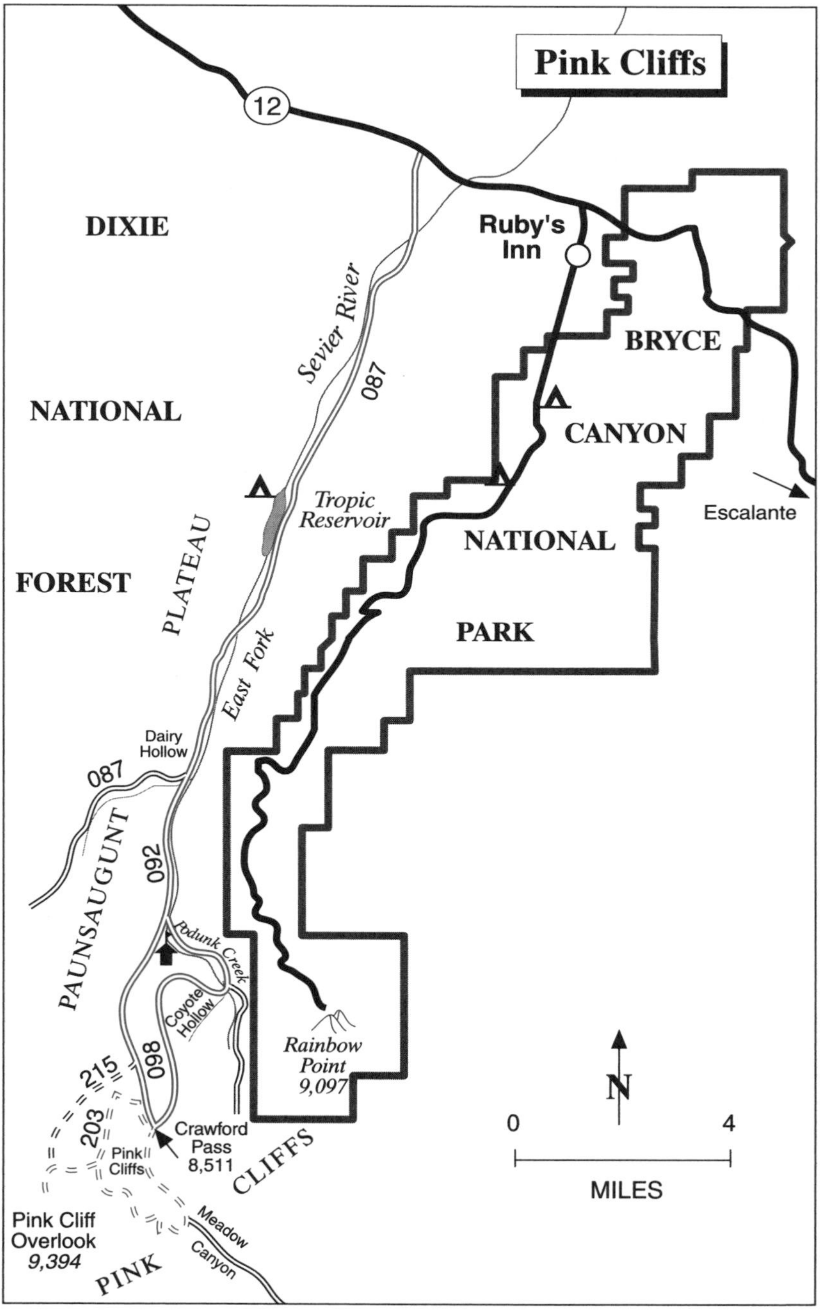
Pink Cliffs
12
DIXIE
NATIONAL
FOREST
Ruby's Inn
BRYCE
CANYON
NATIONAL
PARK
Sevier River
087
Tropic Reservoir
PLATEAU
East Fork
Escalante
Dairy Hollow
087
PAUNSAUGUNT
092
Podunk Creek
Coyote Hollow
098
215
203
Pink Cliffs
Crawford Pass
8,511
Rainbow Point
9,097
N
0
4
MILES
CLIFFS
Meadow
Canyon
Pink Cliff Overlook
9,394
PINK

Hole-in-the-Rock Road

LOCATION: Between Escalante and Lake Powell.

HIGHLIGHTS: Devil's Garden. Chimney Rock. Historic Dance Hall Rock and Hole-in-the-Rock. Vistas across the Escalante Basin and Glen Canyon National Recreation Area from Fiftymile Bench after a 2,000-ft. climb. Rock collecting.

DIFFICULTY: Easy to moderate on the dead-end Hole-in-the-Rock Rd. It's mostly graded dirt & gravel. The last 6 miles are rough. The climb up to and descent from Fiftymile Bench are steep. The bench is easy. I rate the descent on Willow Tank Slide moderate to difficult.

TIME & DISTANCE: 8 hours; 112 miles round-trip. Chimney Rock adds 6.5 miles; Fiftymile Bench adds 11 miles.

GETTING THERE: 4.6 miles east of Escalante on U-12 turn southeast near the scenic turnout. Reset your odometer.

THE DRIVE: In 1879-80 Mormon pioneers established a route between Escalante and Four Corners. Today's road generally follows their route along the edge of the Escalante Basin below the Straight Cliffs, at the rim of Fiftymile Mt., a.k.a. the Kaiparowits Plateau. It ends at a crack — the Hole-in-the-Rock — in a wall of Glen Canyon that the pioneers widened to lower wagons to the Colorado River. 12.3 miles from U-12 detour to the sandstone figures at Devil's Garden. If you're a rock collector, check with the Escalante Interagency Office for locations and restrictions. The Morrison Formation near the base of the Straight Cliffs is a good area. (No collecting in GCNRA.) At mile 33.4 a two-track goes left about 2.5 miles to a spire, Chimney Rock. The main road continues through Willow Tank, where there's a water tank and tiny cabin. 3 miles farther a huge sandstone block hollowed by wind erosion, Dance Hall Rock, is on the left. The pioneers held dances here while members of the expedition scouted a route ahead. A monument 3 miles farther in Carcass Wash recalls the deaths of seven Boy Scouts and six adults in a road accident there in 1963. 4 miles farther you'll see on the right the spur up to Fiftymile Bench. Soon you'll enter GCNRA. The road is rough to Hole-in-the-Rock. To return via Fiftymile Bench, take the spur you passed earlier up Sooner Slide toward the cliffs. Go right at the T for the 10-mile drive to Willow Tank Slide's steep and rough descent to Hole-in-the-Rock Rd.

REST STOPS: Picnic at Devil's Garden; no other facilities. Primitive camping on BLM lands. Some good sites on Fiftymile Bench. Bring a portable toilet. No fires in GCNRA. Fires are allowed but not recommended on BLM lands. If you want one, bring wood; use a fire pan.

GETTING HOME: Return to Escalante. U-12 to U.S. 89.

MAPS: BLM's *Escalante Resource Area Recreation Map* and the *Hole-in-the-Rock Trail* brochure.

INFORMATION: Escalante Interagency Office, 826-5499.

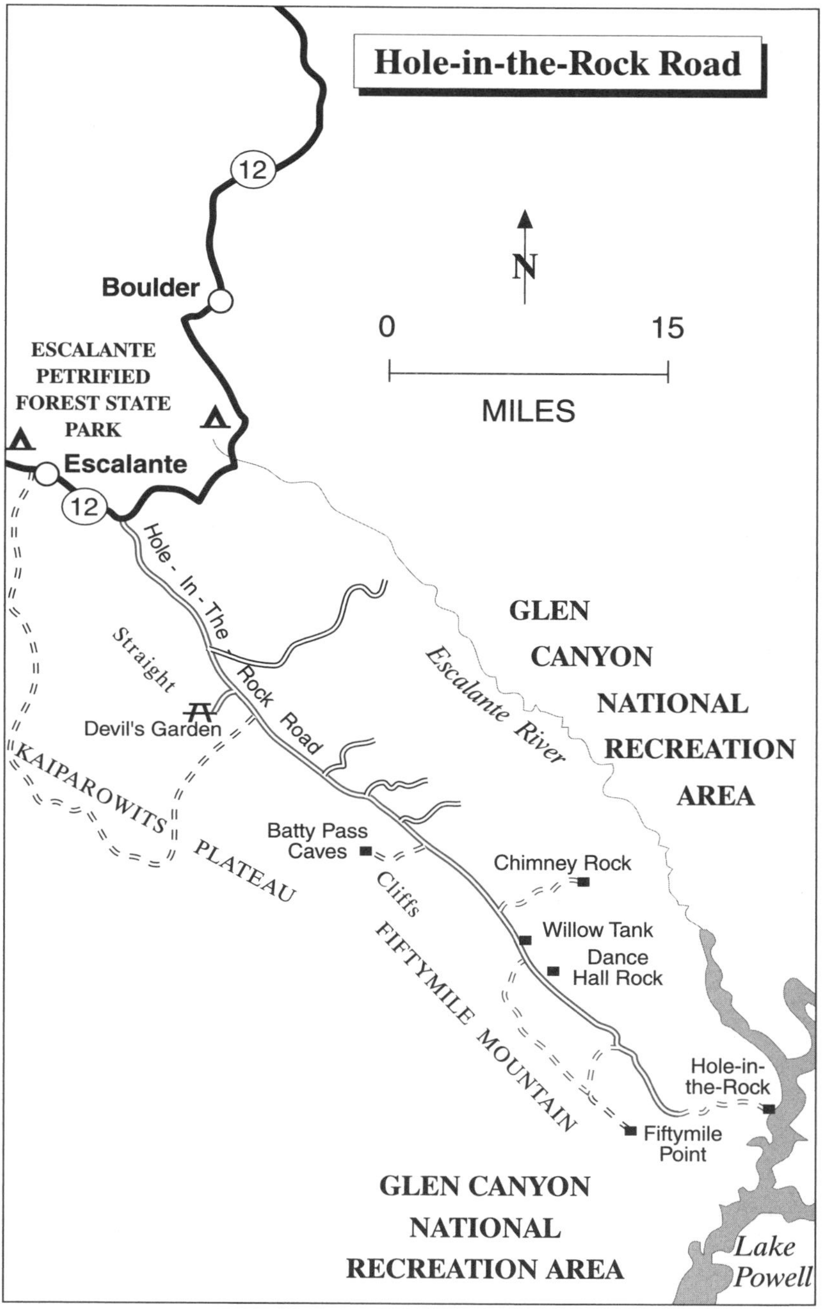
Hole-in-the-Rock Road
12
Boulder
N
0
15
MILES
ESCALANTE
PETRIFIED
FOREST STATE
PARK
Escalante
12
Hole - In - The - Rock Road
Straight
Devil's Garden
Escalante River
GLEN
CANYON
NATIONAL
RECREATION
AREA
KAIPAROWITS
PLATEAU
Batty Pass
Caves
Cliffs
Chimney Rock
Willow Tank
Dance
Hall Rock
FIFTYMILE MOUNTAIN
Hole-in-
the-Rock
Fiftymile
Point
GLEN CANYON
NATIONAL
RECREATION AREA
Lake
Powell

TRIP
54

Comb Wash

LOCATION: Southeastern Utah, southwest of Blanding.

HIGHLIGHTS: A spectacular north-south ridge and 800-ft.-high cliffs bursting from the Earth's crust like a geologic maw. Area of what may have been the last skirmish in the U.S. between Indians and white settlers. The area was populated by ancestral Puebloan (Anasazi) Indians. Comb Wash is where writer Edward Abbey's fictional "Monkey Wrench Gang" sabotaged road-building heavy equipment (Chapter 6, *The Raid at Comb Wash*).

DIFFICULTY: Easy. A periodically maintained dirt road.

TIME & DISTANCE: 1 hour; 18.6 miles.

GETTING THERE: Go north or south. I go north. Turn north off U.S. 163 onto county road 235 about 2.8 miles west of the junction with U.S. 191 southwest of Bluff. The turn is just west of the bridge over Comb Wash.

THE DRIVE: The dramatic humps (hogbacks) of Comb Ridge mark the eastern edge of the Monument Upwarp, an huge arched fold in the Earth's crust, or anticline, that extends west to Glen Canyon. Comb Ridge runs north from Kayenta, Ariz., for about 90 miles to the Abajo Mountains. At Comb Ridge the upwarp's strata suddenly nosedive deep into the Earth. The dramatic cliffs are mostly dune Wingate sandstone, with stream-deposited Kayenta Formation, and a crest of Navajo sandstone from what may have been the Earth's greatest desert. All are from the early Jurassic (144-208 MYA)-late Triassic (208-245 MYA) periods. In 1923, friction between whites and Piute Indians flared into armed conflict. Chief Posey and another Piute were killed. The other Piutes were jailed. Following the wash north, 2.3 miles from U.S. 163 road 237 goes left (west) along the route of the 1879-80 Mormon Hole-in-the-Rock expedition (see *trip 53*). Follow Comb Wash north.

REST STOPS: Scan the cliffs for footsteps in the rock, used by the Anasazi. Waterless BLM campground near the north end. Don't miss nearby Butler Wash Anasazi Ruins.

GETTING HOME: U-95 east to U.S. 191 or northwest toward U-24 and I-70.

MAPS: ACSC's *Indian Country*; Trails Illustrated's *Grand Gulch Plateau*; Recreational Map of Utah.

INFORMATION: BLM, San Juan Field Office, 587-2141.

ALSO TRY: Long (about 8 miles one-way) Arch Canyon, famous for arches, Anasazi ruins and real four-wheeling (moderate to difficult). At U-95 go west 100 yards, then north 2.25 miles. Go left at the campground just before the creek, dip into the wash, angle left and proceed to the sign-in box. 21-mile Butler Wash Road east of Comb Ridge is a great easy route, too.

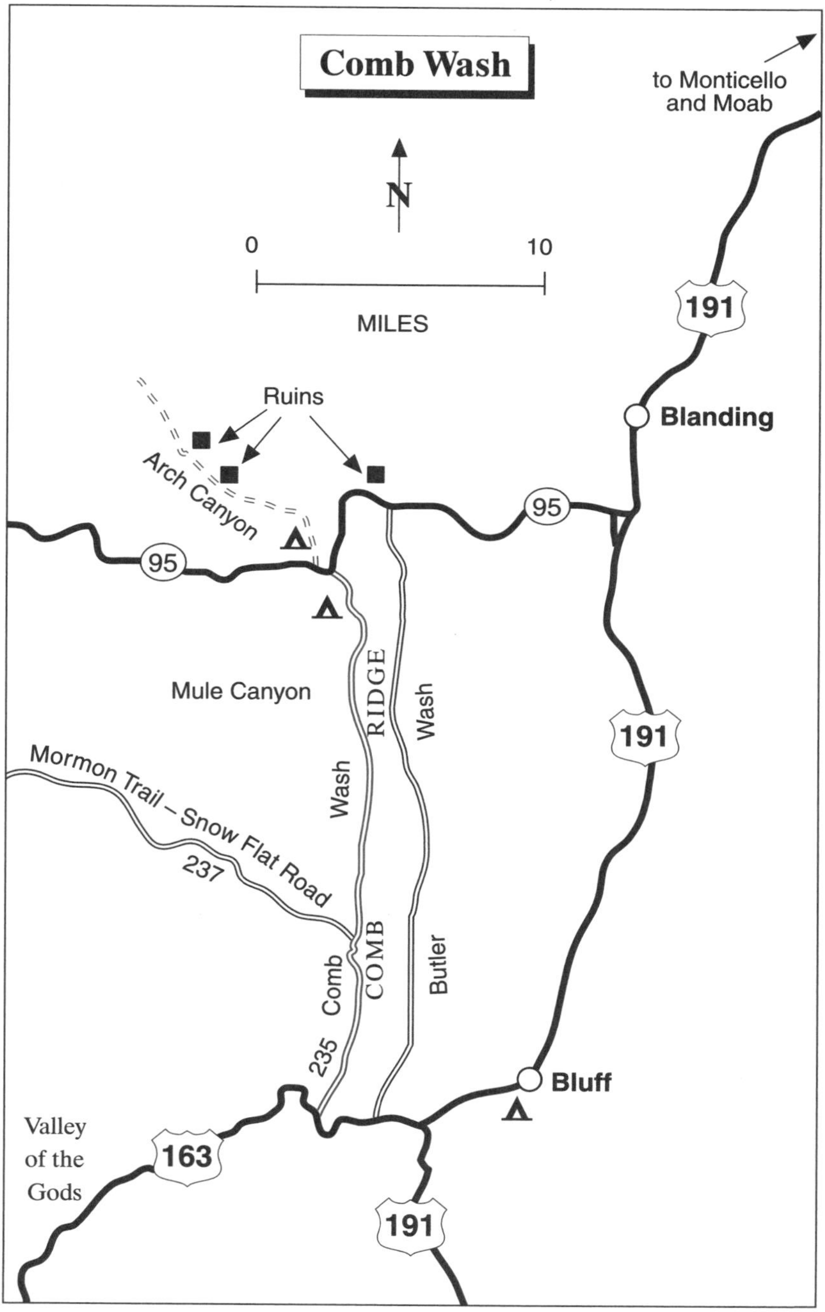
Comb Wash
to Monticello and Moab
N
0
10
MILES
Ruins
Arch Canyon
Blanding
95
95
191
191
191
163
Mule Canyon
Mormon Trail – Snow Flat Road
237
RIDGE
Wash
Wash
COMB
Comb
Butler
235
Bluff
Valley of the Gods

TRIP
55

Kolob Terrace Road

LOCATION: East of I-15 between U-14 and U-9. Passes through a portion of Zion National Park.

HIGHLIGHTS: A picturesque drive through a range of plant zones, including grassy hills, pinyon-juniper woodlands and forests of aspens, firs and towering ponderosa pines. Fantastic views of the Great Basin and Zion National Park's west side.

DIFFICULTY: Easy. Road surface ranges from dirt and gravel to two-lane asphalt. Dirt segments can be impassable in wet weather. Closed late November to May or June.

TIME & DISTANCE: 2 hours; 48.4.

GETTING THERE: I go south, but you can take this north-south road in either direction, beginning or ending at Virgin. Take U-14 east from Main Street in Cedar City for 4.9 miles. Turn south at the sign for Kolob Reservoir. Reset the odometer.

THE DRIVE: Most of the road passes through private land. The first 8 miles coming from the north are paved and forested as you ascend Kolob Terrace, a plateau of Cretaceous (66.4-144 MYA) seabed deposits. The name Kolob derives from the star in the center of the universe which, according to Mormon Church doctrine, is closest to the throne of God. As you curve around the west side of Lone Tree Mountain and cross Cedar Mountain, you'll have tremendous views of the vast Great Basin, with its still waves of ghostly ranges and expanses of pale desert. Rolling hills, aspen groves, grazing sheep and log fences add to the charm of this undulating country road as it climbs to over 9,300 feet. It narrows to a single serpentine dirt lane at mile 19.1 as it descends through a pretty canyon. By 23 you're approaching Kolob Reservoir, where the road improves. In about 3 miles asphalt resumes. You'll enter Zion National Park at mile 30 (only to leave, re-enter and leave again), passing through meadows and aspen stands. You'll have views of Kolob Canyons' red walls in Zion's northwestern corner. Continuing south, gaze across its beige and pink Navajo Sandstone canyons, cliffs and domes, once the dunes of a great desert in late Triassic-early Jurassic time (190-136 MYA). By mile 36 you're on a two-lane paved road, descending through pinyon-juniper woodland to U-9 at Virgin.

REST STOPS: Fish at Kolob Reservoir. Picnic and camp in Zion National Park. Springdale has all services.

GETTING HOME: U-9 or U-14 west to I-15.

MAPS: ACSC's *Indian Country*; Dixie National Forest, Pine Valley & Cedar City Ranger Districts.

INFORMATION: Iron County, 586-8652; Washington County, 634-5736; Zion National Park, 772-3256.

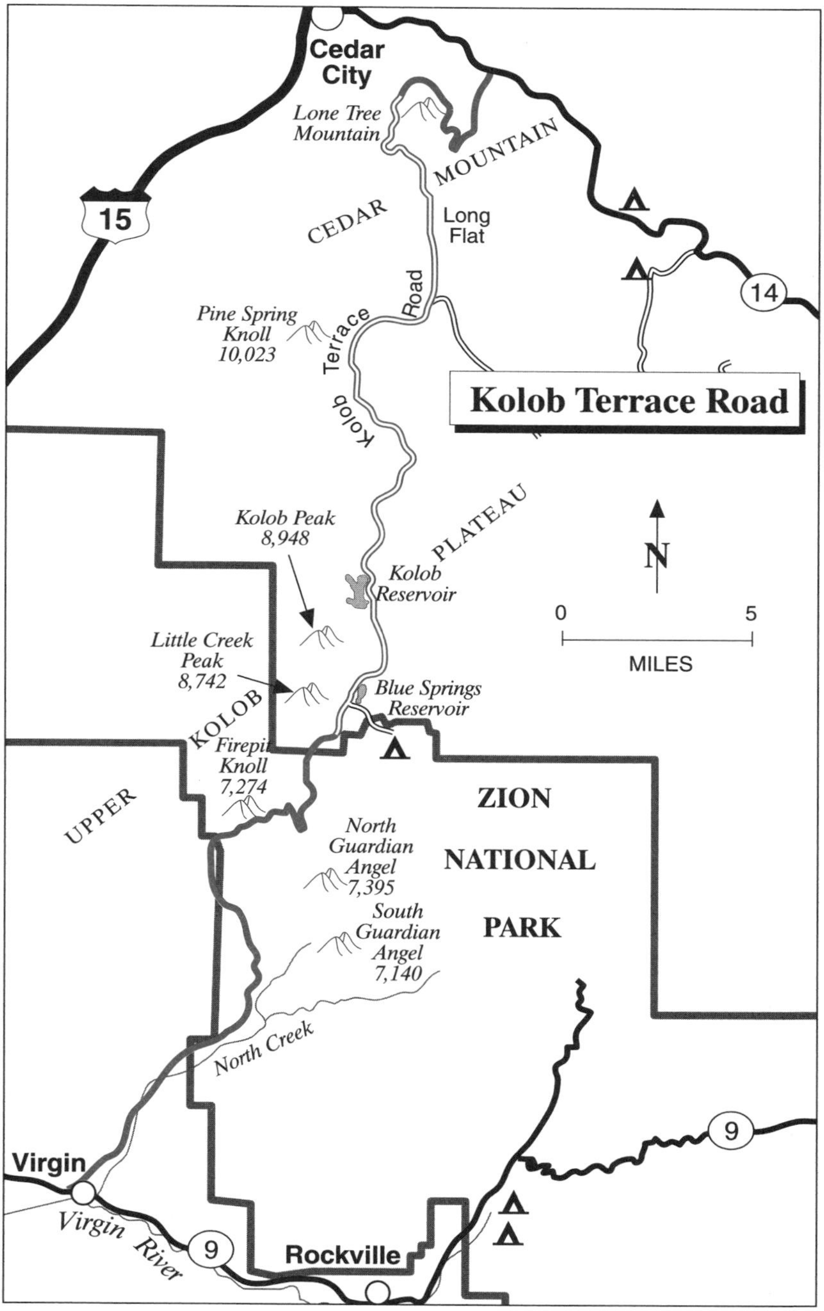
Cedar City
15
Lone Tree Mountain
CEDAR MOUNTAIN
Long Flat
14
Pine Spring Knoll 10,023
Kolob Terrace Road
Kolob Terrace Road
Kolob Peak 8,948
PLATEAU
N
Kolob Reservoir
0
5
MILES
Little Creek Peak 8,742
Blue Springs Reservoir
UPPER KOLOB
Firepit Knoll 7,274
ZION NATIONAL PARK
North Guardian Angel 7,395
South Guardian Angel 7,140
North Creek
9
Virgin
Virgin River
9
Rockville

TRIP
56

Smoky Mountain Road

LOCATION: A north-south road between U.S. 89, at Lake Powell, and Escalante, on U-12.

HIGHLIGHTS: Wild, remote region proposed for federal wilderness protection. 1,400-ft. ascent/descent on switchbacks. Views of Lake Powell, Bryce Canyon, Navajo Mountain.

DIFFICULTY: Easy to moderate. Hot, dusty in summer. Impassable in winter and if wet. No services.

TIME & DISTANCE: 4 hours; 78 miles.

GETTING THERE: You can go north or south. In Escalante, turn south off U-12 at the Utah Scenic Backway sign. I go north from Big Water on U.S. 89 west of Glen Canyon NRA. Reset your odometer at U.S. 89, and follow the Utah Scenic Backway sign and the sign for state Highway 12.

THE DRIVE: The asphalt ends in 2 miles; the roadbed becomes nicely graded, two-lane dirt and gravel. This red and yellow desert, the Warm Creek badlands, is forbidding, harsh and barren. Yet the beauty is overwhelming, the pastel hues almost infinite in variety. To the left (north) rise the sandstone promontories of Nipple Bench. To the south, the taupe desert reclines to the horizon beyond Lake Powell. Ahead are the ramparts of Smoky Mountain, named for its burning underground coal deposits, and the Kaiparowits Plateau, a focal point in the fight over how much of Utah should be protected as wilderness. At mile 3.7 you'll pass through a moonscape of yellow-gray bentonite hills featured in a number of sci-fi films, including "Planet of the Apes." At 12.9 go right at a Y. (The left goes to the area of a proposed coal mine.) At 13.9 pass a spur on the right. At 16.7 begin the thrilling climb up Smoky Mountain and the Kaiparowits Plateau on the Kelly Grade. By 21.7 you're on Smoky Mountain. To the west is the Grand Staircase, a series of cliffs that march north from the Grand Canyon. You'll cross the rocky, wild, pinyon-juniper expanse of the Kaiparowits Plateau, climbing gradually to 7,000 feet. Then you'll descend through pretty valleys toward Alvey Wash and, 6.5 miles farther, reach U-12 at Escalante.

REST STOPS: Primitive campsites. At about mile 36.7 picnic among shady cottonwood trees at Last Chance Creek.

GETTING HOME: In Escalante, take U-12 west to U.S. 89 or north to U-24 near Capitol Reef National Park.

MAPS: ACSC's *Indian Country*; Recreational Map of Utah.

INFORMATION: BLM, Kanab Field Office, 644-2672; BLM, Escalante Field Office, 826-4291.

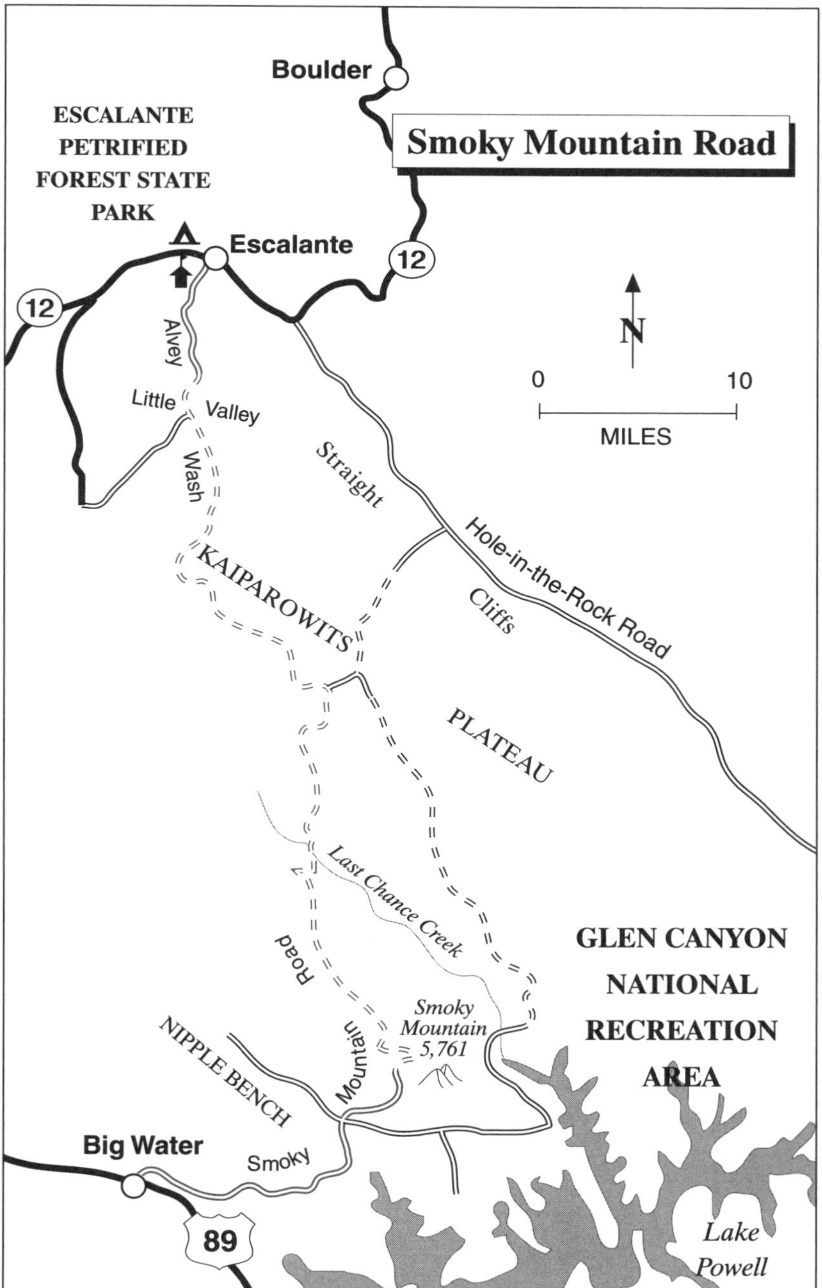
Smoky Mountain Road
Boulder
ESCALANTE
PETRIFIED
FOREST STATE
PARK
Escalante
12
12
N
0
10
MILES
Alvey
Little
Valley
Wash
Straight
Hole-in-the-Rock Road
Cliffs
KAIPAROWITS
PLATEAU
Last Chance Creek
Road
GLEN CANYON
NATIONAL
RECREATION
AREA
Smoky
Mountain
5,761
Mountain
NIPPLE BENCH
Big Water
Smoky
89
Lake
Powell

TRIP 57

San Juan River Goosenecks

LOCATION: Just north of the San Juan River; northwest of Mexican Hat off U.S. 163; east end of Glen Canyon National Recreation Area.

HIGHLIGHTS: The San Juan River's deep, meandering gorge; petroglyphs; high cliffs of Cedar Mesa. Good mountain bike road. Also take the beautiful 16.9-mile drive through nearby Valley of the Gods. Monument Valley is to the south as well.

DIFFICULTY: Easy first 15 miles; moderate beyond that.

TIME & DISTANCE: 2 hours; 15 miles. I end at John's Canyon. Beyond that the scenery is repetitive and the road is rougher, although there are more roadside petroglyphs. It ends at a trailhead.

GETTING THERE: North of Mexican Hat, take U-316 a half-mile west of U-261 toward Goosenecks State Park. Turn north onto dirt San Juan County road 244.

THE DRIVE: The first 3.5 miles cross a broad bench below Muley Point, atop the saffron-colored cliffs of Cedar Mesa to the right. To the left are the deeply entrenched meanders, or loops, carved by the San Juan River. The river snakes through a gorge in Pennsylvanian (280-320 MYA) rock deposited in shallow seas, with the Honaker Trail Formation on the upper slopes and the Paradox Formation below. Deep side canyons force the road to the base of Cedar Mesa, and by mile 5.5 you're on a dramatic terrace. At 6.8, at the brink of a side canyon, go through a gate and close it. 1.7 miles farther scan the boulders to the right about 75 yards from the road for a horizontal slab with a blue-black patina, or varnish. It bears wonderful petroglyphs, including triangular human-like figures with bird heads. (Don't touch them!) As you continue, watch carefully for more petroglyphs on similar flat surfaces. At 11.3 a spur branches left. It ends shortly, but you can walk to a rocky point overlooking the gorge. Soon the main road angles right up John's Canyon along a gorge. At mile 14.9 or so you'll reach a creek at the head of the gorge. This is a good place to stop. The road continues along the opposite side of the gorge, ending in 7.5 miles at a trailhead to the Grand Gulch Wilderness Study Area, where mechanized travel is prohibited.

REST STOPS: Picnic at the creek. Dry camping, pit toilets at Goosenecks State Park. Great vista from Muley Point off U-261, near the top of Moki Dugway.

GETTING HOME: U.S. 163 north or south.

MAPS: Trails Illustrated's *Grand Gulch Plateau*; ACSC's *Indian Country*.

INFORMATION: BLM, San Juan Field Office, 587-2141.

San Juan River Goosenecks

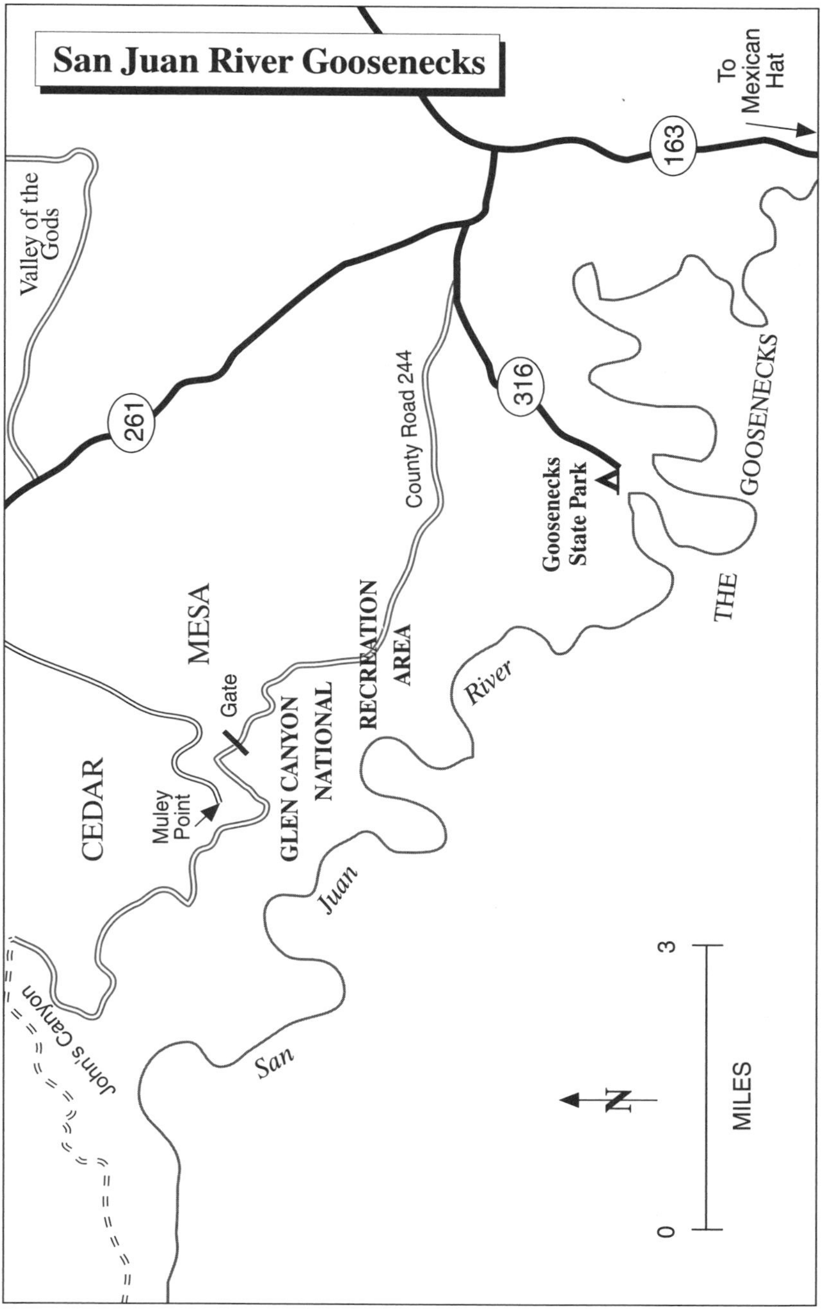

Cottonwood Canyon

LOCATION: Between U.S. 89 & U-12 northeast of Kanab.

HIGHLIGHTS: A geologic showcase that includes Kodachrome Basin State Park, Grosvenor Arch and Cottonwood Canyon, along an absolutely spectacular monocline, The Cockscomb.

DIFFICULTY: An easy dirt and gravel road. Dusty and washboarded after dry periods. Impassable when wet; flash floods possible during storms. Busy in summer as a shortcut between Bryce Canyon and Glen Canyon. Best spring and fall.

TIME & DISTANCE: 2 hours; 46 miles, including the 2-mile (round-trip) spur to Grosvenor Arch. Add 4.6 miles and additional time to visit beautiful Kodachrome Basin.

GETTING THERE: Go either north from U.S. 89 east of Kanab, or south from U-12 at Cannonville. I go north.

THE DRIVE: This route is a geologic showcase where the Earth is torn open to expose colossal sandstone domes, narrow canyons, knobs and sawtooth "reefs." The undulating road passes below the cliffs of Brigham Plain as it meanders toward the Paria River. (Recreational rock hounds find fossil oyster shells and shark's teeth in the shales along Cottonwood Canyon Road.) The sprawling Kaiparowits Plateau lies to the east. To the west and north is the Grand Staircase: the Vermilion Cliffs, White Cliffs, Gray Cliffs and Pink Cliffs. As you drive through The Cockscomb you're following a "strike valley" in relatively soft, more easily eroded shales and clay flanked by high "hogbacks," or humps, of harder Navajo, Page and Straight Cliff sandstones. Triassic and Jurassic rock (144-245 MYA) looms west of Cottonwood Creek; Cretaceous and Tertiary (60 MYA, more or less) rock towers to the east. At mile 26.4 you enter a small basin of hoodoos, spires and reefs. Stop here and walk through narrows just west of the road. In 3.3 miles turn right to Grosvenor Arch. Cross Butler Valley, ford Rock Springs Creek, and in 2 miles pavement resumes near Kodachrome Basin. U-12 is 7.3 miles.

REST STOPS: Kodachrome Basin has camping, showers, picnic tables, supplies. Small campground at Grosvenor Arch. Take the short but utterly spectacular drive from U.S. 89 north to the movie set and old Pahreah townsite, at the Paria River.

GETTING HOME: U-12 west to U.S. 89; at the south end, U.S. 89 south to Arizona or west toward Kanab and I-15.

MAPS: ACSC's *Indian Country*; Recreational Map of Utah.

INFORMATION: BLM, Kanab Office, 644-2672; Kodachrome Basin, 679-8562. Paria Ranger Station 3 miles west of the Cottonwood Canyon turnoff on U.S. 89 (no phone).

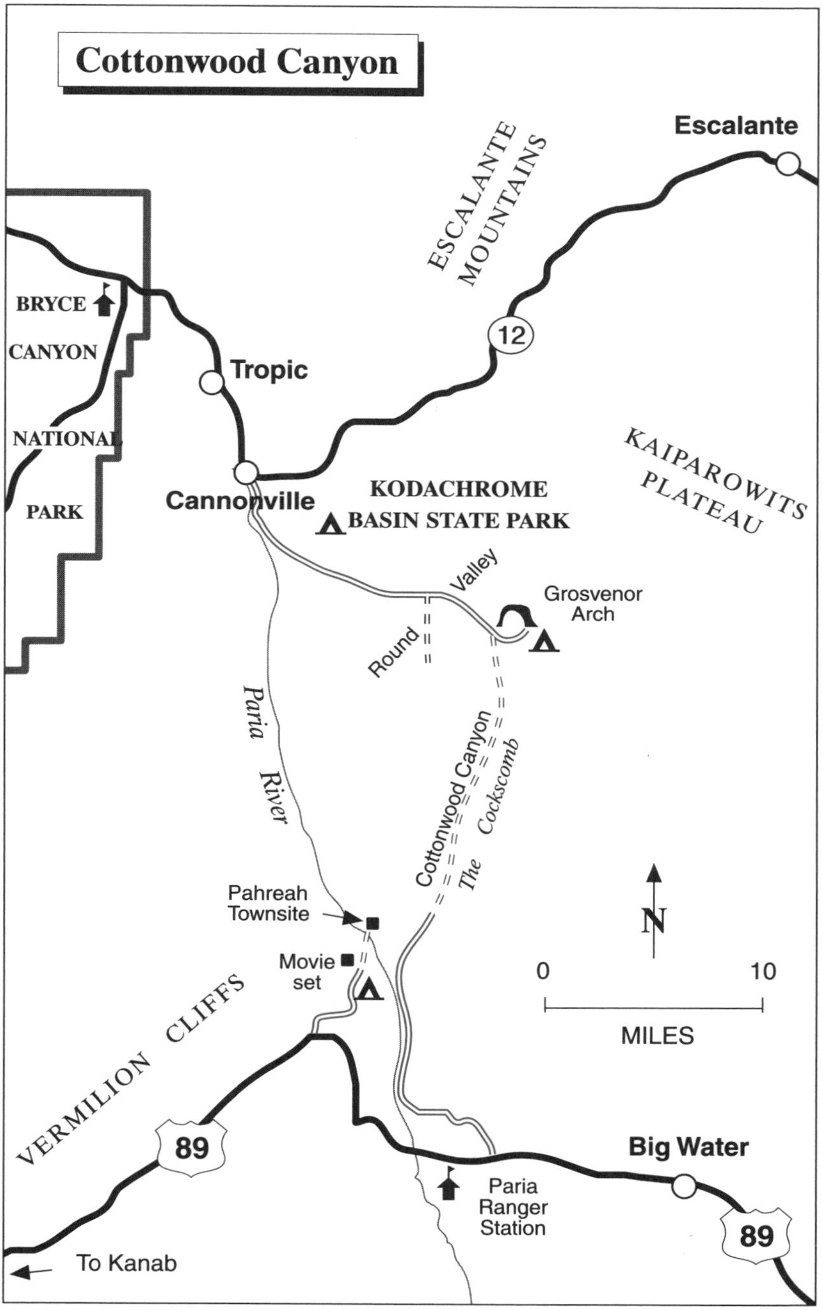
Cottonwood Canyon
Escalante
ESCALANTE MOUNTAINS
12
BRYCE CANYON NATIONAL PARK
Tropic
KAIPAROWITS PLATEAU
Cannonville
KODACHROME BASIN STATE PARK
Valley
Grosvenor Arch
Round
Paria River
Cottonwood Canyon
The Cockscomb
Pahreah Townsite
N
Movie set
0
10
MILES
VERMILION CLIFFS
89
Big Water
Paria Ranger Station
89
To Kanab

TRIP
59

Smithsonian Butte

LOCATION: South of Zion National Park, east of I-15. Between U-9 at the north end and U-59 at the south end.

HIGHLIGHTS: Views include the park's Zion Canyon and East & West Temple, the Virgin River Valley, Canaan Mountain, Vermilion Cliffs and other features. Smithsonian Butte, named by explorer John Wesley Powell, rises to 6,632 ft. along this National Back Country Byway. Grafton ghost town, used in the film *Butch Cassidy and the Sundance Kid*; the nearby pioneer cemetery.

DIFFICULTY: Easy. Can be impassable when wet.

TIME & DISTANCE: Half-hour to an hour; 13.1 miles including the 4-mile (round-trip) spur to Grafton.

GETTING THERE: To go south, take U-9 to Rockville, 3 miles west of Zion. Go south on Bridge Rd. Cross the Virgin River on Old Rockville Bridge, a one-lane steel girder bridge built in 1926. To go north (for the best views) turn north onto the byway from U-59 about 14.2 miles southeast of Hurricane or 7.8 miles northwest of Hildale. I describe it going south.

THE DRIVE: After crossing the old bridge the road bends right (west) and parallels the river valley through fields and orchards. 0.9 mile from U-9 the pavement ends. Views across the scoured red, white and tan sandstone world of Zion begin to expand. At mile 1.6 the route angles left (south), but go right to Grafton. In 1.5 miles go left at a Y to the old cemetery, where the dead include settlers killed by Indians in 1866. Grafton, founded that year, was abandoned in 1907 after hard times. An adobe schoolhouse, a brick house and the ruins of log buildings are all that remain. (It's private property, so be respectful.) The main road climbs steeply through red beds of the Moenkopi and Chinle formations (Triassic Period, 208-245 MYA) whiskered with pinyon pines and junipers along a ridge between two washes, toward the Vermilion Cliffs. Soon Smithsonian Butte looms to the left. Once atop a broad flat you'll see the turnoff for the optional 10-mile (round-trip) spur along Gooseberry Mesa, to a point overlooking the Virgin River region. Continue south to U-59.

REST STOPS: Primitive camping on BLM land. Campgrounds in Zion National Park. Springdale has all services.

GETTING HOME: U-9 west toward I-15 or east through the park to U.S. 89. Or U-59 northwest to Hurricane or south into Arizona via Arizona Highway 389.

MAPS: Recreational Map of Utah; ACSC's *Indian Country*.

INFORMATION: BLM, Cedar City Field Office, 586-2401.

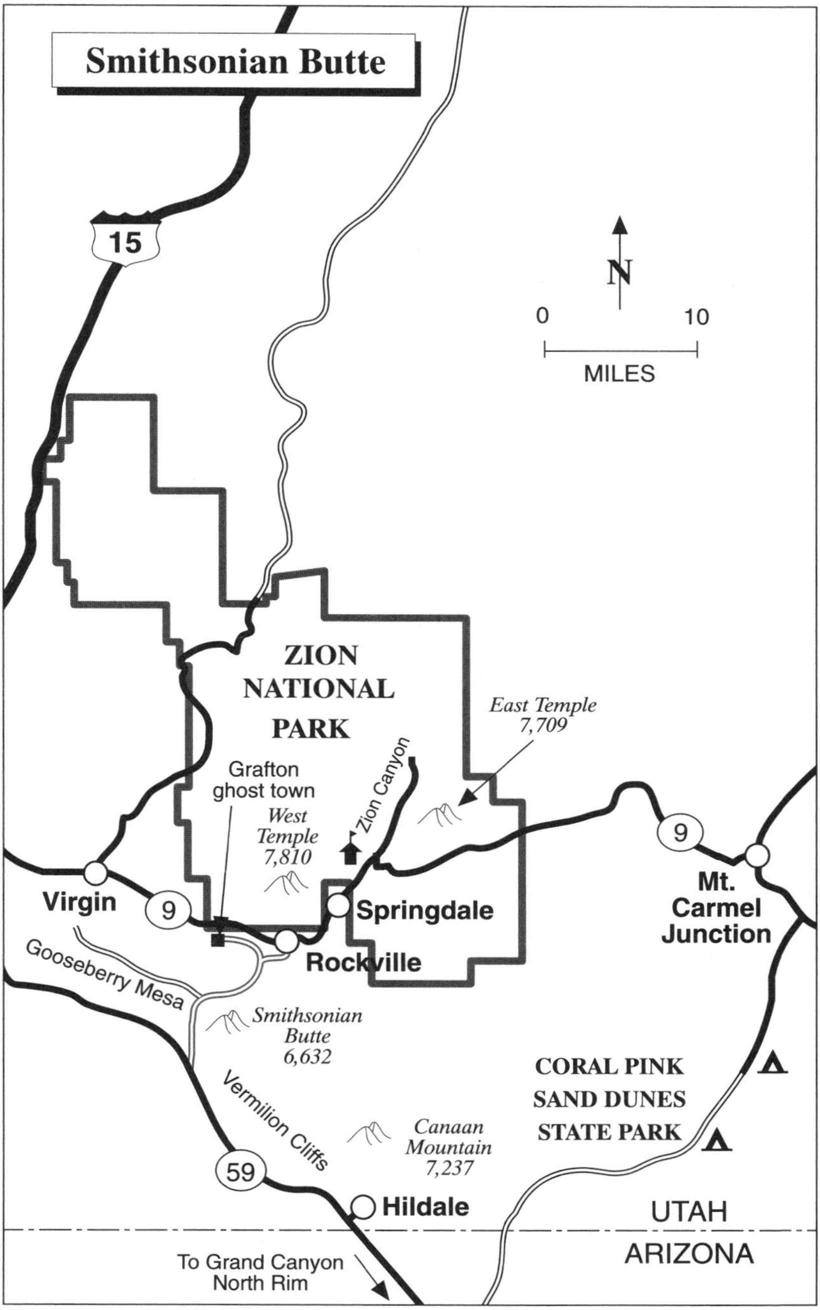
Smithsonian Butte
15
N
0
10
MILES
ZION
NATIONAL
PARK
East Temple
7,709
Grafton
ghost town
Zion Canyon
West
Temple
7,810
9
Virgin
9
Springdale
Mt.
Carmel
Junction
Gooseberry Mesa
Rockville
Smithsonian
Butte
6,632
Vermilion Cliffs
CORAL PINK
SAND DUNES
STATE PARK
Canaan
Mountain
7,237
59
Hildale
UTAH
ARIZONA
To Grand Canyon
North Rim

TRIP
60

Mojave Desert & Joshua Tree Road

LOCATION: Near the Arizona border in Utah's southwest corner, in the Beaver Dam Mountains west of St. George.

HIGHLIGHTS: Mountains where the Mojave Desert, Great Basin and Colorado Plateau meet; vistas of brilliant red cliffs, and of Zion National Park. The northernmost place where Joshua trees grow in large numbers. Woodbury Desert Study Area, set aside for the desert tortoise and other desert life.

DIFFICULTY: Easy. Watch for mine trucks.

TIME & DISTANCE: An hour; 19 miles.

GETTING THERE: Take the north-south route in either direction, beginning or ending on old U.S. 91. I go south. In St. George, take St. George Blvd. west to Bluff Street; go right. Turn left on Sunset Blvd. toward the Shivwits Indian Reservation. Drive through Santa Clara. On the reservation, on old U.S. 91 almost 2 miles from the turnoff to Gunlock, the dirt and gravel road branches left toward Apex Mine.

THE DRIVE: Drive up a broad valley bordered by desert mountains vegetated with sagebrush, pinyon pines and junipers. Deep shades of gray mixed with hues of red make these metamorphic mountains quite pretty. By mile 5, as you skirt the base of Jarvis Peak, you'll have outstanding views of vaulting red cliffs to the north, formerly Jurassic (144-208 MYA) desert sands. By 6.5 a panorama of brilliant red desert, the pale Navajo Sandstone monoliths of Zion and the endless sprawl of southern Utah opens up before you. At mile 7.9, at Cedar Wash, pass the road to Apex Mine, on the right. Here the route diminishes to a single rocky lane requiring high clearance. At mile 9.6 you'll cross Bulldog Pass, then descend to Bulldog Canyon. A couple of miles farther you'll begin to see Joshua trees, named by Mormon pioneers who thought they resembled the prophet's outstretched arms, and other Mojave Desert plants. Soon the Mojave spreads out to the south, dotted with countless Joshua trees. From here you'll descend along the edge of Beaver Dam Mtns. Wilderness (to the south) and through the Woodbury area. Joshua Tree National Natural Landmark is north. You'll reach the highway by mile 19.

REST STOPS: St. George has all services.

GETTING HOME: I-15 north or south.

MAPS: ACSC's *Indian Country*; Recreational Map of Utah.

INFORMATION: Interagency Offices & Information Center in St. George, 628-4491.

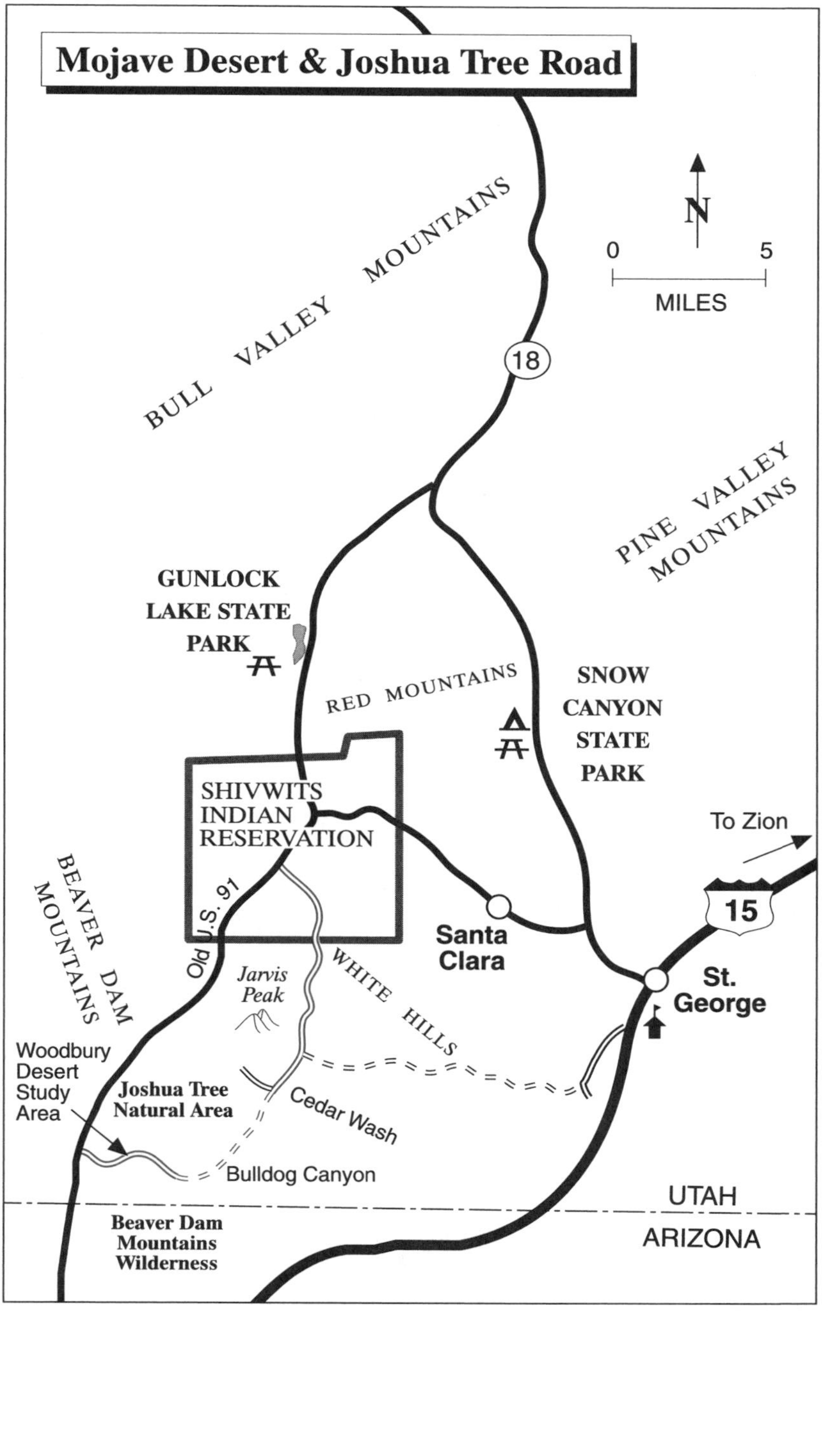
Mojave Desert & Joshua Tree Road
N
0
5
MILES
18
BULL VALLEY MOUNTAINS
PINE VALLEY MOUNTAINS
GUNLOCK LAKE STATE PARK
RED MOUNTAINS
SNOW CANYON STATE PARK
SHIVWITS INDIAN RESERVATION
To Zion
15
BEAVER DAM MOUNTAINS
Old U.S. 91
Santa Clara
St. George
Jarvis Peak
WHITE HILLS
Woodbury Desert Study Area
Joshua Tree Natural Area
Cedar Wash
Bulldog Canyon
UTAH
ARIZONA
Beaver Dam Mountains Wilderness

White Rim Road, Canyonlands National Park

APPENDIX

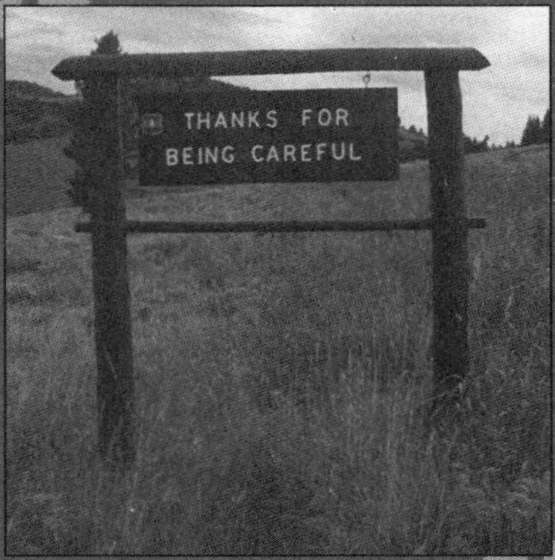
THANKS FOR
BEING CAREFUL

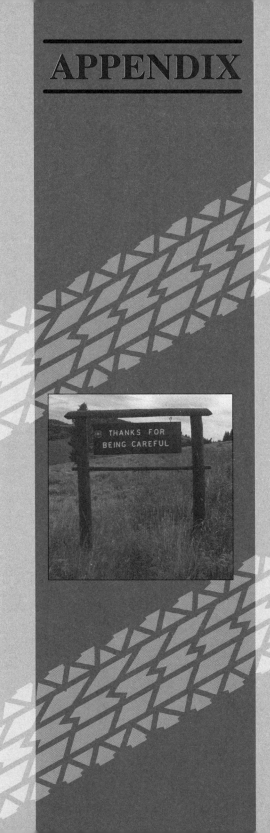

Sources of information

All of Utah is telephone area code 801.

Anasazi Indian Village State Park
P.O. Box 1329
Boulder, UT 84716-1329
335-7308

Arches National Park
P.O. Box 907
Moab, UT 84532
259-8161 (voice)
TTY 259-5279

Arizona Strip Interpretive Assoc.
345 East Riverside Dr.
St. George, UT 84790
628-4491

Ashley National Forest

Duchesne Ranger District
85 West Main St.
P.O. Box 981
Duchesne, UT 84021
738-2482

Flaming Gorge Ranger District
P.O. Box 279
Manila, UT 84046
784-3445

Roosevelt Ranger District
244 W. Hwy. 40
P.O. Box 333-6
Roosevelt, UT 84066
722-5018

Supervisor's Office
355 N. Vernal Avenue
Vernal, UT 84078
789-1181

Vernal Ranger District
353 N. Vernal Avenue
Vernal, UT 84078
789-1181

Automobile Club of Southern California (AAA)
Travel Publications Dept.
2601 S. Figueroa St. H075
Los Angeles, CA 90007
(213) 741-4183

Bryce Canyon National Park
Bryce Canyon, UT 84717
834-5322

Bryce Canyon Natural History Assoc.
Bryce Canyon National Park
P.O. Box 17001
Bryce Canyon, UT 84717
834-5322

Bureau of Land Management

Arizona Strip District Office
345 East Riverside Drive
St. George, UT 84790
673-3545

Cedar City Field Office
176 East D.L. Sargent Drive
Cedar City, UT 84720
586-2401

Dixie Field Office
225 North Bluff St.
St. George, UT 84770
628-4491

Escalante Field Office
P.O. Box 225
Escalante, UT 84726
826-4291

Fillmore Field Office
P.O. Box 778
Fillmore, UT 84631
743-6811

Henry Mountains Field Station
P.O. Box 99
Hanksville, UT 84734
542-3461

John Jarvie Historic Property
885-3307
Vernal Field Office
170 South 500 East
Vernal, UT 84078
781-4400

Kanab Field Office
318 North First East
Kanab, UT 84741
644-2672

Moab Field Office
82 East Dogwood
Moab, UT 84532
259-6111

Price Field Office
125 South 600 West
P.O. Box 7004
Price, UT 84501
636-3600

Richfield Field Office
150 East 900 North
Richfield, UT 84701
896-8221

Salt Lake Field Office
2370 South 2300 West
Salt Lake City, UT 84119
977-4300

San Juan Field Office
P.O. Box 7
435 North Main St.
Monticello, UT 84535
587-2141

State Office
324 S. State St., Suite 301
P.O. Box 45155
Salt Lake City, UT 84111-2303
539-4001

Vernal Field Office
170 South 500 East
Vernal, UT 84078
781-4400

Camp Floyd-Stagecoach Inn State Park
P.O. Box 446
Riverton, UT 84065-0446
768-8932 (April to Nov.)
or 254-9036

Canyon Country Publications
P.O. Box 963
Moab, UT 84532
259-6700

Canyonlands National Park
2282 South West Resource Blvd.
Moab, UT 84532-8000
259-7164 (for general information)
NOTE: The brochure "Canyonlands National Park Backcountry Trip Planner" is packed with important information.

Reservations Office
2282 S. West Resource Blvd.
Moab, UT 84532-8000
259-4351

The Needles District
259-4711

Island in the Sky District
259-4712

Canyonlands Natural History Assoc.
3031 South Highway 191
Moab, UT 84532
259-6003 voice
259-8263 fax

Capitol Reef National Park
HC 70, Box 15
Torrey, UT 84775
425-3791

Capitol Reef Natural History Assoc.
HC 70, Box 15
Torrey, UT 84775-9602
425-3791

Cedar Breaks National Monument
82 North 100 East
Cedar City, UT 84720
586-9451

Coral Pink Sand Dunes State Park
P.O. Box 95
Kanab, UT 84741-0095
874-2408

Dead Horse Point State Park
P.O. Box 609
Moab, UT 84532
259-2614

Deer Creek State Park
P.O. Box 257
Midway, UT 84049-0257
654-0171

Dinosaur National Monument
4545 Hwy. 40
Dinosaur, CO 81610
(970) 374-3000

Dinosaur Nature Association
1291 East Highway 40
Vernal, UT 84078
789-8807

Dixie National Forest

Cedar City Ranger District
82 North 100 West
Cedar City, UT 84720
865-3200

Escalante Ranger District
755 West Main
P.O. Box 246
Escalante, UT 84726
826-5400

Pine Valley Ranger District
196 East Tabernacle St.
St. George, UT 84770
652-3100

Powell Ranger District
225 East Center
P.O. Box 80
Panguitch, UT 84759
676-8815

Supervisor's Office
82 North 100 East
P.O. Box 580
Cedar City, UT 84720
865-3700

Teasdale Ranger District
P.O. Box 99
Teasdale, UT 84773
425-3702

Edge of the Cedars State Park
P.O. Box 788
660 West 400 North
Blanding, UT 84511-0788
678-2238

Escalante Interagency Office
P.O. Box 246
Escalante, UT 84726
826-5499

Escalante State Park
P.O. Box 350
Escalante, UT 84726-0350
826-4466

Flaming Gorge Dam & Reservoir
Bureau of Reclamation
Box 278
Dutch John, UT 84023

Flaming Gorge National Recreation Area
USDA Forest Service
Box 278
Manila, UT 84046
784-3445

Fishlake National Forest

Beaver Ranger District
575 South Main St.
P.O. Box E
Beaver, UT 84713
438-2436

Fillmore Ranger District
390 South Main St.
P.O. Box 265
Fillmore, UT 84631
743-5721

Loa Ranger District
138 South Main St.
P.O. Box 129
Loa, UT 84747
836-2811

Richfield Ranger District & Forest Supervisor's Office
115 East 900 North
Richfield, UT 84701
896-9233

Fish Springs National Wildlife Refuge
P.O. Box 568
Dugway, UT 84022
831-5353

Forest Service, U.S. Intermountain Region Office
324 25th Street
Ogden, UT 84401
625-5306
Campground reservations:
1-800-280-2267
For the hearing-impaired:
1-800-879-4496

Fremont Indian State Park
11550 West Clear Creek Canyon Rd.
Sevier, UT 84766-9999
527-4631

Glen Canyon National Recreation Area
P.O. Box 1507
Page, AZ 86040
(520) 608-6200
Carl Hayden Visitor Center:
(520) 608-6405
National Park Service:
826-4315
Bullfrog Visitor Center:
684-2243

Glen Canyon Natural History Assoc.
32 North 10th Ave., Suite 9
P.O. Box 581
Page, AZ 86040
(520) 645-3532

Goblin Valley State Park
P.O. Box 637
Green River, UT 84525-0637
564-3633

Golden Spike
National Historic Site
P.O. Box 897
Brigham City, UT 84302
471-2209

Goosenecks State Park
P.O. Box 788
Blanding, UT 84511-0788
678-2238

Great Basin National Park
Baker, NV 89311
(702) 234-7331

Great Basin Natural History Assoc.
Great Basin National Park
Baker, NV 89311
(702) 234-7270

Green River State Park
P.O. Box 637
Green River, UT 84525-0637
564-3633

GTR Mapping
(publishes Recreational Map of Utah)
P.O. Box 1984
Canon City, CO 81215-1984
(719) 275-8948

Interagency Offices &
Information Center
(BLM & Forest Service)
345 East Riverside Drive
St. George, UT 84790
628-4491

Iron Mission State Park
585 N. Main
Cedar City, UT 84720-1079
586-9290

John Wesley Powell
River History Museum
885 East Main
Green River, UT 84525
564-3526

Kodachrome Basin State Park
P.O. Box 238
Cannonville, UT
84718-0238
679-8562

Manti-La Sal National Forest

Ferron Ranger District
115 West Canyon Road
P.O. Box 310
Ferron, UT 84523
384-2372

Moab Ranger District
2290 S. West Resource Blvd.
P.O. Box 386
Moab, UT 84532
259-7155

Monticello Ranger District
496 East Central
P.O. Box 820
Monticello, UT 84535
587-2041

Price Ranger District &
Forest Supervisor's Office
599 West Price River Dr.
Price, UT 84501
637-2817

Sanpete Ranger District
540 N. Main 32-14
Ephraim, UT 84627
283-4151

Millsite State Park
P.O. Box 1343
Huntington, UT 84528-1343
687-2491

Minersville State Park
P.O. Box 1531
Beaver, UT 84713-1531
438-5472

Moab/Green River
Information Center
Center & Main
Moab, UT 84532
259-8825
1-800-635-6622

Monticello Multi-Agency
Visitor Center
117 South Main Street
P.O. Box 490
Monticello, UT 84535
587-3235 or 1-800-574-4386

Natural Areas Association
(Interagency Natural Areas of Utah)
P.O. Box 645
145 Zion Park Rd.
Springdale, UT 84767
772-2445

Natural Bridges National Monument
Box 1
Lake Powell, UT 84533
692-1234

Needles Outpost
(mid-March through October)
P.O. Box 1349
Moab, UT 84532
979-4007 (store)
259-8545 (message)

Red Fleet State Park
4335 North Hwy. 191
Vernal, UT 84078-7800
789-4432

Scofield State Park
P.O. Box 166
Price, UT 84501-0166
448-9449

Snow Canyon State Park
P.O. Box 140
Santa Clara, UT 84765-0140
628-2255

Southwest Parks & Monuments Assoc.
221 North Court Ave.
Tucson, AZ 85701
(520) 622-1999

Starvation State Park
P.O. Box 584
Duchesne, UT 84021
738-2326

Steinaker State Park
4335 North Hwy. 191
Vernal, UT 84078-7800
789-4432

T.I. Maps, etc.
29 East Center
Moab, UT 84532
259-5529

Timpanogos Cave National Monument
Visitor Center
RR 3, Box 200
American Fork, UT 84003
756-5238

Trails Illustrated
P.O. Box 4357
Evergreen, CO 80437-4357
1-800-962-1643

Uinta National Forest

Heber Ranger District
2460 South Hwy. 40
P.O. Box 190
Heber City, UT 84032
654-0470

Nephi Suboffice
740 S. Main St.
Nephi, UT 84648
623-2735

Pleasant Grove Ranger District
390 North 100 East
Pleasant Grove, UT 84062
785-3563

Spanish Fork Ranger District
44 West 400 North
Spanish Fork, UT 84660
798-3571

Strawberry Visitors/ Information Center
Heber, UT 84032
548-2321

Supervisor's Office
88 West 100 North
Provo, UT 84601
342-5100

U.S. Geological Survey Earth Science Information Center
2222 West 2300 South
Second Floor
Salt Lake City, UT 84119
975-3742
1-800-872-6277 for the ESIC nearest you.

Utah Division of Parks & Recreation
1636 West North Temple #116
Salt Lake City, UT 84116-3156
538-7221
Campground reservations:
322-3770 (Salt Lake area) or
1-800-322-3770

Utah Department of Transportation
4501 South 2700 West
Salt Lake City, UT 84119
965-4000

Utah Field House of Natural History
235 East Main
Vernal, UT 84078
789-3799

Utah Geological Survey
1594 W. North Temple
Salt Lake City, UT 84114
537-3320

Utah Highway Patrol
4501 S. 2700 W.
West Valley City, UT 84119
965-4518

Utah Idaho Supply/Map World
(They have a number of stores.)
1151 S. Redwood Rd. No. 101
Salt Lake City, UT 84104
974-3144

Utah Road Conditions
492-2400

Utah Travel Council
Council Hall/Capitol Hill
Salt Lake City, UT 84114
538-1030/1-800-1160

Utah Tourism & Recreation Information Center
Council Hall/Capitol Hill
Salt Lake City, UT 84114
538-1467

Vernal Welcome Center
(In the Utah Field House of Natural History)
235 East Main
Vernal, UT 84078
789-4002

Willard Bay State Park
650 North 900 West #A
Willard, UT 84340-9999
734-9494

Wasatch Mountain State Park
P.O. Box 10
750 West Snake Creek Rd.
Midway, UT 84049-0010
654-1791

Wasatch-Cache National Forest

Bear River Ranger Station
(June-October)
642-6662

Evanston Ranger District
1565 Hwy. 150, Suite A
P.O. Box 1880
Evanston, WY 82930
(307) 789-3194

Kamas Ranger District
50 East Center Street
P.O. Box 68
Kamas, UT 84036
783-4338

Logan Ranger District
1500 East Highway 89
Logan, UT 84321
755-3620

Mountain View Ranger District
Lone Tree Road, Hwy. 44
P.O. Box 129
Mountain View, WY 82939
(307) 782-6555

Ogden Ranger District
507 25th Street Suite 103
Ogden, UT 84401
625-5112

Salt Lake Ranger District
6944 South 3000 East
Salt Lake City, UT 84121
943-1794

Supervisor's Office
8236 Federal Building
125 South State Street
Salt Lake City, UT 84138
524-5030

Union Station Information Center
2501 Wall Avenue
Ogden, UT 84321
625-5306

Zion National Park
Springdale, UT 84767
772-3256

Zion Natural History Assoc.
Zion National Park
Springdale, UT 84767
772-3265 or 772-3264

References & recommended reading

A Collector's Guide to Rock, Mineral & Fossil Localities of Utah, by James R. Wilson. Utah Geological Survey, Salt Lake City, UT. A county-by-county listing of places to search for and collect specimens. Includes introductory geological information. Handy and easy to read. (1995)

A Naturalist's Guide to the White Rim Trail, by David Williams & Damian Fagan. Wingate Ink, Moab, UT. A 58-page booklet packed with excellent mile-by-mile background. Don't tour the White Rim without it. (1994)

Canyon Country Off-Road Vehicle Trails; Arches & La Sals Areas, by F.A. Barnes. Wasatch Publishers, Salt Lake City, UT. Detailed descriptions for those seeking extensive experience. (1978)

Canyon Country Off-Road Vehicle Trails; Canyon Rims & Needles Areas, by F.A. Barnes. Canyon Country Publications, Moab, UT. Detailed descriptions for those seeking extensive experience. (1990)

Canyon Country Off-Road Vehicle Trails; Island Area, by F.A. Barnes. Wasatch Publishers, Salt Lake City, UT. Detailed descriptions for those seeking extensive experience. (1978)

Canyonlands Country; The geology of Canyonlands and Arches National Parks, by Donald L. Baars. University of Utah Press, Salt Lake City, UT. Instructive, easy to read, even fun. (1995)

Dark Canyon Trail Guide, Canyonlands Natural History Association, Moab, UT. Useful tips and background for visiting Dark Canyon Wilderness. Includes a map. (1994)

John Jarvie of Brown's Park, by William L. Tennent. U.S. Bureau of Land Management Cultural Resources Series. The story of Brown's Park and its most noted resident, with photographs. (1984)

Mountain Biker's Guide to Utah, by Gregg Bromka. Menasha Ridge Press, Birmingham, AL, and Falcon Press, Helena, Montana. Part of Dennis Coello's *America by Mountain Bike* series. Many routes are driveable in an SUV. (1994)

Roadside Geology of Utah, by Halka Chronic. Mountain Press Publishing Co., Missoula, MT. Explanations of the fantastic geology seen from the highways. (1990)

The Monkey Wrench Gang, by Edward Abbey. Avon Books, New York. Bandits/heroes do good/bad things to thwart progress/environmental degradation in southern Utah. (1985)

The Sierra Club Guides to the National Parks; **Desert Southwest**, published by Stewart, Tabori & Chang. One of the best guides to some of America's crown jewels. Great text and color photographs. (1984)

Tour of The Waterpocket Fold, by Ward J. Roylance. Capitol Reef Natural History Association, Torrey, UT.

Tour of The Valley of Cathedrals, by Ward J. Roylance. Capitol Reef Natural History Association, Torrey, UT.

Utah Handbook, by Bill Weir & Robert Blake. Moon Publications, Inc., Chico, CA. An excellent comprehensive guidebook. (1995)

Utah Place Names, by John W. Van Cott. The University of Utah Press, Salt Lake City, UT. A comprehensive guide to the origins of geographic names. (1990)

Utah Scenic Byways & Backways, by the Utah Travel Council, U.S. Bureau of Land Management, U.S. Forest Service, Utah Department of Transportation, Utah Travel Regions, Associations of Governments, National Park Service. Lists and briefly describes some of Utah's most scenic and historic paved and unpaved roads. Great color photography.

Glossary

Here are explanations of terms and abbreviations that I use to describe what you'll see along the drives in this book.

Anticline — A convex, or arched, fold in layered rock.
Bentonite — A soft, colorful rock formed by the decomposition of volcanic ash.
BLM — Bureau of Land Management, an agency of the U.S. Department of Interior. It manages almost 23 million acres of publicly owned land in Utah.
Cairn — Rocks deliberately piled up to serve as a trail marker.
CG — Campground.
Desert varnish — A dark coating of iron and manganese that commonly covers desert rocks.
Fault — A fracture in the Earth's crust accompanied by a displacement of one side of the fracture with respect to the other and in a direction parallel to the fracture.
Fold — A curve or bend in rock strata, or layers.
Igneous rock — Rock formed of magma, or molten rock.
Magma — Molten rock.
Meander — A looping bend in a river channel.
Monocline — A fold in stratified rock in which all the strata, or layers, dip in the same direction.
NF — National forest.
NP — National park.
MYA — Million years ago.
Petroglyph — A design deliberately etched into the thin, dark varnish that commonly covers desert rock.
Pictograph — A design deliberately painted on rock faces.
Reef — A ridge of sharply upturned rock that 19th century pioneers, traveling in "prairie schooners," saw as obstacles.
Sandstone — Rock composed of sand grains cemented together.
Sedimentary rock — Rock formed by accumulated sediments.
Shale — Solidified muds, clays and silts that split into sheets.
SP — State park.
Strata — Layers of sedimentary rock.
Stratified — Layered, or sheetlike, rock or earth of one kind lying between beds of other kinds.
Travertine — A light-colored porous calcite deposited from solution in ground or surface water.
Trilobite — A general term for a group of extinct marine animals (anthropods) with three-lobed, oval-shaped bodies found as fossils in rocks from the Paleozoic (245-570 MYA) Era.
Upwarp — A broad area where layered rocks have been uplifted by internal forces.
Wash — A dry streambed.
Wilderness — Once just a sparsely or unpopulated place dominated by nature, the 1964 Wilderness Act made it a legislative designation as well. It is now defined, in part, as land that appears to be in a natural state, where the impact of humans is essentially unnoticeable. They are protected from consumptive uses, such as mining and logging, by humans. No forms of mechanized travel are allowed.

Index

Bold page numbers indicate photographs

F

G

H

I

J

K

L

M

River Ford to Cathedral Valley

Swasey Cabin, San Rafael Swell

"I WANT MORE!"

Let Tony Huegel's expanding series of backcountry driving guides show you the way to even more off-highway adventure. Just fill out and clip this coupon — <u>and mail it today!</u>

- ❑ **Sierra Nevada Byways;** Backcountry drives for the whole family. ____ Copies ($10.95* each)
- ❑ **California Coastal Byways;** Backcountry drives for the whole family. ____ Copies ($14.95* each)
- ❑ **California Desert Byways;** Backcountry drives for the whole family. ____ Copies ($16.95* each)
- ❑ **Idaho Off-road;** Backcountry drives for the whole family. ____ Copies ($10.95* each)
- ❑ **Utah Byways;** Backcountry drives for the whole family. ____ Copies ($16.95* each)

Make check or money order payable to the Post Company.

Mail to:

Guidebooks
Post Company
P.O. Box 1800
Idaho Falls, ID
83403

*** Prices may change without notice. Please include $3 for the first book ordered, and 50 cents for each additional book to cover postage and handling.**

$__________ Total

❑ **Adventure Byways:** A seasonal backcountry touring guide. (Information will be sent to you.)

Mail to:

Adventure Byways
442 East 13th Street
Idaho Falls, ID 83404

Name: ____

Street: ____

City: ______________________ State: _______________

Zip: __________________